Inclusive Scholarship: Developing Black Studies in the United States

A 25th Anniversary Retrospective of Ford Foundation Grant Making, 1982–2007

With Introduction and Commentary by
Farah Jasmine Griffin, Ph.D.

Ford Foundation
New York, N.Y.

Acknowledgments

The Ford Foundation wishes to thank Janice Petrovich, director of Education, Sexuality, Religion (ESR); Irma McClaurin, program officer for Education and Scholarship in ESR; Ejima Baker, consultant for ESR; and Janus Adams of Janus Adams Inc., consultant, for their assistance in bringing this project to completion.

Table of Contents

Preface

The Ford Foundation is primarily known for its grant-making in the United States and in 12 overseas locations. Over the last decade, Ford has awarded more than $3 billon to support innovative institutions and individuals committed to strengthening democratic values, reducing poverty, promoting international cooperation, and advancing human achievement. Worldwide, the foundation makes more than 2,000 grants a year.

With such a large and highly diverse portfolio of international grant-making, we believe it is crucial to assess the impact of our work over sustained periods of time. Thus, besides making grants, part of the foundation's core mission is to continually share lessons learned from these efforts. We assess projects and more comprehensive initiatives in a variety of ways, typically including using standard evidence-based methodologies and evaluation techniques drawn from the social sciences. From time to time, however, we also ask distinguished scholars, policy experts, seasoned practitioners, and community-based activists to review a body of work and provide qualitative commentaries on what they think has been accomplished and what challenges remain.

In the past 25 years, no arena of higher education grant-making has received more sustained attention from the foundation than scholarship and curriculum development in African American Studies. Our grant-making in African American Studies is carried out within the program area entitled "Knowledge, Creativity, and Freedom" and within the field of education and scholarship. In 1982, Dr. Sheila Biddle, a program officer at the foundation, commissioned Professor Nathan Huggins of Harvard University to prepare a report on the state of African American Studies at selected colleges and universities. Biddle also asked Huggins to comment on how Ford could work effectively to strengthen this interdisciplinary field. Huggins' report provided a road map for Biddle and other program officers in the 1980s. It also proved to be controversial in some quarters of academe because it did not advocate the establishment of separate faculty lines for "Afro-Am" programs, as they were then known.

Five years after the Huggins report was published in 1985, a second review of African American Studies was issued by the foundation. This time, three distinguished scholars—Professors Darlene Clark Hine, Nellie McKay, and Robert L. Harris Jr.—surveyed the field and offered fresh conclusions and recommendations. In 1994, the foundation asked two other outstanding researchers, Professors Robert O' Meally and Valerie Smith, to conduct an assessment of the foundation's work in African American Studies. And, most recently, Professors Richard Yarborough and Diane Pinderhughes completed a superb review of this critical interdisciplinary field in 2000.

Now, for the first time, and thanks to the hard work and invaluable insights of Professor Farah Jasmine Griffin of Columbia University, the foundation is making all four reports available in a single volume. We believed that Griffin was the right choice because she represents the first generation of scholars who were thoroughly exposed to, grew up with, and became committed to African American Studies as a significant interdisciplinary field. Importantly, too, Griffin began her career as a student of Professor Huggins. This publication—compiled with the assistance of the current program officer, Dr. Irma McClaurin—spans a quarter-century of provocative analysis about African American Studies and its place on American college campuses. While we do not necessarily agree with every conclusion contained in these reports, we are convinced that all of these remarkable scholars and public intellectuals offer important observations about a field of study that is transforming how we think about history—who deserves to be remembered, studied, and celebrated? Most important, African American Studies has offered and continues to offer a critical perspective on what constitutes the "American experience," let alone the experiences of Africans in diaspora. We ignore this history at our peril. These reports provide valuable insights into African American Studies in the last decades of the 20th century, a century that W.E.B. Du Bois correctly characterized as one in which race would be the dominant problem. Sadly, the aftermath of Hurricane Katrina confirmed that the struggle for racial justice continues unabated in the 21st century.

Alison R. Bernstein
Vice President
Knowledge, Creativity & Freedom

Janice Petrovich
Director
Education, Sexuality, Religion

Margaret Wilkerson
Director
Media, Arts & Culture

Introduction
(2006)

Farah Jasmine Griffin, Ph.D.

African American Studies[1] is a vibrant intellectual enterprise that has helped to transform the way we think about the United States and the world. For instance, scholars of African American Studies have called upon us to consider the centrality of the international slave trade to the development of modern capitalism. They have asked that we understand U.S. immigration policy since 1965 in relation to the Civil Rights and Black Power Movements.

African American Studies ought to be of interest to anyone seeking to understand the world's most powerful nation. In order to fully understand the United States, it is imperative that we also comprehend the political and cultural traditions created by a population that has consistently challenged it to live up to its democratic ideals and principles, while at the same time offering the world a vision of hope and freedom through a dynamic culture that is universal.

Indeed, the field[2] of African American Studies has been influential internationally, and the scholarship produced has enhanced and expanded traditional academic disciplines, especially literary studies, history, and sociology.

Although a number of scholars have been critical of the involvement of major foundations in the development of African American Studies, few would argue the Ford Foundation's significance in helping to assure the long-term stability and academic legitimization of the field.[3]

With its ongoing commitment to the discipline and the need to assess the impact of its grant making, beginning in 1982, the Ford Foundation commissioned a series of four African American Studies reports: *Afro-American Studies: A Report to the Ford Foundation* by Nathan I. Huggins (1985); *Black Studies: Three Essays* by Robert L. Harris, Jr., Darlene Clark Hine, and Nellie Y. McKay (1990); *Evaluation of Ford-Funded African American Studies Departments, Centers, and Institutes* by Robert O'Meally and Valerie Smith (1994); and *A Review of African American Studies Programs for the Ford Foundation* by Diane Pinderhughes and Richard Yarborough (2000).

Although the first two reports were released to the public, the second two remained unpublished. The present volume collects all four reports for the first time. Together they present an extraordinary portrait of the growth and development of African American Studies as a discipline in American higher education over a period of more than 30 years.

Entering the public domain as part of the proliferating scholarship on African American Studies, this retrospective provides an appropriate occasion to assess the Ford Foundation's role in the institutionalization and legitimization of African American Studies in the academy, to offer a critical review of the four Foundation-sponsored reports, to assess the responses of the Foundation to the suggestions of the authors as regards future support, and to consider the consequences of the foundation's funding decisions over the last 25 years on the future of African American Studies. From this review, the conclusions drawn suggest how the foundation might continue its historic role in helping to support the field through its next stage of development.

Background: Ford and the Institutionalization of Black Studies

In the spring of 1968, the Black Student Alliance at Yale University organized a scholarly symposium to explore the debates surrounding the emergence of African American Studies at majority White institutions. The Yale students invited a cross-section of leading scholars and intellectuals, including Harold Cruse, Nathan Hare, Maulana Ron Karenga, and Martin Kilson to debate the politics and scholarly legitimacy of this controversial topic.[4] Top-level Yale administrators and faculty, as well as students, attended the event. The Ford Foundation funded the symposium.

Throughout the country universities had been responding to student demands for Black Studies programs in a highly politicized atmosphere. Following almost two years of student protests and strikes, the first department of African American Studies was founded at San Francisco State in 1968. Although a number of highly visible and important departments, including those at Cornell, Harvard, and University of California, Berkeley, were also established in the midst of confrontations between students and administrators, a number of schools readily established interdisciplinary African American Studies programs. Few efforts were characterized, however, by the collaboration and debate among students, scholars, and administrators evident in the Yale endeavor. The Yale program went on to become one of the most successful and prestigious in the country.[5]

For the next 30 years the Ford Foundation supported the development of the field through strategic grant making to key institutions. By committing significant resources to a number of programs and departments, to scholarly efforts, and to graduate student support, the foundation has helped to shape the direction of African American Studies since the Black Studies movement's formal inception.[6]

The Ford Foundation's commitment to Black higher education dates back to 1945. An internal report problematically titled *The Ford Foundation Grants and Projects Related to the Development of the American Negro* (1966) documents more than $34 million in grant funds to support undergraduate education, curricula, programs, and faculty and staff development at historically Black colleges and universities. The foundation also contributed funds to the United Negro College Fund and the National Merit Scholarship Corporation. Of the grants made to educational institutions, the vast majority was made to "Negro colleges."[7] A number of these grants augmented faculty salaries at these institutions.

When McGeorge Bundy became president of the foundation in 1966, he brought with him a commitment to solving "the nation's most pressing social problem . . . the struggle for Negro Equality."[8] A graduate of Yale College, Bundy had been a professor of government and dean of the faculty at Harvard University before entering the administration of President John F. Kennedy as a special assistant for National Security Affairs and joining the foundation. Bundy saw the university as a primary site of social change; he was especially interested in the work of student activists and found compelling their calls for the transformation of institutions of higher education.[9]

The emerging Black Studies movement was a central component of this new activism and became one vehicle Bundy deployed to address his concerns about both race relations and the university. When the foundation began to engage in issues related to Black Studies, it landed in the middle of long-standing ideological debates between "integrationists" and "separatists" as they manifested themselves in this new arena.[10]

In the weeks preceding the Yale symposium, Bundy met and corresponded with Ulric Haynes Jr., about Black Studies. Haynes had been a member of the National Security Council staff in 1965 and 1966. By 1969 he was a well-respected businessperson who went on to become U.S. ambassador to Algeria from 1977 to 1981. At the invitation of James Armsey, the foundation's officer in charge of special projects in education, and F. Champion Ward, vice president, Division of Education and Research, Haynes, along with several other African American scholars and business leaders, met at the foundation to discuss "the Black curriculum." Following that meeting Haynes encouraged Ward to "seek the counsel of the Charles Hamiltons, the Nathan Hares, the Robert Greens and others of the younger Black academicians who are in tune with the desires and needs of Black students."[11] By doing so, Haynes was suggesting that the foundation seek the involvement of a range of representatives within the larger movement to create Black Studies.

By 1969, a year after the Yale meeting, foundation representatives were familiar with the diverse range of ideological positions concerning the creation of Black Studies. In a series of internal memos Ward, Armsey, and others outlined the ideological orientations of the different types of Black Studies programs and encouraged Bundy to avoid the more separatist, Black Nationalist programs. In a memo to Bundy dated February 10, 1969, Ward declared:

> I would favor such programs as Yale's in part because they assume that the subject of Africa and the Black experience in the New World is important and teachable knowledge, valuable for any American student, White or Black. For the same reason, I would not favor support for the notion that only Blacks can teach or understand this subject, and that therefore the Department of Black Studies must be separately organized. . . . I fear it will become a cultural war camp, marked by myth-making and collective self-deception.[12]

When the first grants were awarded, almost a year after the Yale meeting, the foundation "recognized that . . . the Black experience is a worthwhile subject for scholarly inquiry . . . [but] do not concede . . . that the Black experience is the exclusive preserve of Black scholars and that its principal role in the curriculum is to help Black students find their identity."[13] There seemed to be a consensus among Foundation officers not to fund the more separatist programs, but there was at least one dissenting voice.

Roger Wilkins, officer in charge, Social Development, encouraged Bundy to create a review committee of "distinguished Black educators" who would be given the time and opportunity to modify future grants as long as these individuals provided "good reasons for doing so." He underscored the importance of a diverse advisory board, insisting that it include not only representatives of "the older and more settled elements of the academic community" but also "younger and angrier Black scholars." According to Wilkins, "The tension that comes from diversity ought to stretch us." Finally, Wilkins wisely wrote, "I understand and share the psychological and experiential bases for the demand that Blacks develop Black Studies." He goes on to suggest that the foundation support "at least two institutions where the central thrust is the development by Black scholars of the definition, the content, and the development of standards for academic excellence in the field of Black Studies."

While McGeorge Bundy sought the advice of foundation officers, he also solicited the advice of Sir Arthur Lewis, the Caribbean-born economist from Princeton University. Lewis won the Nobel Prize in Economics in 1979 for his "pioneering research into economic development research with particular consideration of the problems of developing countries." At the request of Bundy, Lewis reviewed the first set of grants and wrote an informal position paper on the emerging field. "Notes on Black Studies" (1969) appears to have influenced the foundation's grant making for years after the first grants to establish African American Studies programs.

The author encourages the foundation to focus its attention on helping to build a strong academic field by supporting scholarly and pedagogical initiatives that adhere to the standards of traditional disciplines. The more nationalist programs were to be avoided and White students encouraged to take courses in Black Studies. "The foundation should presumably support only programs intended for both Black and White students." Even though Lewis recognized the importance of addressing the academic needs of undergraduate students, he noted that there was, and would continue to be, a shortage of professors trained to teach in the newly developing field. To address this issue, he encouraged the foundation to shift its focus to graduate programs and the training of future scholars and teachers. "Those who care for Black students and Black Studies should support only genuine intellectual inquiry, of the kind which the militants do not want."

According to Lewis, such programs would outlast "political fads" and would stimulate institutions to provide continued support for them. Indeed, Lewis's document maps the philosophical route the foundation traversed for the next 30 years.

Starting in 1969 and throughout the next decade, Ford Foundation program officer James Scanlon would make a number of grants to help sustain African American Studies programs that met Lewis's criteria at historically Black colleges and universities (HBCUs), as well as at predominantly White institutions. Grants for Black Studies initiatives at HBCUs were made to Fisk, Howard, and Lincoln Universities, Morgan State, and the Atlanta University Center. Grants to help establish fledgling programs at White institutions went, most notably, to Princeton, Rutgers, Stanford, and Yale Universities.

In the 1980's, under program officer Sheila Biddle, both the number and monetary size of grants would greatly increase. Biddle's grant making provided consistent support for a number of programs at institutions throughout the nation.

Between the mid-1980's and 2003, under the leadership of program officers Sheila Biddle, Margaret Wilkerson, and Gertrude Fraser, the foundation made a series of strategic grants that helped develop and sustain a number of key programs throughout the country. For the most part, they focused on predominantly White, major research institutions, both private and public.

Produced during this period, the four Ford Foundation-commissioned Black Studies reports chronicle critical years in the growth of African American Studies, and Ford's commitment to and impact upon the field.

The Reports: African American Studies and the Role of the Ford Foundation

In 1982, the late historian Nathan I. Huggins was chair of the Department of Afro-American Studies and director of the W. E. B. Du Bois Institute at Harvard University when Ford program officer Sheila Biddle commissioned his essay on the "present state and future prospects of Afro-American Studies." Dr. Huggins's report was much more than an overview or survey. Twenty-five years into those "future prospects," his assessment has proven prescient with two surprising lapses.

To author its second report, the Ford Foundation chose three intellectual and administrative leaders in the field of African American Studies:

Robert L. Harris, Jr., director of the Africana Studies and Research Center at Cornell University; Darlene Clark Hine, John Hannah Professor of History at Michigan State University; and Nellie Y. McKay, professor of American and Afro-American literature at the University of Wisconsin. Commissioned in 1987, Harris, Hine, and McKay set out to evaluate diverse institutions with the intention of keeping their report confidential (as would be necessary if it were to contain an honest assessment). When many within the field expressed interest in the findings, the foundation compiled and published their essays in a report titled *Black Studies in the United States* in 1990.

The report begins with Dr. Harris's "The Intellectual and Institutional Development of Africana Studies," an overview of the field dating back a century to the late 1890's. Today, 20 years since Dr. Harris was commissioned to write that essay, his contribution remains one of the most extensive histories of the field.

In her essay, "Black Studies: An Overview," Dr. Hine explores the nomenclature of the field: African American, Afro-American, Africana, Black Studies—titles reflecting the diversity of the field, its varied curricula, and geographic reach. Indeed, Hine's exploration is echoed in this volume; from Huggins' "Afro-American Studies" report to Harris, Hine, McKay's "Black Studies" essays and O'Meally-Smith's and Pinderhughes-Yarborough's final two reports' "African American Studies," the term now officially used by the foundation.

From 1987–1989, when the Harris, Hine, McKay essays were commissioned and completed, Hine found that White college administrators enthusiastically supported African American Studies as the site that has racially diversified the university population and curriculum.

Yet, as Dr. McKay notes in her essay, "Black Studies in the Midwest," despite the commitment among predominantly White institutions to strengthen African American Studies, there was reason to doubt the extent to which the discipline had been accepted in the scholarly community.

While the first two Ford reports—Huggins' *Afro-American Studies: A Report to the Ford Foundation* (1985) and Harris-Hine-McKay's *Black Studies in the United States* (1990)—provide historical overviews and survey the landscape of the field, the next two reports document the health of the field by focusing on specific Ford-funded programs. Seen through this lens, the later reports demonstrate the diversity of the field and the complexities of the challenges confronting it.

For its third report, *Evaluation of Ford-Funded African American Studies Departments, Centers and Institutes* (1994), the foundation commissioned two scholars of African American literature, Robert O'Meally, Zora Neale Hurston Professor of English and Comparative Literature, and Valerie Smith, then professor of English at UCLA, and currently Woodrow Wilson Professor of English and director of the Center for African American Studies at Princeton.

The Ford Foundation had initiated a large-scale grant program in 1988. Three-year, $300,000 sum grants were made to support "leading Departments, programs and centers." The O'Meally-Smith report follows up these grants to "leading departments, programs and centers" at Cornell, Harvard, Indiana, Michigan, Michigan State, Pennsylvania, Wisconsin, Yale Universities and the University of California at Berkeley and Los Angeles.

With its site study approach, the report documents the impact of Ford Foundation funding on these departments and programs. Significantly, the report acknowledges the impact of the field on traditional disciplines and the resulting creation of newer interdisciplinary methodologies.

November 1996 ushered in a major shift in public policy. California passed Proposition 209, which prohibited affirmative action programs in state hiring, contracts, and education.[14] That same year a Texas federal court banned the affirmative action program at the University of Texas Law School (which did not admit Black students until 1950). Within a year Black enrollment dropped more than 90 percent; Mexican American enrollment dropped approximately 60 percent.[15]

In these changing times for American higher education, African American Studies programs were hit hard by budget crises prevalent throughout higher education. Program officer Margaret Wilkerson commissioned political scientist Dianne Pinderhughes of the University of Illinois, Urbana Champaign, and literary scholar Richard Yarborough of the University of California, Los Angeles, to research the fourth and final report of this volume. *A Review of African American Studies Programs for the*

Ford Foundation was completed in 2000. In tandem with the field it surveys, the Pinderhughes-Yarborough report warns about serious challenges threatening its stability. The authors observe "a whole-scale brutal assault both on the goal of increasing educational access through such mechanisms as affirmative action and also on the most obvious institutional signs of that hard won access, Ethnic Studies."

Against this backdrop, the Pinderhughes-Yarborough report revisits institutions considered in the O'Meally-Smith study, evaluates the field at the turn of the 21st century, and offers suggestions on how best to help strengthen and sustain the discipline.

The Response: Grantmaking in African American Studies by the Ford Foundation

Since the first Ford grants to the field of African American Studies in 1969, the field of African American Studies has grown and matured from idea to movement to a thriving intellectual field in the academy. It is an institutionalized part of the academic structure, replete with degree-granting departments and programs, refereed publications, tenured professorships, and endowed chairs.

Starting in 1969 through the next decade, Program Officer James Scanlon's initial grants to HBCUs and fledgling Black Studies departments in predominately White institutions helped institutionalize the field.

From 1983–1987, program officer Sheila Biddle made grants totaling $1.2 million to Cornell University, Harvard University (the Du Bois Institute), and the University of Virginia (the Carter G. Woodson Institute). At Cornell and Harvard, the grants supported visiting scholars programs; at Woodson, predoctoral and postdoctoral fellowships.

Between 1988 and 1996, the foundation granted more than $600,000 to the National Council for Black Studies (NCBS) for summer institutes that provided administrative training workshops. The Association for the Study of Afro-American Life and History (ASALH) received a total of $600,000.

Since publication of the Huggins report in 1985, the foundation has consistently funded a core set of institutions and expanded its reach. Although each of these may have been identified as programs that offered the most promise in terms of curricular innovation and scholarly production, foundation support certainly helped to sustain them as the most prestigious programs in the country.

In a draft of her report, Professor Hine wrote, "In the past, funding agencies have all too often pursued activities without consulting [the] principals subsequently affected. It would be wise for the foundation to listen to what they have to say about the future needs of the discipline."[16] Following the submission of her report, in August 1987, the foundation convened leading figures in the field (see photo, p. xviii). A number of programs that had never received funding from Ford were invited to present proposals; however, several other programs had received funding in the past.

In keeping with the recommendations in the O'Meally-Smith report, program officers Sheila Biddle, Margaret Wilkerson, and Gertrude Fraser made grants to consortiums and archives, as well as to individual programs and departments. One of Dr. Biddle's grants provided support to Harvard's W. E. B. Du Bois Institute as it sought to strengthen links between the African American Studies Department and the Committee on the Study of Africa.[17] The two units recently merged into the Department of African and African American Studies. The vast majority of Dr. Fraser's grants helped to institutionalize projects at the University of Wisconsin, Madison, UCLA, and University of California, Berkeley. The foundation's long-term commitment to its grantees assisted UC Berkeley, for example, in becoming one of the first institutions to offer the Ph.D. in African American Studies.[18]

Convening of Black Studies Scholars
at the Ford Foundation, 1988

Front Row: Thomas Holt, Sheila Biddle, Darlene Clark Hine, Russell L.
Adams, Claudia Mitchell-Kernan, Clayborne Carson, Kennell Jackson.

Middle Row: John Blassingame*, George Wright, Milfred Fierce, Henry
Louis Gates, Nellie McKay*, Robert L. Harris, Jr., Delores Aldridge,
Molefi Asante.

Top Row: Alfredteen Harrison, Armstead Robinson*, Karen Fields,
Ronald Bailey, Charles Henry, Joseph Scott, Nathan Huggins*,
John Wright.

*Person is now deceased.

Convening of Black Studies Scholars at the Ford Foundation, August 2005

Seated: Irma McClaurin, Farah Griffin, Valerie Smith.

Standing (middle row): Ejima Baker, Darlene Clark Hine.

Standing (back row): Janice Petrovich, Robert L. Harris, Richard Yarborough, Robert O'Meally, Dianne Pinderhughes, Alison Bernstein, Margaret Wilkerson.

As the current volume documents, since its first African American Studies grants in 1969, the Ford Foundation has supported those programs having the most mainstream legitimacy and those that worked within the methods of traditional disciplines—even as they helped to hone the interdisciplinary field of African American Studies.

For the most part, the foundation has committed resources to select programs and departments over a period of time in order to ensure continuity and stability. By also funding consortiums and large national organizations, the foundation has spread limited resources to a wider range of institutions and individuals than is readily apparent. With each funding cycle, a broader range of institutions receives funding.

The Implications

In the 25 years since the first Ford Foundation report on African American Studies was commissioned, the foundation has made almost $31 million in grants to African American Studies programs, departments, and organizations. As evidenced in the four reports included in this volume, it has contributed immeasurably to the institutionalization of this important intellectual discipline.

Notes

[1] Throughout this introduction the term *Black Studies* connotes the historical efforts to bring this subject matter into the academy. *Afro-American* and *African American Studies* are used interchangeably to discuss the academic field that has been institutionalized in the last 20 years. *Africana Studies* refers to specific programs with a diasporic focus. It should also be noted that the Ford Foundation has generically and traditionally used *African American Studies* when referring to the field. A further discussion of the nomenclature appears on pages 118–120 of the essay by Dr. Hine.

[2] An ongoing and long-standing debate within African American Studies revolves around whether it is a field or a discipline. The documents in this volume use the terms *discipline* and *field* somewhat interchangeably without referencing the debate.

[3] These critiques tend to fall into two categories. The first, which has been stated in print a number of times, charges large foundations, especially Ford, with having emptied Black Studies of its radical political implications. As early as 1974, Robert Allen wrote: "By selecting certain programs for funding while denying support to others, government agencies and foundations could manipulate the political orientation of these programs and the direction of their academic

research. With hundreds of such programs competing for limited funds, effective control of the future of Black Studies was thereby shifted from Black scholars and students, and instead . . . to the funding agencies—college administrations, government and foundations. Departments which were thought by the establishment to be dangerously independent or radical could thus be crippled and destroyed without the necessity of resorting to violent repression." See Robert L. Allen, "Politics of the Attack on Black Studies," *Black Scholar*, vol. 6 (September 1974) p. 2. In *White Money/Black Power: The Surprising History of African American Studies and the Crisis of Race in Higher Education* (Boston: Beacon Press 2006), Noliwe M. Rooks argues that although the Ford Foundation provided much needed funding to the development of African American Studies, its strategies, which saw African American Studies as a vehicle for integrating predominantly white campuses and curricula, ultimately undermined the field's own intellectual identity and agenda.

[4] Black Nationalist social critic Harold Cruse was the author of *The Crisis of the Negro Intellectual* (1967), a book that had tremendous influence on younger African American intellectuals and activists. At the time of the Yale meeting he taught at the University of Michigan, Ann Arbor. Sociologist and psychotherapist Nathan Hare became the coordinator of the first Black Studies program at San Francisco State College in 1968. By the next year, he'd left the college to become founding publisher of *The Black Scholar: A Journal of Black Studies and Research*. Maulana Ron Karenga was a leading Black Cultural Nationalist and director of the Kawaida Institute of Pan-African Studies in Los Angeles. Martin Kilson was a professor of government at Harvard University. In 1968 he became the first African American granted tenure by that institution. Kilson objected to establishing Afro-American Studies as a separate research and curricular unit.

[5] For a comprehensive historical overview of Black Studies see Manning Marable, "Introduction: Black Studies and the Racial Mountain" in *Dispatches from the Ebony Tower: Intellectuals Confront the African American Experience* (New York: Columbia University Press, 2000).

[6] It should be noted that a number of important intellectual and organizational projects that contributed to the development of African American Studies received little or no funding from major foundations.

[7] *The Ford Foundation Grants and Projects Related to the Development of the American Negro (All Fiscal Years Through June 10, 1966)*, unpublished paper in Bundy papers.

[8] Ford Foundation Annual Report, New York: Ford Foundation, 1967.

[9] For a critical discussion of the Ford Foundation's relationship to and influence upon the efforts of student activists, see Julie A. Reuben, "Consorting with the Barbarians at the Gate: McGeorge Bundy, the Ford Foundation, and

Student Activism in the Late 1960s," unpublished paper. According to Reuben, current Black Studies programs do not represent the triumph of radical student activists, but instead that of liberal administrators who "took advantage of the crisis [created by student activists] to gain the upper hand in academic politics. [These programs] represent the successes of a group of liberal academics (or former academics) instituting their own reform agenda with the help of a powerful patron." That patron was the Ford Foundation.

[10] These two categories oversimplify the actual diversity of perspectives; however, they are useful in describing the distinction between those programs that encouraged the involvement of non-Black scholars and sought to integrate the traditional curriculum and those that did not. To these two categories, separatism and integration, scholars Leith Mullings and Manning Marable have added "transformation," which they define as the "collective efforts of Black people neither to integrate nor self-segregate but to transform the existing power relationships and the racist institutions of the state, economy and society." See Marable, *Dispatches from the Ebony Tower*, and Mullings and Marable, "Introduction" in *Let Nobody Turn Us Around: Voices of Resistance, Reform and Renewal*, (New York: Rowman & Littlefield, 2003).

[11] Memo from Ulric Haynes to Champion Ward, August 13, 1968. Bundy Papers Box 23, Folder 274.

[12] Ward to Bundy, February 10, 1969. Bundy Papers, Box 4, Folder 44.

[13] John Scanlon to James Armsey, May 21, 1969. Box 4, Folder 44.

[14] http://vote96.ss.ca.gov/Vote96/html/BP209.htm.

[15] http://tarlton.law.utexas.edu/hopwood/effects.html.

[16] Hine Report, unedited version, p. 45.

[17] This is an especially significant development since the Foundation ordinarily funds African Studies and African American Studies separately. Recent revelations from the Melville J. Herskovits (www.library.northwestern.edu/africana/herskovits.html) papers suggest the foundation refused to fund projects that joined the study of Africa with that of the African diaspora.

[18] In 1988, Temple University became the first institution to offer the Ph.D. in African American Studies. The University of Massachusetts at Amherst followed. In 1997 the department at Berkeley welcomed its first entering Ph.D. class. Today there are five institutions that award a Doctor of Philosophy in African American Studies; in addition to the three mentioned above, Yale University (2000) and Harvard (2001) can be added. As of July 2006, Indiana University indicated it was working to implement a Ph.D. program.

PART ONE

The American University in Crisis and Transition: The Huggins Report

An Introduction to the Huggins Report
Farah Jasmine Griffin

Afro-American Studies:
A Report to the Ford Foundation
Nathan I. Huggins
Preface by Susan V. Berresford, Vice President, Ford Foundation

The American University in Crisis and Transition:

An Introduction to the Huggins Report

The late historian Nathan I. Huggins was chair of the Department of Afro-American Studies and director of the W. E. B. Du Bois Institute at Harvard University when Ford Foundation program officer Sheila Biddle commissioned his essay on the "present state and future prospects of Afro-American Studies." Professor Huggins's report is much more than an overview or survey. He used the opportunity to contextualize the historical and political conditions that gave birth to Black Studies on predominantly White campuses. He explores the explosive growth and changing nature of the American academy following World War II and the contemporaneous movement Black Americans waged for political rights and social justice. Their convergence set the stage for the emergence of Black Studies.

Because Huggins's point of origin is the immediate postwar years, his history of the field is less an intellectual history and more an institutional one. He does not evaluate the quality of a century-old scholarly project but, instead, is primarily concerned with the various institutional forms a field born of political turmoil takes on predominantly White campuses. According to Huggins, "three basic concerns lay behind the demand for Afro-American Studies—the political need for turf and place, the psychological need for identity and the academic need for recognition." Huggins shares the latter concern, and he sees it as the most legitimate quest of the new field. Throughout the report, Huggins is clear about his preferred models, and he advocates the foundation fund these efforts.[1]

Huggins writes the history of Black Studies by focusing on six campuses: three Ivy League institutions—Cornell, Harvard, and Yale; two public institutions—University of California, Berkeley, and San Francisco State; and one small liberal arts college—Wesleyan University.[2] In addition, he uses these individual cases to explore diverse ideological and methodological issues and to document how these issues impacted upon the field's institutionalization. Among the patterns of ideology, Huggins identifies integrationists and separatists (separated into advocates of Black Power and advocates of Cultural Nationalism). According to Huggins, "Integrationists . . . insisted that Blacks had to succeed in terms of . . . imperfect [White] institutions and people the better to function in the even less perfect world outside." Furthermore they "preferred to see Black Studies courses offered in conventional departments," such as African American History courses in history departments. In distinguishing between advocates of Black Power and advocates of Cultural Nationalism, he writes: "The Black Power argument was . . . one of self-reliance. . . . Black people had to become self-reliant economically and politically before they could bring genuine power into play. . . . Once they had power, however, coalitions with Whites and others would not only be possible and desirable but effective." On the other hand, Cultural Nationalists, who had more influence on the rhetoric of Black student activists than they did on the actual formation of programs at many colleges, "assumed two nations and two cultures." They believed the university should assume a stance of "nonintervention in Black communities . . . but should deliver financial and technical aid as Black people demanded it."

Finally Huggins also identifies the typical academic-unit forms that these ideologies helped to establish: the program, the college, the department, and the research center or institute. According to Huggins, the program is an interdisciplinary project drawing upon scholars from a variety of departments. The "most radical kind of Afro-American Studies program" is a separate college. The department is an autonomous unit with its own budget and the ability to hire, promote, and tenure its own faculty. Depending upon the institution, research institutes and centers support advanced scholarship in the arts and sciences and rarely have a pedagogical function within the university. Of these, Huggins privileges the program and the research center because both seem best suited to ensure the legitimization of the field through the production of new knowledge and by maintaining contact and relationships with established disciplines. Because the program shares its faculty with established departments, those scholars and teachers would be advocates for the field in their home departments and also inform the curriculum of the mainstream disciplines. Huggins felt that Yale University (at which Black Studies has since become a department) and the Institute of the Black World at Atlanta University were two successful models. At its founding in 1969 the Institute of the Black World (IBW) was funded in part by the Ford Foundation, but by the 1980's, it was forced to close due to lack of resources. The IBW has been called "the most progressive model of what Black Studies could have been."[3]

Huggins believed the integration and transformation of traditional disciplines was the fundamental goal of African American Studies. Because of this mix, his model programs are those that privilege scholarly production, meet the already existing standards of review and promotion, and work in conjunction with departments within the arts and sciences:

> It seems to me that the movement to make academically legitimate the study of a wide range of issues and questions having to do with the Black experience in America has been the most valuable outcome of the struggles during the last decade. Afro-American Studies will achieve greater impact and influence the more it is permitted to resonate in the conventional disciplines. Standard offerings in history, American literature, economics, political science, and so on should be informed and enriched by scholarship in African American Studies.

Within a decade, scholarship in African American Studies did indeed inform a number of disciplines. Huggins recognized the changing political climate as a reason to institutionalize the field within current academic structures and the continued production of high-quality scholarship as factors to help insure its longevity and survival.

Huggins identifies one of the greatest challenges facing the young field as a problem of the pipeline. As more and more students (of all races and ethnicities) sought to enter professional careers, consequently choosing law, medical, and business careers over academic ones, the declining number of Black academics "portends more serious problems for the field than small class enrollments do." Indeed, the pipeline ensuring a steady flow of new Ph.D.s in the areas of African American Studies continues to be one of the greatest challenges facing the field. The production of groundbreaking scholarship has indeed influenced the fields of history and American literature. It has yet to transform more conservative disciplines such as political science and economics, except where they converge in public policy centers. Finally, Huggins did not foresee the rise of Black Women's Studies or the rise and influence of Afrocentricity, two intellectual formations that would greatly affect the future directions of African American Studies.

Developments in the Field

During the years immediately following the publication of the Huggins Report, the field of African American Studies underwent major changes that would result in its further institutionalization and legitimization within the academy, as is evident by the establishment of the Ph.D. at Temple University in 1988 under the leadership of Dr. Molefi Asante; the publication of a number of major works in the field; and the emergence of a cadre of public intellectuals who aligned their intellectual projects with African American Studies.[4] Henry Louis Gates's appearance on the cover of the *New York Times Magazine* (April 1, 1990) and *Newsweek*'s coverage of Molefi Asante (September 23, 1991) both signaled the mainstream media's recognition of the field as a site of important intellectual and political work. The same might be said of *Atlantic Monthly*'s cover story, "The New Public Intellectuals" (March 1995), featuring a number of diverse Black intellectuals, including Cornel

West, Michael Eric Dyson, bell hooks, and others. Significantly, these three stories presented different perspectives on African American Studies: Gates represented a kind of liberal multiculturalism, Asante Afrocentrism, and the various scholars featured in the *Atlantic Monthly* range from the conservative Glenn Loury to the more leftist Cornel West or the feminist bell hooks.

Even though these more visible developments greatly affected the way the field was seen by the world outside of the academy, major tremors were taking place within as well. On the one hand, Black women scholars challenged the field's masculinist biases and in so doing helped to bring together critical discourses of race and gender. On the other hand, with the founding of the first Ph.D. in African American Studies, Afrocentric scholars secured a foothold in the academy. Although Afrocentricity was little felt within the elite academy, it exerted a major influence on African American Studies nationwide and in nonacademic Black institutions, such as Afrocentric charter schools (and public school curricula), spiritual and religious rituals, and rites of passage programs for young people.[5] Although a few Black public intellectuals received positive media coverage, Afrocentric scholars were often harshly criticized and caricatured in the mainstream press, which gave a great deal of attention to the most extreme and controversial stances and figures in the field.

The Pipeline

Although the field gained more visibility within and outside of the academy, there was still a dearth of young African Americans pursuing Ph.D.s. In 1985, the Ford Foundation committed resources to address the pipeline problem by adding predoctoral and dissertation fellowships to their postdoctoral fellowship programs for underrepresented minorities. This program, administered by the National Academy of Sciences, joined a long line of Ford Foundation initiatives devoted to Black faculty. Earlier programs provided resources for faculty development at historically Black colleges and universities, but by 1969 eligibility was expanded to include Black faculty at any institution of higher education. Also in 1969, a doctoral program was established offering up to five years of support to Black students holding the bachelor's degree. The following year, both programs were expanded to include applicants from three other minority groups underrepresented in higher education: Mexican Americans, Native Americans, and Puerto Ricans. In 1973, the two programs were combined into the Graduate Fellowship Program. Fellowships for Black students were administered by the National Fellowships Fund of the Council of Southern Universities in Atlanta; for the other three groups, by the Educational Testing Service in Princeton, New Jersey. That program continued through 1981.

In 1979, the foundation funded a postdoctoral program for underrepresented minorities, administered by the National Academy of Sciences. The first awards were made in 1980. The three-year predoctoral and one-year dissertation fellowships were funded in 1985 and first awarded in 1986. In 2004 the name of these fellowships was changed from Ford Foundation Fellowships for Minorities to Ford Foundation Diversity Fellowships; all U.S. nationals who are committed to diversity are now eligible to apply. The more contemporary Ford fellowships have made it possible and economically feasible for a number of young people of color to pursue academic careers and have lent prestige to those careers.

To date, more than 2,000 scholars have received support from the Foundation. Because many of the Black and non-Black scholars work in humanities, sciences, and social sciences, fields other than African American Studies, it is important to note that through its fellowship program Ford has not conflated diversity in higher education with the development of African American Studies but instead has maintained a commitment to both.

Farah Jasmine Griffin
(2006)

Notes

[1] For critiques of the "liberalism" of the Huggins' Report see, Manning Marable, "Introduction: Black Studies and the Racial Mountain," p. 13; Maulana Ron Karenga, "Black Studies and the Problematic of Paradigm: The Philo-

sophical Dimension," *Journal of Back Studies,* vol. 18, no. 4 (June 1988). For Marable "the Huggins report reflected the triumph of the liberal multiculturalist version of Black Studies" (p. 13).

[2] I do not know how many programs Huggins researched or if he did site visits.

[3] Marable, *op cit,* p. 23.

[4] I want to make a distinction here between the publication of major works of scholarship and the creation of an agreed-upon canon for the field. Even though recent surveys have shown that W. E. B. Du Bois's *The Souls of Black Folk* is the only agreed-upon canonical text to be found on most introductory syllabi, few would argue that the last 20 years have witnessed the publication of major, sophisticated and rigorous works in the field. These include but are not limited to works by Henry Louis Gates, Molefi Asante, Hazel Carby and Patricia Collins, among others.

[5] Throughout the 1990's a number of public school systems including Baltimore and Detroit began to utilize Afrocentric curricula. Also relevant is the growth in the numbers of individuals, families, and communities that recognized and celebrated Kwanza, a week-long holiday observance founded by Maulana Ron Karenga.

Afro-American Studies:
A Report to the Ford Foundation
(1982, 1985) [*]

Nathan I. Huggins

---

[*]The Huggins Report, presented to the foundation in 1982, was first published in 1985.

The Huggins Report
Contents

Preface to the Huggins Report

Since 1969 the Ford Foundation has granted almost $30 million for the study of Afro-American, Hispanic, and Native American history and culture. This support reflects our belief that the rich experience of these groups has played an important part in the evolution of American society and that students as well as the larger public would benefit from knowledge of it.

The foundation began by helping a few strong institutions—among them Howard, Princeton, Rutgers, Stanford, and Yale—to develop undergraduate programs in Afro-American studies. Subsequently, support was expanded to include Hispanic and Native American studies, and the grant focus shifted to the graduate level to train minority scholars and to add to scholarship about minority cultures.[A] Currently, the foundation makes grants to advance the careers of minority scholars at the postdoctoral level and to strengthen selected research centers and ethnic archives.

Since Afro-American studies has accounted for nearly 50 percent of the total granted by the foundation for ethnic studies, it seemed appropriate for the foundation to review developments in the field. In 1982 therefore, the foundation asked Nathan Huggins, director of the W. E. B. Du Bois Institute for Afro-American Research at Harvard University, to survey

---

[A]An account of these earlier programs is contained in *Widening the Mainstream of American Culture*, a Ford Foundation Report on Ethnic Studies, available upon request.

the current status of Afro-American studies on American campuses in light of the early experience and future needs of the field. The report that follows is the result of that investigation.

A distinguished Afro-American scholar (his books on Frederick Douglass, on American slavery, and on the cultural flowering of Harlem are widely used references), Professor Huggins begins his report by placing the rise of the Black Studies movement within the context of the huge postwar growth of American higher education and of Black demands for social justice. He describes the effort to gain a place for Black Studies in the curriculum as part of a broader movement to integrate Black students and faculty into a traditionally White educational system. Strong programs were established in a number of institutions, with the result that by the 1980's few scholars any longer questioned whether the field was a legitimate subject for study. The aim now, Professor Huggins tells us, is to bring more sophisticated methodologies to bear on the study of Black issues and to expand the presence of Black Studies in conventional disciplines.

Professor Huggins's report makes a valuable contribution to our understanding of an important chapter in American academic history, and the foundation is pleased to publish it. We hope that it will serve as a guide and stimulus to other donors interested in aiding a scholarly initiative now well under way.

Susan V. Berresford
Vice President, United States and
International Affairs Programs
Ford Foundation.[B]

[B] Susan V. Berresford became president of the Ford Foundation in 1995.

Afro-American Studies

Nathan I. Huggins

This essay—on the present state and future prospects of Afro-American studies—addresses what twenty years ago would have been considered two separate spheres of social concern: first, the growth and change taking place at American colleges and universities and, second, the struggle of Blacks for social justice. During the late sixties these two spheres became interrelated; to some, indeed, inseparable. To understand Afro-American studies, a product of that period and of the interaction of those spheres, it is thus necessary to consider both American higher education and the American civil rights movement.

The American University in Transition

In the quarter-century following World War II, the American university underwent enormous growth and a remarkable transformation. Both were unexpected. As late as 1941, Archibald MacLeish, referring to Harvard University, predicted "a period of organization within existing frontiers, rather than a period of extension of existing frontiers."[1] In less than a decade, all discussion of higher education in America was attempting to comprehend unprecedented expansion and transformation. By 1963, Clark Kerr's Godkin Lectures were defining the American university in new terms: as the multiversity or the federal-grant university.[2] Not only had it ballooned in size—numbers of students, faculty, and scale of physical plant—it had changed dramatically in character and purpose, departing both from Cardinal Newman's idealism and from the shaping influence of the German university.

Kerr merely articulated what had come to be commonly recognized: that the American university was no longer an academic cloister but was a major force in modern society—vital to industry, agriculture, medicine, government (in war and in peace), and social health and welfare. It was the major producer in what Kerr called the "knowledge industry," and crucial as such to economic and social progress and to national security. Perceiving itself (and generally being perceived) as essential to social and political change, the university naturally became an instrument for those demanding such change, Blacks among them. To better understand the broader context of demands for Black Studies and the institutional response, we should consider aspects of this transformation of the university.

Growth

Between 1955 and 1965, the number of students (undergraduate and graduate) enrolled in U.S. colleges and universities more than doubled. The total of three million students enrolled during that one decade more than equaled the total number of students enrolled during the previous three centuries of American higher education. This extraordinary growth reflected more than the coming-of-age of the children of the postwar "baby boom." It was also a consequence of the democratization of higher education, a long-term trend in the United States but one that made a quantum leap when the G.I.s came home following World War II. Ex-G.I. students embodied two important changes: the massive influx into higher education of people for whom such education had previously been possible (if even conceivable) only through city colleges and night schools, and direct federal support for tuition and expenses through the G.I. Bill. By the sixties, Americans shared two very new assumptions: that nearly everyone could benefit from some postsecondary education and that everyone—without exception—was entitled to access to higher education. Chronic social inequities—in particular, the failure of one particular ethnic group, Blacks, to move into the middle class might, many thought, be explained by that group's systematic exclusion from most American colleges, universities, and professional schools.

While southern society in general, and southern, White universities and professional schools in particular, were early targets of the civil rights movement, northern institutions had been far from exemplary on racial matters. The liberal response to the demand of Blacks for racial justice was, in part, to try to bring more Black students into northern, White colleges and universities. The growth and democratization of the American university thus had racial consequences as well as those of class and scale.

Black migration northward and the G.I. Bill increased Black enrollment in northern schools following World War II. From 1940 to 1950, the percentage of Blacks residing outside the South increased from 23 to 32. C. H. Arce estimated that Black enrollment in White colleges outside the South in 1947 was 61,000 (47 percent of all Black enrollment but 3 percent of the total enrollment in those institutions). Black college enrollment was 6 percent of the total national enrollment that year, a rate not reached again until 1967.[3]

Between 1967 and 1971 Black college enrollment increased enormously, by the latter year reaching 8.4 percent of total college enrollment. The numbers leveled off for two years and then began once again to grow, so that by October 1977, Black enrollment accounted for 10.8 percent of total enrollment, a remarkable figure considering that in 1976 Blacks made up 12.6 percent of the nation's 18- to 24-year-old, college-age population.[4] These increases were the result of aggressive recruitment by northern institutions and vastly increased financial aid, mainly from the federal government.

In the fifties, modest support for Black students was available through the National Scholarship Service and Fund for Negro Students. The funds of this group were later augmented by those of the National Defense Student Loan Program (1958) and the National Achievement Program (1964). The Higher Education Act of 1965 (Work Study, Educational Opportunity

Grants, Guaranteed Student Loan Program) made additional funds avail-able. These programs were followed in 1972 by the Basic Educational Op-portunity Grant Program, which vested funds in individual students who could take them to the institutions of their choice. In 1976–77, $1.5 billion were awarded under this program, to nearly two million students. In addi-tion to federal funds, state aid also became available. In 1977–78, for in-stance, there were $756 million in state aid programs.

These figures point to an important characteristic of the growth of Black student enrollment in the sixties. Not only did many more Black stu-dents attend predominantly White schools in the mid-sixties; those who did were a different social slice of the Black population than those who had attended those schools in the fifties and before. Administrators deliberately set out to recruit poor youngsters from the inner city (so-called ghetto youth), imagining that the university might rectify failures in the second-ary school system and redeem these students so they might enter main-stream life. This policy implied a changing (or at least a rethinking) of standards for admission as they applied to these youngsters. It implied the establishment of remedial programs, a faculty and a student body gen-uinely sympathetic both to the means and the ends of this policy, and inner-city Black students who would be grateful for the opportunity. These assumptions were only partly to be realized, contributing to the general malaise among Black students in the mid-sixties and leading in turn to much of the Black contribution to student unrest in those years.

Being a Black student at a predominantly White institution had never been easy. Before the sixties, such students had always been few in number, hardly more than a dozen undergraduates at any time on any college cam-pus. Sports and other extracurricular activities were sometimes closed to them. Little deference was given them, and they were likely to feel them-selves alternately exemplars of their race and altogether ignored. Unlike those who arrived in the mid-sixties, however, they had not been specially recruited. Those who went to these institutions had made conscious, de-liberate choices to be there, and had undoubtedly made important per-sonal sacrifices. There had been no special admissions considerations, and they probably assumed (following conventional Black wisdom) that they had to be better than Whites to do as well. They expected to overcome obstacles and discrimination based on race. There could be a source of pride in that. It was pride as well (and their limited numbers) that made them unwilling to call attention to themselves by complaining even about real grievances.

After 1965, Black college students were less likely to share these assumptions. Proportionately fewer were motivated in quite the same way; proportionately fewer had the educational background or the study habits to do well in these colleges. In addition, events outside the colleges—the war in Vietnam and, particularly, the continuing struggle for racial justice—were distracting from conventional academic pursuits. To some students—Black and White—it seemed that the goals and values of those outside occurrences were in conflict with the university as it defined itself. Ironically, the growing number of Black students contributed to their own malaise. There came a point, as their numbers grew, when their isolation became conspicuous. In earlier years, the handful of Black students managed to fit in, badly or well, nursing as private matters any hurts they felt. With larger numbers, it became possible (indeed, almost inevitable) to consider being Black on a White campus a collective condition. Private hurts became public grievances.

The extraordinary mid-century growth of the American university only partly explains the demand for Black Studies programs. Equally important were the assumptions about the new role of the university—assumptions about the university as a force extending social justice and its benefits to disadvantaged groups by means of higher education. The university would find it difficult to serve both traditional values and its new role of social reformer.

Shifting Academic Emphasis

The American university had changed not only in size and purpose but in substance. The explosion of information, of new knowledge, had prompted Clark Kerr's metaphor of scholarship as "the knowledge industry." The new university was, of course, producing much of that new information; it was also training the engineers, technicians, and scientists who would put that knowledge to practical use in industry and government. One aspect of the university—science and technology—was experiencing dramatic growth, while the rest was being carried in its wake. The university was becoming, more than ever, the port of entry into the professions. The social sciences could help train young people to serve the expanding bureaucracies of government and industry. A natural consequence of these developments was the growing pre-professionalism of the undergraduate curriculum.

As faculty members and administrators saw the university in the terms defined by Kerr, as undergraduate teaching by research-preoccupied specialists became more problematic, and as the general public increasingly came to see higher education as training for careers, the pressure to make the undergraduate curriculum efficient to those ends became even more compelling. That efficiency, however, came at the expense of the liberal arts tradition. Public institutions, most having land-grant origins, from the beginning had appealed to their legislatures for funds by citing their immediate contribution to agriculture, mining, and business. They had always found it easy to design undergraduate curricula that allowed students to avoid "useless" courses in the humanities. In the postwar period, however, even the prestigious private universities tolerated an erosion of the liberal arts core.

Kerr's utilitarian emphasis was echoed by most university administrators, most notably by James A. Perkins, president of Cornell.[5] By the end of the sixties, administrators and faculty were forced by both White and Black students to defend themselves against charges of complicity in the evils of society and nation. Their defense relied heavily on the university's traditional posture of detachment and disinterest. "Relevance," a word often used by Kerr and Perkins to distinguish the modern university from the "ivory tower," became a student clarion call. Black students wanted courses and programs "relevant to our Blackness," relevant to the lives of Blacks in the ghettos and in the rural South. They wanted to make the university useful in ending racism in America (as others wanted to make it useful in ending poverty and the war in Vietnam). They would begin by confronting and excising the evil at the institution's heart. By the end of the hubristic sixties, university administrators and faculty were more than willing to recognize limits to their usefulness.

It is important to understand, however, that the emphasis on utility and relevance had already struck discordant notes among faculties, notes discordant with traditional views of the college and its curriculum. Utilitarianism seemed merely to emphasize the increasingly secondary place of the humanities in the university. Physics, and later biology and chemistry, were experiencing marked growth. (In those fields, far more than in any of the humanities, public and private funds were available for research and development, and national reputations could be made.) As the university was increasingly seen as the place for the creation of new knowledge and new techniques, the humanities were seen as less and less central. Social scientists and even humanists would mimic the physical and natural sciences, focusing ever more on methodologies and narrowing themselves into smaller and smaller specialties.

One of the principal characteristics of the liberal arts had always been *inutility*. The college graduate, according to the traditional conception, was not supposed to be able, on the basis of his education, to do anything; his education was, rather; supposed to do something to him. While faculty arguments over general education requirements often sounded suspiciously like squabbles over course enrollment (i.e., budget), matters of principle were at stake. Defenders of the liberal arts tradition found something superior in education for its own sake. John Henry Newman, in his *Idea of the University Defined* (1873), had characterized "useful knowledge" as a "deal of trash." The very process of distancing oneself from private concerns, of transcending mundane matters to glimpse the universal, was itself, he and many others felt, educational. Time enough later to train to make a living; some part of the postsecondary years should be given to training for life.[6] In contrast, James Perkins imagined that much of what passed for general education would, in the future, be taught in secondary school, where he thought it belonged.[7]

Given the new democratic and utilitarian direction of the American university, a defense of the humanities in terms of their inutility seemed perverse. That the strongest proponents of the liberal arts were to be found in expensive private schools tended to confirm the elitism of the humanities. It was difficult, also, to shake the Veblenian assessment that the pursuit of the liberal arts was merely an example of the conspicuous display of wealth; who else but the rich could afford to spend four years in pursuit of an education having no practical end? Humanists also easily drew the charge of elitism because they tended to think of their work as having a *civilizing* influence, and because their work (particularly in literature, the fine arts, and music) called upon them to make judgments as to quality. Some works were better than others; some writers, artists, and musicians were better than others. Those artists and works of art not studied, discussed, and evaluated were, by implication, inferior.

In practice, the liberal arts curriculum reduced itself to courses concerned with not just civilization, but Western civilization. Sometimes emphasis was placed on the "disciplines," sometimes on interdisciplinary approaches to "great issues," sometimes on the "great books" approach. The object was always the same: Matthew Arnold's "acquainting our selves with the best that has been known and said in the world." Though the "world" of Matthew Arnold was small, it probably did include "acquaintance" with Islamic and Asian culture. Compared to Arnold's, the "world" of postwar American scholars in the humanities—products of university Ph.D programs—was Lilliputian. It certainly did not encompass Asia, Africa, and Latin America. Most American teachers in the humanities assumed our heritage (their students' as well as their own) to be the history and culture of the West. They could hardly imagine an American youngster of whatever ethnic background challenging that assumption.[8]

Most supporters of the liberal arts probably did not really believe that what they taught comprised the "world" or "civilization." Rather, they supposed certain concepts, ideals, principles, values, to be universal rather than particular to any people or culture. Those values were, nevertheless, accessible through certain texts and other cultural artifacts of a Western tradition, a tradition that could be studied as coherent and whole. *King Lear, Medea,* Machiavelli, Plato, Kant, Locke, Mill, Jefferson posed questions as relevant to a Chinese, a Malayan, a Ugandan, or a Nigerian as to an American of any ethnic background.

When, in the late sixties, Black students challenged the curriculum, their main target was the parochial character of the humanities as taught. They saw the humanities as exclusive rather than universal. They saw humanists as arrogant White men in self-congratulatory identification with a grand European culture. To those students, such arrogance justified the charge of "racism."

The woeful ignorance of most humanists about all cultures and traditions other than their own made it difficult for them to respond to the charge in a constructive way. Nothing in the training of American scholars in the humanities—scholars who were becoming more and more specialized even within the tradition they knew and accepted—prepared them for the challenge. Not surprisingly, their response was dogmatic: what they taught was the best that could be taught; it was what truly educated men and women needed to know; it trained (that is, disciplined) the mind; it was *our* heritage.

The same defense had been raised against the utilitarians in the university. It is important to understand that Black students were taking aim at the segment of the college that was already the most frequently attacked; theirs was merely the latest in a series of frontal assaults. To the embattled humanists, Black students arguing for courses "relevant to our Blackness" sounded much like engineering students demanding that they be exempted from courses not "relevant" to their professional training. Humanists thus saw themselves as holding the line against a new wave of Philistines. This time, however, the Philistines were poor and Black, and, when not denouncing their courses as worthless, a deal of trash, they were demanding both remedial courses to help them read and write and the redesign of admission standards to make college more accessible to inner-city Blacks with inadequate high school training.

The social science faculties were less central, but they, too, came under attack. Political scientists, sociologists, and economists had for some time been modeling themselves after the natural and physical scientists. Historical and "institutional" study had diminished in importance in these fields. Systems and model analysis had become dominant, and even theory had ceased to be broadly philosophical, becoming instead a matter of model definition and analysis. As positivists, social scientists tended to avoid a priori assumptions and value judgments; their mastery of sophisticated methodologies defined the objective condition of the subject under study, implying solutions.

Few social scientists took up questions having directly to do with Afro-American life and circumstances, and few courses offered could be said to have to do with Blacks. Events outside the university nevertheless spoke loudly to the fact that questions regarding race were at the heart of American social, political, and economic problems. When social scientists discussed Blacks at all, Black students found, they often did so in pathological terms, asking why Blacks had failed to move into the social mainstream more quickly. The most flagrant example was Daniel P. Moynihan's The Negro Family—the so-called Moynihan Report—which seemed to place the blame for continued poverty among Blacks on a dysfunctional Black family.[9]

Black students and scholars thus began to challenge the "objectivity" of mainstream social science. In most "scientific" discussions of "problems" a norm was assumed, that of the White middle class; the social scientist, himself, was at the center, defining all variation as deviation and "blaming the victim," as critics liked to say. The demand of Black students was for a discussion of what they saw to be the inherent racism in these normative assumptions and for a shift in perspective that would destigmatize Blacks and reexamine the "normalcy" of the White middle class.

Black students and their allies imagined that out of these demands—for the introduction of non-White subject matter into the curriculum and for the shift of normative perspective—would come a revolutionary transformation of the American university. It was a transformation that neither Clark Kerr nor James A. Perkins anticipated; but then they could not have predicted the course of the civil rights movement and its impact on the university.

The Black Student Movement

There are those who claim that the general unrest on college campuses in the sixties had roots in the movement of southern Black students to bring about reforms for racial justice. Whether or not that is true, the general social protests of that decade shared assumptions and tactics with the Black student movement: (1) the evils to be corrected were endemic to society and its institutions; (2) individuals who worked within society's institutions (within "the system") were, consciously or unconsciously, controlled by attitudes, conventions, and bureaucratic constraints that made reform either impossible or painfully slow ("freedom now" was the slogan); and (3) therefore, direct confrontation was necessary to bring Americans to see the urgency of radical change and to act.

The early tactics of such organizations as the Student Nonviolent Coordinating Committee (SNCC) and the Congress of Racial Equality were difficult to ignore. Young people putting their bodies and their lives in jeopardy for the cause of civil rights touched a central nerve of American idealism. The mass media brought their protests into every home, broadcasting to the world the ugly and persistent problem of racism in America. These students were agents of disorder; their nonviolence exposed the evil of their adversaries. The civil rights movement attracted Whites as well as Blacks from throughout the country, and much of its financial support came from northern White contributors.

The demand of Black students for reform on college campuses was in their view an extension of the civil rights movement, transported from the South to the North (where racism was less overt but just as pernicious) and onto predominantly White college campuses. By the mid-sixties, when the movement manifested itself on northern college campuses, its tactics and assumptions had changed in important ways. The northern Black students had come to question nonviolence. Change had been much too painful and slow, and achievements had been ambiguous. Most of the Black students were from northern cities and thus were far removed from the influence of Christian stoicism in the southern Black church. They attended the words of Malcolm X more than those of Martin Luther King, Jr., or of student nonviolent leaders. SNCC, itself, had changed by the middle of the decade. Its membership had come to question nonviolence as a tactic, resulting, by 1966, in a change of leaders from John Lewis to Stokely Carmichael. The change reflected the membership's growing militancy, their being tired of turning the other cheek, and a growing race-centered emphasis. Carmichael popularized the slogan "Black Power" and stressed the desire to place the movement in the hands of Blacks. The removing of Whites from leadership positions, the indifference to their presence and even their financial support, became the general attitude of Blacks throughout the organization. In February 1968 three South Carolina State students were killed by police in Orangeburg; they had been using nonviolent tactics to desegregate a bowling alley. In April 1968, Martin Luther King, Jr., was assassinated. These events, and the rapidly changing mood and character of the Black student movement, had more to do with the style and attitude of Black students in northern schools than did the specific actions (or inaction) of individual administrators or faculty members.[10]

By the early sixties, most administrators and faculty members at northern universities willingly extended their assumptions about the social role of the university and its democratizing principles to include Afro-Americans. Few questioned assertions of the historic and systemic nature of racism in America, doubted the need for the admission of Blacks to colleges and universities in order that they be incorporated into the American mainstream, or challenged the view of higher education as a principal instrument of upward mobility. Faced with the glaring inequities exposed by sit-ins and other protests, many, too, were willing to accept the necessity and efficacy of compensatory treatment of Blacks (that is, modification of admission standards and expansion of remediation programs).

Recent experience supported the notion that high motivation could compensate for a weak secondary education. Many G.I.s had proved that to be the case. The postwar experience of Blacks in predominantly White schools proved it also. While they had been few in number, the Blacks who went to northern schools in the forties and fifties had done well. Their dropout rate was much lower than the average, and their grade level was at least as high as their White peers. Those of that generation who responded to a survey generally described their college life as gratifying, often as the most important experience of their lives. They reported little racial antagonism or hostility, and they considered their treatment by administrators and professors to have been fair.[11]

One would have expected much the same from those Black students arriving in increasing numbers after 1967. College was a great opportunity being opened to this class of Americans for the first time.[12] But if faculty members and administrators expected these students to be grateful and appreciative for the opportunity, they were disappointed. Increased numbers—the recruitment effort itself—effected a change in attitude and expectation. Fairly or unfairly, many Black students attributed the institutions' efforts to increase their numbers to an attempt to assuage guilt for past and present racism. Many expressed themselves to the effect that their presence on campus benefited Whites and their institutions rather than the other way around; many detected an attitude of condescension in the efforts of White liberals to uplift ghetto youth. Furthermore, as Black students on a campus achieved a "critical mass," racial problems that might previously have been accepted as matters of private adjustment could be dealt with collectively. Larger numbers made another difference: Black students saw Whites—students, faculty, and community—as being threatened by their numbers, by their very lifestyle. It was a time, after all, of open and symbolic displays of militancy. Hair styles, clothing, language, name changes all conspired to challenge and intimidate. The White response to Black student demands was too often shocked and fearful uncertainty, which did little but increase the anxiety felt by Blacks. Thus, one detects a similar cycle in every situation where there were confrontations by Black students: alienation expressed in terms of racial grievance, followed by ever more strident demands, answered by fearful and uncertain response, in turn provoking greater anxiety and alienation.

Between 1965 and 1970, Black undergraduates became increasingly militant. Events outside the university had much to do with it, but it also seemed that each new freshman class was more militant than the one before, especially as students were increasingly drawn from the inner city. It is also the nature of student life always to be changing in leadership; each year, seniors with the wisdom of experience are lost at the top and replaced at the bottom by persons who have never before dealt with a complex bureaucracy. Perversely, however, it was the underclassmen who, in the sixties, challenged the leadership of seniors, demanding of them greater militancy.[13]

Crisis of Establishment

Between 1966 and 1970, most American colleges and universities added to their curricula courses on Afro-American life and history, and most made efforts to include Blacks on their faculties and administrative staffs. The fact that schools like Macalester, Bowdoin, Colby, Reed, Dartmouth, and Carleton (to pick just a few names), which were relatively free of pressure, joined the rush argues that there was something more to explain it than the threat of students disrupting academic life. Like all other aspects of the movements for peace and civil rights, the demand for university reform by Black students was national in its impact as well as local in particular manifestations. In some sense, the urge for change was everywhere; whether or not a campus had militant Black students making demands, the urge for reform was in the air.

I suggest three motives, independent of immediate student pressure, that compelled college administrators and faculty to join the march for change. First, there was, particularly among liberal-minded academics, a genuine sense of American higher education's complicity in the social inequities resulting from racism-indifference to Black undergraduate enrollment, insensibility to non-White subject matter in the curriculum, and the discouragement of Black scholars. Second, it had become fashionable to bring Blacks onto staffs and faculties, just as it had earlier become fashionable to recruit "hardcore, inner-city kids" for admission. The sense of competition among institutions should not be discounted; the legitimate purpose of the act too often was joined by the wish to do at least as well as comparable institutions. Third, in their effort to attract the "best" applicants from a generation of teenagers noted for their social consciousness, college administrators felt it important to look reasonably open to change, to appear to be progressive without compromising integrity. A course or two on Black history or culture could achieve that end.

The great majority of institutions added courses pertinent to Afro-Americans and, as a direct result or not, experienced little or no student disruption; most changes involved merely a course or two and could hardly be called a program in Black Studies. Yet, from 1966, student disorders were increasingly common, and no college or university could be indifferent to, or uninfluenced by, events at San Francisco State, Cornell, Harvard, Wesleyan, and so on. It was widely assumed that disruptions of the sort that had occurred at those institutions could be avoided, if at all, only by swift and significant reform.

With the spurt of Black enrollment in 1966, students and administrators began a process of negotiation aimed at correcting the problems perceived by Black students. One problem was that many Black students felt themselves to be educationally disadvantaged compared to their White peers; they wanted remedial programs that would compensate for their poor high schools (poor because White society made them so) and poor study habits. Problems also arose because of a deep sense of alienation from the institutions and their goals. This alienation was often expressed by defining schools as "White," as a part of a "White, racist system." Blacks' success and achievement within these institutions could come only if they "Whitewashed their minds" and alienated themselves from "their people" and "their community." In this view, while college may have been a necessary route to upward mobility, success within the college would be purchased through the denial of one's "Blackness" and through co-optation by the system. This was the Black version of the widespread (and, among many young Americans, the rampant) alienation from mainstream, conventional, middle-class America. For Black undergraduates, the solution to this dilemma was an assertion of Blackness: beauty, culture, community, etc. The newly developing Black student associations, therefore, pressed to make the college environment congenial and hospitable to what they described as Black values and culture. They wanted student activities for Black students, Black cultural centers. Sometimes they asked for separate dormitories (or Black floors or sections of dormitories); they established Black tables in dining halls and treated White students with the same hostility and contempt they assumed Whites had for them. They almost always pressed for the appointment of Black faculty and for the introduction of courses "relevant to us as Black people."

Black student leaders found some sympathetic ears among faculty members, administrators, and White students, but their demands also created hostility among the same groups. To some, the demand for remediation only supported the belief that standards were being lowered to admit Black students who were bound either to fail or to undermine the quality of education. The new Black assertiveness could only antagonize those who held to the ideal of integration and of a color-blind system of merit. Black students were, in their view, racists who merely wanted to turn an evil on its head. Antagonism over these issues set the tone for the debate over Black Studies when it became a central issue, and it also affected the reception of these programs when they were established by the end of the decade.

For the most part, negotiations went quietly. Colleges like Bowdoin, Carleton, Macalester, and Dartmouth, removed from crosscurrents of student radicalism, were able to move at their own pace to increase Black enrollment, appoint Black faculty and staff, and introduce a few courses on topics of interest to Afro-Americans.[14] In some conspicuous instances, however (Cornell, San Francisco State, Wesleyan), the students armed themselves, and the threat of riot and violence was quite real. At other institutions, calls for Black Studies courses and programs merely added to a general atmosphere of conflict and upheaval. To the most vociferous activists, Afro-American academic programs were likely to be of incidental or secondary importance; what they were really interested in was not an academic but a political revolution.

San Francisco State University

On September 29, 1968, the trustees of the California State College System voted 85 to 5 to fire one G. M. Murray from his post as an untenured lecturer at San Francisco State College. Murray, a member of the Black Panthers, had been hired as part of an attempt to increase Black faculty; he had been teaching courses that were, according to Murray, "related to revolution." The firing set in motion a series of shocks to the campus, including student strikes, violence from civilians and police, the closing of the school, and the final enforcement of order under the newly appointed president, S. I. Hayakawa.

The institution came as close to anarchy as one could possibly imagine, with college faculty and students, the mayor and citizens of San Francisco, Governor Ronald Reagan, and President Hayakawa engaged in strategies alternating between charges, threats, demands, the use of violence, naked power, and, from time to time, efforts at arbitration. Lines were firmly drawn, and few were willing to negotiate. In time, backed by Governor Reagan, Hayakawa succeeded in reopening the school much on his own terms.

Black Studies, as an issue, was one element (but by no means the most important) in the dispute. On December 7, 1968, the Black Student Union rejected Hayakawa's offer to establish a Black Studies department under the direction of Dr. Nathan Hare. The Black Student Union wanted a program with more "autonomy" than Hayakawa would permit, and there were elements in the union's demands suggesting a racially separatist model. Conflict between Blacks and Hayakawa continued for nearly two years. On March 1, 1969, Hare announced that he had received a letter from Hayakawa stating that he would not be rehired in June. In June, four of the college's six Black administrators resigned, charging Hayakawa with racism. On November 2, 1969, Hayakawa accused the Black Studies department of a "reign of terror" and threatened to disband it, claiming that it was both authoritarian and anarchistic. By Christmas 1969, he had again threatened to close it and to put worthy courses under other departments. The bickering continued until March 3, 1970, when the entire Black Studies faculty was ousted because the department's hiring, retention, and tenure committee reports were turned in only an hour before the deadline.[15]

Cornell University

The first evidence of serious racial discord at Cornell came as early as January 1968, when a Black student successfully challenged the validity of a psychiatric examination that had been administered by a White person. In April of that year, Black students protested the "covert racism" of a visiting professor of economics, Michael McPhelin. Getting no results from the economics department or the dean, the students disrupted McPhelin's class by reading a statement. This brought about a judicial action against the students, protests of the resulting punishments, and, finally, the occupation by a hundred Black students of the student union building. The occupation of Willard Straight Hall occurred in April 1969, a full year after the initial event. In the course of this occupation, the students armed themselves and made a series of demands, placing the negotiations with the faculty and administration in an atmosphere of imminent violence. The occupation ended as the students, armed with rifles, shotguns, and belts of ammunition over their shoulders, marched out of the building.

These were the most public and most notorious events; the struggle to establish a Black Studies program was going on simultaneously, as if it were a separate and independent matter. On September 15, 1968, the university agreed to establish an Afro-American studies program with a budget of $250,000 a year, and announced a search for notable Black scholars to staff it. In early December, however, students from the Afro-American society met with the acting director of the program and insisted that the program be turned over to Black students. Within a week they demanded that Afro-American studies be established as an autonomous all-Black college.

President Perkins reaffirmed his support for an Afro-American studies program but rejected the idea of an all Black college. The faculty-student committee appointed James Turner, a graduate student, as director. In time, Turner was able to convince the faculty and administration that a separatist Black-studies program made sense. By mid-May 1969, in the wake of the most potentially explosive racial conflicts ever on a northern campus, Cornell acquiesced. While the program was neither autonomous nor all-Black, it was one of the most separatist and most political in the country.

University of California, Berkeley

By the spring of 1969, the University of California at Berkeley had been shaken by a series of student protests, few having to do with minority issues. Yet increased numbers of minority students, and their heightened consciousness of special needs, brought pressure on the university to reform its curriculum and increase minority faculty. These demands (in a context of broad student demand for reform) resulted in the creation that spring of a department of ethnic studies, which was divided into Afro-American, Chicano, contemporary Asian, and Native American studies divisions. The student instigators of this reform, behaving in keeping with the alienation they felt, insisted that the department remain outside the College of Letters and

Sciences. In effect, they wanted to be a separate college, dealing on budgetary and other matters directly with the chancellor. They were especially concerned that the traditional disciplines (that is, the university faculty) should have no say about course content or faculty appointments.

Each division within the Department of Ethnic Studies developed differently. Native American studies has remained quite small. Chicano and contemporary Asian studies, while larger, has never developed a strong academic emphasis; the latter, in fact, has concentrated on "community outreach" rather than scholarly programs. The department's history has been marked by internal conflict among its divisions and, in its relations with the university, by conflicts over budget and autonomy. In all of the department's divisions, student participation in policy and management was assumed to be necessary. The Afro-American studies faculty, after some tumultuous years marked by internecine fighting (in 1969, faculty and students came armed to meetings) and an undefined academic program, left the ethnic studies department in 1974 and joined the College of Letters and Sciences.

In 1972, the university forced a change in the leadership of Afro-American studies by replacing its nontenured director with William M. Banks, a psychologist who was appointed with tenure. It was through Banks's leadership (despite student boycotts of Afro-American studies courses) that Afro-American studies elected in 1974 to join the College of Letters and Sciences as a normal university department. It has since become one of the stronger departments of its kind in the country, with several notable tenured faculty. It has been aided in this by the fact that some other departments at the university (notably, history) have long been offering courses on aspects of Afro-American life.[16]

Yale University

By all accounts, the Afro-American studies program at Yale is the strongest and most respected in the country. It has been a healthy program from the beginning, and that fact has much to do with the way it came into being: intelligent and wise leadership from faculty, students, and administration and a genuine spirit of cooperation among them. From the fall of 1967, the

Black Student Alliance at Yale had been working, without much success, to convince the college of the need for courses in Afro-American history and culture. Early in the spring of 1968, they decided to sponsor a conference that would draw nationally upon White and Black intellectuals having something to say about the subject. One of the student organizers, Armstead Robinson, has written: "We viewed this symposium as an opportunity to create an atmosphere in which those persons who were in pivotal positions . . . could engage in active and open intellectual exchanges on questions related to Afro-American studies."[17]

Supported by funds from the Ford Foundation, this symposium to educate the educators brought together a wide spectrum of opinion (all favorable to some form of Afro-American studies). Some, like Nathan Hare and the "cultural nationalist" Maulana Ron Karenga (of UCLA), were deeply anti intellectual and hostile to the academy. These were offset by such self-conscious intellectuals and committed academics as Martin Kilson, Harold Cruse, and Boniface Obichere. The result was a provocative conference that gave the Yale community a chance to compare several differing concepts of Black Studies and to identify the one that might work best at Yale.

The development of the Yale program was helped most by the constructive attitude of the university's senior faculty and the deft leadership of its administration, out of which a program emerged that was an integral part of the life of the institution. Several of the major departments (including history, English, and anthropology) supplied faculty and courses to the program, and the administration allocated the funds to make that possible. Such a program required trust and respect by all parties. Whatever the reasons that Yale had those qualities, they were hard to come by at other institutions. The result is that others have had to suffer painful periods of adjustment to get to the point at which Yale was able to start. After more than a decade, some are just now getting there.

Harvard University

Harvard's program might have gone the way of Yale's except for bad timing, bad luck, and perhaps excessive distrust on the part of some of those concerned. Like Yale, Harvard began working on the problem in the spring of

1968. The historian Frank Friedel had organized a successful course on the Afro-American experience.[18] A student-faculty committee under the chairmanship of Henry Rosovsky[19] was organized to report on a wide range of issues related to Afro-American student life and needs at Harvard. The committee made its report to the faculty in January 1969, recommending a program in Afro-American studies (one similar to that later adopted by Yale), increased graduate fellowships for Black students, and a variety of measures to enhance Black student life on campus. The student members of the Rosovsky committee were unable to win for the report the general approval of Harvard's Black students. Nevertheless, the report was adopted by the faculty in February and a committee was established to implement it.

In just two months, however, everything had changed. On April 9, in a totally unrelated matter, student members of Students for a Democratic Society (SDS) and the Progressive Labor Party occupied University Hall demanding the banning of ROTC from the Harvard campus, the university's active commitment to ending the war in Vietnam, and amnesty for certain students who were under disciplinary terms from a previous demonstration. (In all, there were nine "non-negotiable demands," most without lasting significance.) The protesters at University Hall were mainly White students and the "sit-in" had nothing to do with Black Studies, but the dramatic outcome of this demonstration was to radically change the context in which discussion of all reforms was to take place. It was a new ball game.

The police were called to force the eviction of the demonstrators and a general strike by students followed. The faculty met in the ensuing weeks to deal with a range of issues flowing from those student protests. There was justifiable concern among administrators, faculty, and students that the university could be shut down or forced to operate under a state of siege.

The leadership of the Association of African and Afro-American Students, becoming more militant (or more emboldened by the crisis atmosphere), presented the faculty with new demands framed as a thinly veiled ultimatum. They wanted Afro-American studies to be a department on its own and not a program, and they wanted a student voice in the selection and appointment of its faculty. On April 22, the faculty were asked to vote on these propositions without altering them. Although deeply divided, and despite the forceful opposition of Henry Rosovsky, Martin Kilson, and others, the faculty voted for the changes the students demanded. It was a bitter decision, as were many the faculty made in the days following. One could hardly expect an Afro-American studies department, thus created, to have the warm support from administration and faculty that the Yale program enjoyed.[20]

Wesleyan University

Until 1967, the number of Black undergraduates at Wesleyan had been negligible. After that year, the numbers grew significantly. The change in racial composition resulted in serious and disturbing friction between White and Black students in the fall and winter of 1969. In December 1969, the Ujamaa Society (the Black student group) had to be restrained by court order from disrupting campus student events that the Black students considered "White" and thus unrelated to the needs of Black students. At Wesleyan, as at Cornell, the threat of violence was real. To meet the demands of Ujamaa, Malcolm X House was established as a Black cultural center and as a center for Afro-American studies. As we shall see, the program that emerged was confused in academic purpose.

Few academic institutions in the country had experiences as dramatic as Cornell's or Wesleyan's, but all with sizable numbers of Black undergraduates faced similar demands for reform. Keeping peace on campus was everywhere a principal concern of faculty and administrators. Black students everywhere were making similar demands. These included: (1) increased recruitment of Black students; (2) increased financial aid and special support for remedial needs; (3) an increased number of Black faculty and advisers; (4) courses "relevant" to Black and/or Third World peoples; (5) a Black Studies program (or department); (6) a Black or Third World cultural center; (7) course credit or a program for community work. All of these items did not have the same weight everywhere, and institutions responded to them variously. It is important to recognize, however, that Black Studies was only one item in a package. It was not always the most important item to students, and it was not always feasible to implement.

The most difficult problem for all northern institutions was to find qualified (or even marginally qualified) Black scholars. In 1970, a Ford

Foundation survey revealed that less than 1 percent of Americans with doctorates were Black, and that most of that 1 percent were more than fifty-five years old.[21] The sudden demand for Black scholars increased anxiety among educators concerned about the future of southern Black institutions. The fear was that northern schools would "raid" traditionally Black colleges for the Black academics who, for racial reasons, would hardly have been considered for membership in White departments before the 1960s.[22] Northern institutions would find it difficult to discover Black candidates for faculty appointment, but they could and did funnel money to the support of Black students, add Black faculty or staff where they could, offer new courses in Afro-American history and literature, swallow liberal instincts by accepting de facto separate facilities under the guise of Black culture, and put together what might be called a program in Afro-American (or African-American) studies. All of this in response to Black student demands.

It is hard to know how much Black students wanted Afro-American studies as a field for possible academic concentration. Doubtless much of their demand arose from their desire to shake the complacency of their institutions. In that sense, Black Studies was symbolic; its presence was more important than its substance. But it was also a field of legitimate scholarly inquiry, as Black scholars have been saying for more than a century. Black Studies, as fact and symbol, would continue to create tension among Black scholars and student reformers because some Black scholars wanted their scholarship to be taken seriously and were as likely to be put off by anti-intellectualism and hostility to academic work as were their White peers. We should consider more closely some of the reasons advanced for the establishment of these programs.

Assumptions of Reform

In most institutions, Black Studies was part of a larger package of reforms insisted on by Black students and their supporters among the reform-minded faculty and students. The demands for reform began with a general malaise among all students and particularly among Blacks; I would suggest that the remedies they seized on were "in the air" rather than derived from specific needs in particular circumstances. I am persuaded in this by the near-uniformity of the demands nationally and by the adamantly collective character of the protest; there was little if any individual refinement or qualification. It is therefore hard to judge the significance of Black Studies to any particular campus. As we will see, there were many different expectations as to what Black Studies should be. It is worth reviewing some of the assumptions behind the demands. For the sake of clarity, I will discuss three distinct expectations, although they were generally confounded.

"To Have Something That Is Ours"

In striking contrast to the reported experience of Black undergraduates in predominantly White schools in the fifties, Blacks in college in the sixties felt racially alienated and isolated. It might seem that, because the earlier group was so small in number, its members should have felt isolated, but generally they reported fitting in. They differed also in that their admission to college was untainted by suspicions that it was attributable to special standards or compensatory policy. They were highly motivated to succeed in mainstream, middle-class America. They were likely to see their presence, success, and achievement in a White college as a sign of racial progress and thus uplifting. If they had a sense of alienation from Whites or from the Black community, they did not make their feelings public.[23]

Ironically, as the numbers of Black students increased in the late sixties, the students increasingly reported that they were alienated and isolated from the rest of the campus. That, undoubtedly, had to do with a number of factors: (1) a large number of students were drawn from socioeconomic circumstances where the conventional academic expectations and values were weak or lacking; (2) the lowering of admissions standards to increase the number of Black, inner-city youth enrolled was publicly acknowledged, encouraging those so admitted to regard themselves—and to be regarded—as second-class enrollees; (3) many Black students were, in fact, poorly prepared for college, lacking adequate academic preparation, discipline, study habits, or all three; (4) many found college work not only difficult but uninteresting and irrelevant to their lives as Black people; (5) many felt that the ultimate end of success in college would be adaptation to the values of conventional White America, and thus a placing of distance between themselves and other Black people; (6) their larger numbers, rather than making them feel more at home, gave them a collective sense of malaise and made it easy to divide the world into Black and White; (7) greater numbers also meant peer-group pressure on those who otherwise might have adapted easily to join in the general malaise; (8) the institution in all its aspects—courses, student activities, facilities—could easily be divided into "theirs" and "ours."

Black students could call little of what normally existed at predominantly White institutions "ours." Much of the emotional energy of Black student protest was aimed at forcing faculties and administrations (generally liberal and integrationist in values) to accept race differences in ways that guaranteed Blacks a sense of "turf" while refraining from any racial distinctions suggestive of racism. While the student demands might have begun as requests for programs and activities "relevant to Black people," with no implication of being exclusionary, they almost always evolved into de facto Black dormitories, cultural centers, programs, etc. The few curious Whites who ventured in were soon made to feel hostility against them and their alienation. Demands for Black "turf" generally resulted in separatism. Students at San Francisco State (1968), U.C. Berkeley (1968), Cornell (1968–1969), Wesleyan (1970), and Barnard (1970) were, in fact, explicit in their demand for racially separate programs or facilities.

Little wonder that in such an atmosphere demands were heard for "courses relevant to us as Black people." The standard curriculum's indifference to the special problems, concerns, and basic humanity of Afro-Americans and other non-Europeans seemed glaring. Socrates, Plato, Aquinas, Goethe, Kant, Hegel, Milton, Shakespeare, Donne, Eliot, Dylan Thomas, were all theirs, and they celebrated them. "Who are we?" Black students asked. "What is ours?"

It was generally assumed that those questions could best be answered by courses on the African and Afro-American experience: on Black history, literature, music, and "culture." For some, the informational content of such courses was paramount. For others, course content was less important than the mere presence of such courses in the catalog. Students in the former group were likely to be more concerned with the quality of instruction than with the color of the instructors. Students in the latter group were likely to insist that only Blacks were qualified to teach such courses; some even demanded all Black classes or sections.[24] Carrying such thinking to its logical end, some demanded complete academic "autonomy"; a separate college (as was called for at Berkeley, San Francisco State, and Cornell) or a separate department (as was called for at Harvard). The indifference to course content and preoccupation with symbolism rather than substance of those in the latter group caused many Black Studies programs to be ridiculed and eventually abandoned by Black students as well as White.[25]

Quest for Identity

Many Black students on White campuses regarded the college experience as a threat to their sense of ethnic identity, and thus to their sense of personal identity.[26] Ironically, it was the very liberalization taking place in society—residential desegregation, greater prospects of upward mobility—that created the problem. In the past, Blacks had all been pretty much in the same boat regardless of class and education. Now, Black prospects included admission to a good college, a position—if only "token"—in corporate America, entry into the mainstream middle class, a move "out of the ghetto" and into the suburbs, and acceptance by conventional White America. Such "upward mobility," though attractive to many Black students and increasingly common, was repugnant to others, who claimed that it cut Black people off from the vast majority of their brothers and sisters and from their ethnic and cultural roots. The best way to guarantee one's personal identity, it seemed to many Blacks, was to assert one's ethnic identity. The university could be transformed from a potential threat to identity into an instrumentality through which to find a new wholeness—an instrumentality potentially more effective than church, family, and community.

For those Black students, references in reading assignments or lectures that tended to enhance Blacks' sense of identity and self-worth seemed few and far between. In the liberal arts, Blacks (and practically all other non-Whites) scarcely existed. In American history, Blacks were viewed as slaves or as problems, rarely as contributing anything of value, or even as being central, to the American experience. Black authors were seldom included in courses in American literature; such Black characters as occurred in "White" fiction, like Twain's Nigger Jim and Faulkner's Dilsey, often raised difficult questions about Black identity. Social science, with its pose of objectivity, was perhaps most painful of all to Black students, who complained that Blacks were viewed by most sociologists, economists, and political scientists as deviants from a norm arbitrarily defined by White social scientists.

The solution, as many Blacks saw it, was courses in African history and civilization, Afro-American history, Afro-American literature, Afro-American "culture," or Afro-American contributions to American "culture." But most White faculty members knew next to nothing about those topics, and were inclined, not surprisingly, to regard what they did not know about—what none of their colleagues ever talked or wrote about—as being of little or no importance. Few scholars were sympathetic, most were condescending, and some were actively hostile to the suggestion that the Black experience in any of its manifestations was worthy of study. Many were heard to comment that the very idea of Black economics, Black sociology, or Black literature was ludicrous. All of which is to say that the problem implicit in the student complaint—the blind ethnocentrism of American higher education—was for the most part ignored.

A major obstacle for those who wanted courses for identity building was that this was not what most scholars understood their function to be. Courses in history explicitly intended to identify and venerate heroes and heroines, to celebrate a people's "contribution"; to make students feel good about themselves did not command the respect of good scholars. History had a different—a critical and analytical—role to play. Of what good was a literature course taught and attended by people so in awe of the mere existence of certain works that there was little room for criticism and textual analysis? Most teachers were likely to say "You can read anytime; courses are to make you think in a disciplined way." The onus was on Afro-American studies to prove that it did just that.

Students in search of their ethnic and personal identity did not automatically seek separatist solutions, although the hostility or indifference of faculty members tended to move them in that direction. These students generally believed that there was no intrinsic reason to deny Afro-American studies recognition as a bona fide academic discipline. They felt that the major obstacle to Afro-American studies was faculty members who did not take it seriously. The real problem, however, was the students' uncritical acceptance of courses that celebrated the Afro-American past and their hostility to faculty (Black more so than White) who insisted on a critical analysis that showed heroes and heroines to be merely human.[27]

A Field of Study

Apart from the need to define an academic turf in a sea of Eurocentric Whiteness, and beyond the psychological rationale arguing that courses in history and literature and culture would lead to a healthy discovery of "self," there was the claim that the African/Afro-American experience and culture provided subject matter of legitimate academic study in its own right. The African Diaspora, the Black presence in the Western Hemisphere and particularly in the United States, provided, it was argued, a historical reality worthy of study for its own sake as well as for its value in understanding conventional history. Afro-American writers had left a literature, there was an Afro-American musical heritage, and there was folklore, none of which had received adequate academic attention. Courses should be offered in Afro-American studies to fill a gap in scholarship and to spur scholarly interest in a neglected field.

By the sixties, actual scholarship in what was to be called Afro-American studies had a considerable history. The names of W. E. B. Du Bois, Carter G. Woodson, and Arthur Schomburg, whose works date back to the first decade of the twentieth century, are well enough known to illustrate this point. There were others like them whose names are not so well known. Aside from their personal scholarship, they joined with others in support of such scholarly organizations as the American Negro Academy (1897–1915) and Woodson's Association for the Study of Negro Life and History, which was established in 1916 and which is now called the Association for the Study of Afro-American Life and History.

This early generation established a tradition of careful and conventional scholarship. Their work, however, was largely unacknowledged by professional historians. Except for a small group of Blacks (academics in southern schools and amateurs) and a smaller number of Whites, there was little interest in Afro-American life and history. By the fifties one might have identified a subfield of American history called "Negro history," but that was something taught almost exclusively in Black schools. Less could be said for Afro-American literature. Articles on Negro history could not be found in the two major historical journals—*The American Historical Review* and the *Mississippi Valley Historical Review*—unless they could pass as "southern history." As a consequence, the *Journal of Negro History* (Carter Woodson's creation) had its pick of the very best scholarly work being done.

The White scholarly establishment was not hospitable. There was a predisposition among historians, for instance, to believe that Blacks could not be objective about their history, especially since their interpretations were likely to run counter to conventional wisdom.[28] The onus was on the Black scholar to prove himself or herself unbiased; ideally such scholars would produce scholarship that disguised the fact that the authors were Black. Only Whites could be presumed unbiased. In the effort to gain professional respectability, Black scholars were likely to try to make themselves color-blind in their work.

Despite efforts at conformity, such scholars as Du Bois, Woodson, Rayford Logan, and Benjamin Quarles were aware of the entrenched racism in their profession. They were of a "progressive" generation, however, and imagined that reason and demonstrated quality would in time be recognized. Meanwhile, something should be done to educate Afro-American young people to understand and appreciate their past, to see themselves not only through the eyes of White American scholars whose interpretations of slavery, Reconstruction, and the historical oppression of Blacks were by no means disinterested. That was much of the reason behind the establishment of the American Negro Academy and the Association for the Study of Negro Life and History, that is, the creation and dissemination of a useable past for Black Americans. Carter Woodson railed against what he called "the miseducation of the Negro": arguing that conventional schooling in America (the North as well as the South) brainwashed Blacks into a belief in the superiority of Whites and in Blacks' lack of history or culture. To correct that, one needed scholarship. Du Bois, too, came to argue the special responsibility of southern Black colleges to support such scholarship for the purpose of teaching Black youth who, otherwise, would be mis-educated.[29] All of these men, however, called for the soundest scholarship.

In the sixties, the few Black Ph.D.s were likely to echo these beliefs. They were prepared to support Afro-American history courses, willing to advocate their scholarly importance, but insistent on professional standards of scholarship. In the last regard they differed with student advocates of such programs. This older generation of scholars tended also to be distrustful of (or ambivalent about) the students' efforts to politicize the program, to make an academic program the instrument of ideology. They preferred to see such courses taught within conventional departments for two reasons: (1) the department would give a legitimacy and stability to something new to the institution; and (2) such courses would be a foothold, a beginning, in the reform of the scholarly profession. As we will see, these expectations ran counter to what students and some of their faculty allies wanted.

I have written here mainly of historians, in part because they were asked to play a major role in Afro-American studies. (To the extent that there was a field, it depended on them.) Sociology, perhaps, had the largest number of Black scholars interested in the Afro-American. Race relations had, from the 1890s, been a recognized academic field, one in which both White and Black scholars had built reputations. Beginning with the work of Robert Park, the University of Chicago had been a center of this study, supporting such scholars as Eric Reuter, E. Franklin Frazier, Horace Cayton, and St. Clair Drake. Black sociologists like Charles S. Johnson, Ira De A. Reid, Frazier, Cayton, and Drake had built national reputations. But sociology as a field was not ready to supply leadership to Afro-American studies.

In the first place, most of the old scholarship (whether by Blacks or Whites) seemed to view its Black subjects pathologically, with Whites as the exemplary norm. Furthermore, the field of sociology was beginning to splinter. The newer, positivistic, quantifying scholarship was becoming predominant in the field (as it was in other social sciences), and such qualitative and relatively subjective topics as race relations were receiving less respect. The profession began to split over methodology and, as the sixties advanced, it split racially as well. Black sociologists created separate caucuses to establish an independent direction and to criticize what they began to refer to as "White sociology."[30] The deep racial and ideological divisions within sociology were perhaps best illustrated by the rancor and division generated by the so-called Moynihan Report.

It is important to observe that the Black sociologists who took the lead as advocates of Afro-American studies were likely to be at the radical edge in this split. Both Nathan Hare and Harry Edwards were deeply cynical about, and distrustful of, institutions and traditional academic fields. Their tendency was to be anti-intellectual and anti-"Establishment." Edwards saw the Black student movement as providing the "impetus for violent and irreversible revolution in America." And he saw the object of Black leadership and Black Studies as being to "fight the mainstream to establish Black authenticity and to achieve full equality or be overwhelmed in the attempt."[31] It should be said, however, that St. Clair Drake, a senior and respected scholar, early took on the direction of Afro-American studies at Stanford and made it one of the best programs in the country.

The humanities (excluding history) were always the most Eurocentric of American scholarly fields. English literature, philosophy, art history, and music were, in the sixties, the fields least touched by subject matter having to do with Black Americans. Of these fields, literature, music, and the fine arts had the least excuse; American literature was a field where Blacks had played a role. It was a rare college course in a northern school that taught any Black author—until Ralph Ellison and James Baldwin became fashionable. There were, however, a number of senior Black scholars in American literature: J. Saunders Redding, Blyden Jackson, Charles Davis, George Kent, to name a few. Most taught in southern Black colleges. Professionally, the modem languages are so factionalized that it was almost natural for scholars of Black literature to become merely another faction within the professional ranks. As activity in the subject developed, room was made for them, as it would be made, for example, for Chicano literature. Very little room would be made, however, in the canon of American literature or in the mainstream curriculum.

Those who wanted Afro-American studies to be recognized as an academic discipline generally held that it should emphasize three existing academic fields: history, literature, and sociology—especially history.[32] Once one confronted the problem of getting scholars to take Afro-American studies seriously, one also had the task of explaining how such disparate fields could be brought together in it. Those who took the matter most seriously were the most uncomfortable with the character of student demands. As scholar-teachers, they saw their object as being the development of a teaching field that would remain academically respectable to their peers, and they saw as the primary object of any course the giving of an academic competence to students. Those aims could be hostile to demands for a program as a quest for power or personal (racial) identity. These conflicts would plague the supporters of Afro-American studies throughout the seventies.

Three basic concerns lay behind the demand for Afro-American studies—the political need for turf and place, the psychological need for identity, and the academic need for recognition. While they might be discussed as separate questions for the sake of convenience, they were really inseparable. Individuals could be driven by more than one of these needs. As long as matters remained at the reform stage, implicit differences could be ignored. When it came time to build and define programs, compatibility among the various agents of reform became strained. Scholars who once found the "student constituent" useful in establishing the urgency of the program might well find that student views of an academic program did not comport well with their own. Students who had hoped to find psychological and emotional support in new courses might find them both academically difficult and emotionally troubling. Once the programs were in place—the need for "turf" having been achieved—Black students might not even take the courses, or might act as though taking them were a political statement rather than an academic choice. Furthermore, there came in the mid-seventies a generation of students—both Black and White—who were highly career-oriented. Courses that existed largely to make rhetorical and political statements had little appeal to students whose main concern was admission to a professional school. By 1975, the decade of ideology was over.

Patterns of Ideology

The Black student movement, in sharp contrast to the White, was virtually indifferent to Marxist ideology. Doctrinal disputes within the American Left over Marxism had been intense since World War I, and what conflict there was within the White-student left can be seen as a continuation of the tradition.

Most Blacks, if asked, would have defined themselves as sympathetic to the Marxian interpretation of social change (that is, to the view that racial oppression was the result of an exploitative economic system) and to the view that racial justice would most likely be achieved under some form of socialism, but few were committed to an ideological faction. (Angela Davis, of course, had been an exception.) They would have said, rather, that their unity in Blackness transcended political factionalism.

They divided themselves roughly into two camps: integrationists and separatists. This division had to do not so much with desired goals for a future society as with a predisposition to work with Whites in conventional institutions or to focus on self-development among Blacks. The one was not necessarily anti-Black, nor the other necessarily anti-White; they had, rather, to do with efficacy and the relative importance one placed on racial identification. The separatists, also, could be divided into "Black Power" advocates and cultural nationalists.

Integrationists

Few in this group defended American colleges' and universities' past or present policies with regard to race. Few denied the need for courses having to do with Afro-Americans. Hardly any found White faculty and administrators faultless in their attitudes and feelings about race. Integrationists, however, insisted that Blacks had to succeed in terms of these imperfect institutions and people, the better to function in the even less perfect world outside. Nothing could be gained, save the comforts of self-indulgence, by defining oneself outside the system. Black students and their faculty allies, the integrationists felt, made a serious mistake in demanding an "autonomy" that would only result in the creation of an academic ghetto, providing an excuse for Whites to dismiss Blacks as irrelevant or to treat them with patronizing condescension.

The institution, the integrationists felt, was important to Blacks for the skills training it offered—skills Blacks had been denied. It was important also for the experience it offered Blacks in management—the management of White peers and of an institutional bureaucracy as complicated and sophisticated as that of a university. Finally, the institution was a certifying agency whose graduates were assumed to possess intelligence, competence, and discipline, qualities essential to professional training and employment. To the integrationist, separating oneself from the institution or undermining it was self-defeating. Not only must one work through the institution, but one should protect its academic integrity while getting it to adopt Afro-American programs. Any victory would be hollow if its "spoils" were debased in the process of being won. Integrationists, therefore, were seen as defenders of the university and were often attacked by student radicals as having been co-opted.

Of course, integrationists were hostile to student demands for separate facilities. They preferred to see Black Studies courses offered in the standard curriculum, in conventional departments; perhaps, like other interdisciplinary programs, administered by a committee made up of faculty from the several departments involved. They were suspicious that an argument for "autonomy" was really a plea for racially separate (and Black-controlled) programs. While they might concede that Blacks, because of special experience, would bring a unique and necessary perspective to courses in Black Studies, they rejected the idea that such courses should be taught only by Blacks and could not be well taught by Whites. While they advocated the increased hiring of Black faculty (whether or not they supported affirmative action programs), they did not want to see Black faculty strictly tied to Black Studies, or affirmative action goals met by the packing of Blacks into Black Studies programs. They were likely to urge White faculty to teach courses in the program.

Integrationists were the least troubled by alienation from the Black community as they did not see success in the university and professional life as a rejection of Black people. They were, as a result, unlikely to support demands for "community programs" except in such service roles as tutoring in the schools or churches. And they were ambivalent in their relations with Black student groups. The integrationist Black student preferred to be independent (to have White as well as Black friends, for instance), but in the sixties and seventies that role was difficult.

Separatists—"Black Power"

The "Black Power" rhetoric of Stokely Carmichael in 1966 signaled an ideological shift among Blacks generally and the student movement in particular. The new position argued that Blacks, by conforming to the demands of White institutions, White liberals, and even White allies and supporters, were allowing values and strategies to be defined by White people, the most well-meaning of whom were ignorant of, or indifferent to, genuine Black needs. More important, Whites were hostile to the thought of power being in the hands of Black people. They would give Blacks everything except what they needed: power and the self-respect that comes with it. By making alliances with Whites—by allowing them to define issues, strategies, and goals—Blacks were denying themselves the responsibilities of leadership and community building. Furthermore, Blacks in these alliances were being co-opted and removed from their real source of strength, their natural constituency: Black people. Finally, White allies would abandon Blacks whenever it served their interest to do so.

The "Black Power" argument was, therefore, one of self-reliance. It was separatist because it saw community building and race consciousness as essential first steps in the achievement of a program. Black people had to become self-reliant economically and politically before they could bring genuine power into play; without power they would always be dependent. Once they had power, however, coalitions with Whites and others would not only be possible and desirable but effective. In this sense, then, theirs was not an absolutist, separatist strategy. It was more of a tactic intended to lead to a more fruitful interracial cooperation.

The demands for "autonomous" Black Studies programs must be seen in light of this "Black Power" ideology. At bottom, autonomy was a question of power. Would the university give to Blacks (students included) the power imagined to exist in a department or college? In some ways, the answer to this question was more important to those making the demand than was the substance of the program or the efficacy of such "autonomous" agencies in achieving academic objectives. "Black Power" also informed the demand for Black dormitories, student centers, and the like. Community building implied the coming together of Black people on and off campus as a community. In this regard, it is important to observe that these students were unknown to one another before coming to college and were often from places that, at best, were disintegrating communities. They were the more anxious, therefore, to tie themselves to the local Black community as a defense against the perceived co-opting pressures of the institution.

On the positive side, "Black Power" proponents claimed that Blacks had the ability and the obligation to create their own world on their own terms (just as Whites had done). On the negative side, "Black Power" was an attitude deliberately inhospitable to Whites. One wanted Blacks on the faculty, of course, but especially to teach courses in Afro-American studies. Black faculty would have a perspective different from Whites. More important, the appointment of Black faculty and the control of the Afro-American studies program by Blacks would be a delivery of power into Black hands. Some argued that Whites had nothing of value to say about Blacks and that the program should be controlled by Blacks without interference from White faculty and administration.

Some programs—notably at the University of Illinois at Chicago Circle and at Cornell—kept a strong "Black Power" orientation. Since the decline of interest in Black Studies in the mid-seventies, supporters have seldom talked of autonomy, turning, rather, to guarantees of continued university support. Most of those that started with separatist notions either expired or moderated their positions.

Separatism—Cultural Nationalism

This aspect of separatist ideology was of slight real influence on college campuses but should be mentioned to distinguish it from that of "Black

Power." "Black Power" advocates believed it possible to negotiate with and otherwise relate to Whites on the basis of power; cultural nationalists like Maulana Ron Karenga of UCLA did not. Like the "Black Power" advocates, Karenga placed great emphasis on community building among Blacks, but he went further in assuming two nations and two cultures—one White and one Black. Even while attached to the university Karenga was deeply antagonistic to it, especially to its efforts to be helpful to Black people. His model was a colonial one: Blacks, as he saw it, were emerging from colonial status into nationhood. The university's proper role, he maintained, was (1) "nonintervention" in the Black community, with no efforts to influence it or shape it; (2) separation—as an institution of the former colonizing power, the university should deliver financial and technical aid but only as Black people demanded it; and (3) the creation of a movement to civilize White people. While such notions were not central to Black student thought, they did inform some of the rhetoric.[33] As we shall see, such ideological presuppositions defined the form as well as the style the new programs took.

Typical Models

The models on which Afro-American studies programs were built were influenced by ideology and conditions on individual campuses. Naturally, each particular form had intrinsic strengths and weaknesses.

The Program

From an academic point of view, the "program" approach has been the most successful. It acknowledges the interdisciplinary character of Afro-American studies by using faculty from established departments. It relies on the president and the dean to guarantee the program through budget allocations to the departments involved. While a faculty member's appointment may be principally to offer courses and service to Afro-American studies, his or her membership remains within the department of discipline. By definition, all senior faculty in a program are jointly appointed to a department and to the program. Because of this structure, it is relatively easy for the program to exploit the curricula of other departments; it is not necessary for the program to provide all of the courses its students are expected to take.

Most Afro-American studies offerings in the country follow the program model. A good example is the Yale program. Its success had much to do with the willingness of student advocates to accept this plan rather than insist on "autonomy." It has been noted for the broad range of faculty involvement. Names like Sidney Mintz, Charles Davis, Robert Thompson, and John Blassingame have been associated with it. Davis, until his recent death, served as director; his place has been taken by Blassingame. Young scholars of remarkably high quality have been in the program—especially in literature. Names like Robert Stepto, Henry Gates, and Houston Baker come to mind. Apparently from the beginning, association with the program has been judged with approval in academic circles. The Yale program is one of the few in the country offering a graduate program leading to a master's degree.

The strengths of this model are obvious, but principally they reside in its capacity to engage a wide range of departments and faculty in the service of Afro-American studies. This, of course, would not have been a strength to those of markedly separatist persuasion. Its major weakness, as those who argued for autonomy predicted, is its dependence for survival on the continued support and goodwill of others in the university: the president, dean, and the heads of cooperating departments, among others. Yale's program has not been troubled in this regard, but other programs have, especially when enrollments drop or when there is disagreement about standards or goals.

Programs like Yale's are designed to offer undergraduates a major (or field of concentration) for their degree. Not all programs do. Some merely offer a few courses with a focus on subject matter having to do with Afro-American life. Such courses may be accepted for credit by the student's major department (for example, economics) or may serve merely as an elective. Wesleyan, for instance, until recently had a complicated system in which an Afro-American studies major was possible but in which students found it difficult to put the necessary courses together; they thus majored elsewhere and took the one or two Afro-American studies courses as electives. (The

Wesleyan program has undergone changes designed to strengthen and improve it.) The program at the University of Rhode Island is also of interest in this regard. It offers special courses: one, for example, on free-enterprise zones, and another on human resources. Such courses are designed to serve students interested in working in the community or in Third World countries. These courses do not lead to a degree in Afro-American studies, but they serve students in special programs such as a master's program in international development.

The College

The most radical kind of Afro-American studies program was that of the independent college—sometimes an all-Black college—within the university. That was the demand at San Francisco State and at Cornell. The ethnic studies department at Berkeley, existing outside the College of Arts and Sciences, had for a while something of a de facto college status. Afro-American studies, however, defected and became a standing department in Arts and Sciences in 1974. No other major university came close to acceding to this extreme demand.

Local community colleges sometimes became de facto all-Black colleges. That was surely the case with Malcolm X College in Chicago. It is a community college, supported by public funds, but located in an area almost wholly Black. Formerly Crane Junior College, it became Malcolm X in 1968 when it moved to its present location. Its student population is about 80 percent Black, 8 percent Hispanic, and 12 percent other. While it offers a range of Black-oriented courses, it specializes in computer sciences and health services. Whether or not it was planned to be so, circumstance permits it to be the kind of college the separatists demanded. It is difficult to know how many other such community colleges there are.

The Department

The more practical model for those who insisted on autonomy was the department. A department had its own budget, could appoint and dismiss its own faculty and staff, design its own curriculum, and service its student concentrators without any control or oversight by others. It was also assumed to be a more permanent structure than a program. Some institutions established Afro-American studies departments without much ado. In others, like Harvard, departmental status remained a bone of contention years after it was established. The more it was resisted, of course, the more it appeared to be worth fighting for and defending.

The argument against it was mainly that a department normally represented a discipline. Afro-American studies, being interdisciplinary in character, should, critics said, be organized into a program made up of faculty from the various departments serving it. Its defenders most often claimed it was a discipline defined by its particular perspective on a topic none of the other departments offered. In these terms the argument was tendentious. As defined by the nineteenth-century German university, departments were identical with academic disciplines. By 1969, however, that had ceased to be true of American university departments. Interdisciplinary departments had developed within the sciences, and occasionally area studies were departmentally organized. On the other hand, a perspective, which was what Afro-American studies offered, could hardly be thought of as a discipline. Whatever it once was, a department is now largely an administrative convenience. Afro-American studies departments have worked reasonably well in some institutions, Berkeley and the University of Indiana being examples. It did not work well at Harvard, and its problems illuminate some of the weaknesses of the model.

Departmental autonomy, it turns out, is not as absolute as some believed. Such autonomy as exists carries problems. Under a program, the president and dean can, in effect, direct departments to make searches and appoint competent faculty approved by the program's committee. The department has the power and budget to make recommendations for appointment, but, lacking other arrangements, it must find scholars willing to take positions in Afro-American studies alone. In practice, most senior scholars with major reputations insist on joint appointments with the departments of their discipline. So, most often, an Afro-American studies department's appointment is contingent on another department's approval of its candidate. Such arrangements presuppose goodwill and respect among the departments involved. In such ways, autonomy can work against the department's efforts. Furthermore, even when university budgets were more ample, it was impossible for an Afro-American studies department to provide faculty in all of the disciplines thought useful to it. As a result, they are forced to depend on a very limited program (history and literature) or rely on other departments' offerings.

Whatever the expectation of those who struggled to create departments rather than programs, joint appointments are the general rule throughout the country. Sometimes this resulted from administrative fiat, sometimes out of necessity. Ewart Guinier, the first chairman of Harvard's department, had no joint appointment himself and attempted to make the question of departmental autonomy and integrity rest on the power to promote a junior person to tenure from within. The president and the dean, responding to university-wide criticism of the department's program and standards, in 1974 made promotion from within the Afro-American studies department conditional upon joint appointment. Guinier failed in his effort to force this issue in his favor. This case illustrates another important limit to departmental autonomy. Appointment and tenure matters must be concurred in by university-wide and ad hoc committees (in Harvard's case these committees are made up of outside scholars appointed by the dean), and, finally, only the president makes appointments.

The practice of joint appointments is a good thing when it works well. It dispels suspicion about the quality of a department's faculty, especially necessary in a new field in which standards and reputation are in question. Furthermore, it gives Afro-American studies a voice and an advocate within the conventional departments, which is quite useful for communication and goodwill. In this regard, the practice achieves some of the good features of programs. Whether imposed by the administration or adopted as a matter of convenience, however, joint appointments may be the cause of problems and friction. A candidate may fail to win tenure in the second department, its faculty claiming a failure to meet their standards. Since questions of standards are seldom easy to resolve, these decisions are likely to cause antagonism and ill will. Joint appointments also raise questions of service, loyalty, and commitment of faculty to Afro-American studies. Once appointed, a faculty member may find it more congenial working in the field of his discipline; if he is tenured, little can be done. From the faculty member's point of view, moreover, joint appointments can pose problems. It is time-consuming to be a good citizen in two departments. Junior faculty, particularly, are likely to feel themselves to be serving two masters, each having its own expectations.

Graduate Programs

Few Black Studies departments or programs offer work toward a graduate degree. Yale, as has been noted, offers an M.A. in Afro-American studies, which seems to attract student teachers and those who expect to be able to use knowledge thus acquired in community or public service work. The University of Rhode Island offers courses that supplement other master's programs in, for example, human resources and international development. UCLA has a graduate and postdoctoral program and provides no formal undergraduate offering.

The small number of graduate programs is not difficult to understand. Graduate programs in the humanities and social sciences have been shrinking everywhere; some have ceased to exist. Student interest has shifted from academic careers to law, medicine, and business. Furthermore, those who wish to follow scholarly careers are better off working in conventional departments; in universities where they exist, such study could be directed by scholars of Afro-American life. One advantage of this arrangement is that it can help to stimulate scholarship about Afro-Americans in conventional disciplines. In general, however, Afro-American studies faculty lack the advantages that come from having graduate students.

The Undergraduate Center

Sometimes, when there is neither a department nor a program of Afro-American studies, there will be a center, as, for example, the Center for Afro-American Studies at Wesleyan. Such centers have little or no academic program. Mainly, they provide such services to undergraduates as counseling and career guidance. (As at Wesleyan, those services are also available elsewhere in the institution for all students, Blacks included.) These centers sponsor programs of interest to Black students, are a focal point for extracurricular activities, and are, in effect, Black student unions. The existence of such centers reflects the continued sense of exclusion among some Black students from such general student activities as campus newspaper, dramatics, and literary magazines, the sense that the typical campus lecture or program has little to say to them and that they must maintain "turf" that is clearly theirs. In places where student-community programs exist, these centers often serve to coordinate them. If Wesleyan is the rule, the existence of such centers is likely to result in a weak academic program and student indifference to that weakness.[34]

The Research Center or Institute

Institutes have long been a means to encourage and support advanced scholarship in the social sciences and, to a lesser degree, in the humanities. While some are unattached to a university, most major universities have been eager to house such centers because they are a source of prestige and serve as inducements to the best and most productive scholars, who, by means of the institute, can pursue advanced studies among colleagues of kindred interests and talents while sheltered to some extent from teaching obligations. Since examples of successful institutes abound, it is little wonder that persons interested in Afro-American studies would attempt their own. The results have been mixed, at best.[35]

Columbia University, with funds from the Ford Foundation, established the Urban Center in 1968–69. Because none of the funds were invested as endowment, and because the university interpreted the terms of the grant as permitting their use for related projects and programs, the Urban Center had either to seek other funding or to expire when the Ford money ran out. Its first director, Franklyn Williams, served only a short time before taking a position at the Phelps-Stokes Fund. The bulk of the original grant went for staff salaries and university overhead. Except for some community-related programs that were federally funded, the Urban Center did very little. Nothing of an academic or scholarly character was developed in the center, and few of the university's faculty were involved. The funds ran out in 1977, and the center was allowed to expire.

The Institute of the Black World (IBW) was established in Atlanta in 1969. It was originally intended to be part of the Martin Luther King, Jr., Memorial Center and to work in cooperation with the Atlanta University Graduate Center, but in the summer of 1970, for ideological and other reasons, IBW split with the King Center and Atlanta University. The King Center came to focus almost entirely on King's literary and ideological legacy, and its leadership was far more integrationist in its approach than the leadership of the IBW.

From the beginning the IBW attracted many of the most capable among those who followed the "Black Power" mode. Vincent Harding, William Strickland, Howard Dodson, Lerone Bennett, St. Clair Drake, and Sylvia Wynter were among its original board of directors. Claiming to be a "gathering of Black scholar/activists," it remained consistently intellectual and serious in scholarly intent.[36]

IBW's funding came from a variety of sources. In 1969–70, perhaps its most promising year, it received grants from Wesleyan University, the Ford Foundation, the Cummins Engine Foundation, and the Southern Education Foundation. The level of funding was far lower over the next decade, yet the institute managed to generate position papers from scholars and others that were generally of good quality and provocative. In 1983, with its staff much reduced and its principal office now in Washington, D.C., IBW, it is fair to say, has ceased to function as a center for scholarly research. It is now seeking funds for a major film that will provide a Black perspective on American history.

The W. E. B. Du Bois Institute for Afro-American Studies was established at Harvard in 1975 by President Derek Bok. Seen perhaps as a corrective to Harvard's highly political, radical, and contentious Afro-American studies department, the Du Bois Institute was designed for advanced study of Afro-American life, history, and culture. During its first five years, led by a series of "acting directors," the institute supported lectures and other programs, but mainly offered predoctoral fellowships to four or five advanced graduate students a year. The object of the predoctoral program was to identify promising graduate students and to support them through the successful completion of their dissertations. Funding for that program (from the Henry R. Luce Foundation) ran out in 1981. Funds for the balance of the institute's program were provided by the university.

In the past three years, the institute has sponsored major art exhibits, lectures, and concerts. With funds from the Ford Foundation, it has inaugurated an annual lecture series and, since 1983–84, it has supported in residence two senior scholars a year. It has appointed four postdoctoral research fellows each year since 1980–81. Proposals are now being designed for multiyear research projects on criminal justice, economics and public policy, public health, and education. The intention is that the Du Bois Institute will generate major research projects on questions and problems related to Afro-American life and experience, sustaining a broad range of scholarship.

The Carter G. Woodson Institute for Afro-American and African Studies was established by the University of Virginia in 1981 with a mandate to encourage research and teaching in all the geographic components of the Black experience: the African, Afro-Latin, Afro-Caribbean, and Afro-American. Funded by the Ford Foundation, the institute supervises the university's undergraduate Afro-American and African Studies Program; sponsors colloquia, lectures, and conferences; and others both pre- and postdoctoral fellowships in the humanities and social sciences for research and writing in Black Studies.

At UCLA, the Afro-American Studies Program is a quasi-institute in form. It supports research by graduate students and postdoctoral scholars. This program offers no instructional courses.

The research institute seems the most attractive and useful instrument to develop serious scholarship in this field. So far, none have succeeded in establishing themselves. There are several reasons: (1) there are too few high-quality scholars in the field to support several competing centers; (2) ideology has tended to dominate some, weakening their appeal to some of the best scholars; (3) lack of capital funding has forced them all to rely on funds generated year by year and on the generosity of a host institution. Furthermore, most university-based institutions can rely on university faculty to generate their own funds, which then can be funneled through the appropriate institute. Scholarship on Afro-American topics is in no university general enough to offer much help in this way. Afro-American institutes' directors and program officers must both generate their own programs and discover the scholars to do the work.

Varieties of Curriculum

A continuing debate rages as to whether Afro-American studies is a legitimate discipline. Many in the Black Studies movement have taken this question very seriously and have attempted to define the discipline in a core curriculum. The National Council for Black Studies, in a 1981 report, defined the purpose and rationale of such a program: (1) to provide skills; (2) to provide a standard and purposefully direct student choice; (3) to achieve "liberation of the Black community"; (4) to enhance self-awareness and esteem. Black Studies, the report says, "inaugurates an unflinching attack on institutional oppression/racism." It also aims to question "the adequacy, objectivity and universal scope of other schools of thought; it assumes a critical posture."[37]

The National Council apparently understood discipline to mean doctrine, for it goes on to outline in detail a course of study that would cover the four undergraduate years. It would begin in the African past and end in the American present, touching on the non-Black world only to show racism and its oppressive consequences. If students following this program were to take courses in the sciences, or acquire any of the specific analytical skills associated with the social sciences, they would have to take them as electives. There have been other efforts to design a core curriculum in Afro-American studies, for example, at the University of Illinois-Chicago Circle. Such efforts are notable for their attempt to create an undergraduate curriculum totally independent of other departments and offerings.

Limited budgets and the interdisciplinary nature of most Afro-American studies programs make it impossible to staff such a program as the National

Council recommends. For the most part, existing programs stress Afro-American history and culture. That stands to reason, because the great teaching opportunities have been in this area. Afro-American history and literature are fairly well-developed fields, and there has been a notable Black production in music and the arts. It has been harder to create good courses in the social sciences (or to appoint good scholars, for that matter). That is because, except for sociology, none of the social sciences have taken subject matter and problems related to Black Americans to be of such importance in their disciplines as to constitute a specialization. Few economists or political scientists are willing to define themselves as specialists on Afro-American questions.

The recent shift in student interests to business and law, and the universal interest (especially among funding sources) in public policy is pushing Afro-American studies programs to emphasize the social sciences more than they have. I suspect, also, that the growing preoccupation among social scientists with public policy will push them into more questions having to do with Blacks, and they may find it to their advantage to be associated with an Afro-American studies department. Courses on the economics of discrimination, urban politics, social mobility, and the like are logical offerings in an Afro-American studies department.

A word should be said about typical courses in the humanities. Except for those in literature, the tendency of Afro-American programs is to offer courses in the performing arts rather than their scholarly counterparts. Art courses are seldom art history; music is taught rather than musicology and music history; and there are courses in dance. This is important to note because it varies from the traditional liberal arts relegation of performing arts to extracurricular activities.

Afro-American studies programs remain tailored to available talent and other institutional resources. For the most part, they are based on some combination of history and literature with enough additional courses to fill out an undergraduate major. Many closely resemble such interdisciplinary programs as American studies. In practice, however, few students choose to major in Afro-American studies, preferring to select Afro-American studies courses as electives or, when possible, as course credit toward a conventional major in, for example, history. At the University of Illinois at

Urbana/Champaign, for instance, the majority of course offerings in Afro-American subjects are in other departments, with Afro-American studies acting as a service department. Harvard has attempted in the past four years to design an undergraduate concentration similar to other interdisciplinary programs in the college, namely history and literature and social studies. Beginning with a base in Afro-American history and literature, the student is directed through tutorials and selected courses toward achieving an academic competence in more than one discipline. Harvard also permits joint concentrations in the college, so it becomes possible for students to link Afro-American studies with one of the other departments. This has become a popular option. At Harvard, as elsewhere, the current preprofessional emphasis among undergraduates makes many wary of a major which they think might jeopardize admission to a professional schools.[38]

After the initial demand for Afro-American studies courses, there followed a rather sharp decline in interest. The peak years were 1968 through 1970. By 1974, there was general concern that these programs would become extinct for lack of enrollment. The reasons for the decline in student interest were many: (1) students, both Black and White, increasingly turned from political to career concerns; (2) the atmosphere in many courses was hostile and antagonistic to White students; (3) many of the courses lacked substance and academic rigor; and (4) campus communities had been exhausted by the rhetoric, bombast, and revolutionary ideology that still permeated many of these courses and programs. The White guilt many Black activists had relied on had been spent.[39] Born, as these programs were, out of campus crises, in an era of highly charged rhetoric, unconditional demands, and cries for revolution, it was difficult for them to shake that style and reputation.

Institutional Context

The programs that survived naturally reflected the circumstances in which they were created. In the short run, colleges like Yale and Stanford, where programs were adopted in relative calm, seem to be among the soundest and most stable. Furthermore, those that opted for programs—avoiding faculty

conflict over departmental status—have tended to enjoy the easiest relationship in their academic communities. For the others, the legacy of conflict and bickering about status and legitimacy have continued to be
troublesome. Evaluations and judgments about every program must therefore be made in the context of its particular college and history. At schools
like Berkeley, Cornell, Columbia, and Harvard, the events of 1968 through
1970 deeply divided the faculty; bitterness stemming from those divisions
remains, though muted and controlled. Issues and problems related to Afro-
American studies continue to provoke emotional rather than reasoned responses. In most places, however, the programs are accepted as "here to
stay," so both hostility and anxiety tend to be more latent than overt.[40]

The history of the efforts to establish Afro-American studies makes us
aware of how deeply conservative faculties are. Change is usually very slow
in academic institutions, and most conflict is resolved by consensus. In this
sense, Afro-American studies was a shock to the system. In the past, new departments (biochemistry, for instance) were created only after years of development within established disciplines; the production of scholarship
and fresh knowledge was antecedent to, and justification for, the new department. Even so, there was friction and dissent. It was many years before
English departments acknowledged the importance of American literature,
and many advocates of the establishment of American studies programs (or
departments) have failed to overcome resistance to what some see as their
novelty. Little wonder that Afro-American studies had a chilly reception.
Many scholars—some out of ignorance and bigotry, others out of healthy
skepticism—wondered whether there was enough there to make a field of
study. Many have yet to be convinced. Those scholars of Afro-American life,
history, and culture who are careless of and indifferent to the opinions of
Whites and Blacks outside their fields will not convince many skeptics. Others, however, are successfully influencing the scholarly community. Most
often, they are based in the more viable Afro-American studies programs
and, to my mind, constitute the strongest argument for such programs.

With falling enrollments and the budget crunch, there has been considerable anxiety that Afro-American programs will lose support within
the university. Anxiety has been increased by the fact that most such pro-

grams were, in some sense, created in response to the political demands of a constituency that, since the mid-seventies, has largely ceased to exist. Many Black students abandoned these courses because they lacked academic substance. Criticism previously ignored was taken seriously, and the most egregious courses and behavior were excised.

Student enrollments leveled off after 1974. They will probably never again approach the level of 1970, but they seem, at the moment, to be low (in most places) or modest, but stable.[41] Despite the fears (or hopes) that they would be allowed to die, few programs have done so. The fact that they have remained part of the academic landscape is likely to encourage more constructive relationships with other parts of the university. For political as well as demographic reasons, most state institutions are not likely to discontinue support, even in the face of serious budget constraints. The University of Michigan has been forced to eliminate some departments. Geography has been forced out, but Afro-American studies has not been touched so far. The fact is that some departments and programs—those at Berkeley, Harvard, and Wesleyan, for example—are becoming stronger in program and in character of enrollment.[42]

Even with the passing of generations of students, some of the problems that provoked unrest among Black students in the sixties persist. The conservative national trends reflected in White student attitudes are making some Black students feel even more isolated than before. The former liberal consensus is no longer present to lend support and encouragement to Blacks in their struggle for racial justice. Some White faculty and students may be openly hostile to programs like affirmative action and to admissions policies that give preference to Blacks and other minorities. Some may challenge their right to take the place of those assumed to have superior records.[43] In recent years there have been racial incidents involving the denigration of Blacks at schools like Wesleyan, the University of Cincinnati, the University of California at Santa Barbara, and Dartmouth. Blacks are more likely to experience racial hostility now than they were a decade ago. These trends are offset by fifteen years of a sizable Black presence in northern colleges; Blacks are more likely to be taken in stride, and less likely to be made to feel exotic.

Many of the problems Black students complained of then and now are hard to distinguish from the kinds of complaints all students make. The college years are a difficult time of transition for young people. Separation from home and family, acceptance of adult responsibilities, the formation of new friendships and the loss of old ones, the challenging of one's loyalties to family, class, and community, are problems everyone faces in these years. In the more prestigious colleges, individuals who had always been at the top in their classes in high school may suddenly find that they are unremarkable, even mediocre, in the new setting. These problems, common as they are, have a special impact on Black students, who may view them as a "Black experience in a White institution" and seek to interpret as a collective condition what are basically individual and personal problems. As a result, many Black students continue to seek "identity" in courses about Black people, try to establish or maintain Black centers such as Wesleyan's Malcolm X House, and work to effect community outreach programs in the local Black community. Insofar as they insist that Afro-American studies programs be the instrumentalities to achieve these ends, those programs will be weakened in their academic purpose and reputation.[44]

One of the principal arguments against the establishment of Afro-American studies was the claim that such programs would have the effect of "ghettoizing" both the field and Black academics. By establishing such departments, it was said, the traditional departments would be absolved of responsibility for that subject matter. They could remain as lily-White in attitude and faculty as they had always been, now with the assurance that whatever there was to the subject could be taught in Afro-American studies. It was also feared that the challenge of affirmative action could be met simply in the staffing of such departments. In the context of separatist and "Black Power" ideology, these fears were the more compelling. The argument was that, ironically, Black Studies would prevent the broad study of Afro-American life and history in the standard curriculum and offer a way off the hook for faculties and departments reluctant to meet affirmative action criteria.

It is impossible to know with certainty how this problem has been met. It is clear that in colleges following the program model, faculty and courses serving the program are based in departments. This, as I have pointed out, is one of the strengths of that model. Elsewhere it is unclear.

The question, it seems to me, is not whether English departments offer courses in Afro-American literature, but whether works by Black authors are taught in courses on American literature. A similar question can be asked of other departments—political science, economics, history, and so forth: do those faculties feel a lesser need to include within their courses matter pertaining to the Afro-American experience because Black Studies programs exist? I do not know the answer to that question, but my impression is that American history has gone farther in developing Afro-American subject matter than other fields and has been the most affected by recent scholarship. The discussion of Black authors in standard English courses remains rare. Except for Ralph Ellison (and sometimes Richard Wright and James Baldwin), Black authors are largely ignored. Afro-American literature is taken by most White scholars to be a subfield and taught only by those who specialize in it. It is fair to say, however, that there is a much wider knowledge about a few Black authors now than fifteen years ago. While this does not answer the question, it suggests that conventional departments have not leapt into the field; they have been slow and grudging. Yet it cannot be proven that without Afro-American studies they would have done better. The need for integration of this subject matter into mainstream courses is great and should be one of the principal tasks in the years ahead.

Afro-American Studies and Affirmative Action

I have suggested a tendency to confound Afro-American studies with affirmative action. This is partly owing to the tendency of early reformers to combine them in their package of demands. They called for Black Studies programs and for more Black faculty, sometimes, as we have seen, insisting that only Blacks should teach Black Studies. Black candidates who are eligible for academic positions are very few in all fields. Their scarcity has resulted in resentments: one has to offer more to get them (earlier tenure, higher salaries, etc.), departments are burdened by affirmative action procedures adding to departmental administrative chores, departments have a feeling of undue pressure from those administrators who take affirmative action guidelines seriously.

These attitudes affect Afro-American studies programs in giving the general impression that the only Black faculty available are in Afro-American studies. I have found, especially among social scientists, a tendency to believe that the only persons willing (and able) to teach Afro-American studies are Black. Some fail to acknowledge the potential relevance of their own courses to the field.

Problems of Black Scholars

Black scholars, scarce enough in the past, will be even scarcer in the coming years, it seems. They have been in great demand, but they are likely to be ambivalent about membership in Black Studies departments. Their reputations as scholars will have to be made in their scholarly discipline, and they are likely to have to explain to their colleagues their role in such a department. The tumultuous and politicized past of these departments makes it the more difficult and problematic to accept an appointment. An Afro-American studies department has to be strong (or promising) and well located to attract the very best Black scholars.

Black faculty complain that they are burdened by work and responsibilities not normally asked of Whites. Generally, they are a small minority on any campus (often there are only one or two Blacks on a faculty), and Black students bring to them all their problems with the institution. Thus, they take on the burden of counseling, negotiating with officials, and peace-keeping. School officials push these burdens on them by placing them on a great number of committees, and calling on them to advise on crises having to do with Black students or the local Black community. Young faculty get confused signals from the institution: they are seemingly praised and respected for being good and helpful citizens, but promotion and career advancement will depend on scholarship and publications. These are conflicting activities, and Black scholars often complain that they do not receive adequate support for research and writing. Undoubtedly they have been partly to blame. Being supportive of Black students can be appealing, as can the role of peace-keeper. A sharper and more single-minded commitment to scholarship would help them avoid these traps. But these are not easy choices, especially for the young. In any case, many young Black scholars fail to produce much in their early years. And the quality of their scholarship is often disappointing. Frequently, they fail to get tenure and are drawn into administrative positions—if they remain in the academic world at all.

One unfortunate consequence of Black Studies to Afro-American scholars is that it encourages young scholars to train themselves too narrowly. They become Afro-American historians with little sense of American history—not to mention that of Europe, Africa, or Asia. The same can be said of some Black literature scholars.

Student Problems

Afro-American studies presents Black students with the special problem of having to sort out the academic, political, and personal significance of this course of study. It can present students with deep conflicts. Departments and programs, as they define themselves, may encourage one or the other of two tendencies: those that become distinctively academic in character will discourage and alienate students searching for identity or desiring to make political statements. Those that serve psychological and political needs will not attract the career-oriented or scholarly student. It will take time for academic programs to establish their natural constituency. That will come, however, as those students interested in careers that address public issues discover that Black Studies courses are important to their professional training.

A more immediate question for students has to do with how a major in Afro-American studies will affect their chances for admission into graduate and professional schools. Many students and their advisers suspect that admissions committees will not respect an Afro-American studies undergraduate major, but little evidence exists to support that. A good student from a good school will do well regardless of undergraduate major. Graduate training in academic disciplines, however, does require an adequate background in the field the student wishes to follow. With proper foresight, that expectation can easily be met.

One must continue to ask whether particular Afro-American studies programs provide students with a sufficiently broad education and train them to an adequate level of academic competence in a combination of disciplines. Competency in reading and writing is hardly enough to justify a college education. One hopes that students would be helped to develop skills in critical analysis and encouraged in their respect for the intellect their own as well as others'. Obviously, the critical pose assumed in the National Council for Black Studies' dictum—that it "questions the adequacy, objectivity, and universal scope of other schools of thought"—is adequate. One would hope that such programs in Afro-American studies would submit their own programs, pedagogy, and assumptions to as harsh a critical gaze as they level at those of others. The time is past when questions about the rightness or wrongness of Afro-American studies are constructive. Afro-American studies exists and has established itself well enough to continue to exist. Accepting that, it is important to require it to meet standards comparable to those of any other undergraduate major. It should produce students with specific knowledge, and the skills to make use of it, but at the same time a broad enough view of the world and of human experience to place their special knowledge in a meaningful context. It is my impression that very few Afro-American studies programs do this well. There is nothing about the subject matter of the field, or its focus, that makes these criteria impossible.

Conclusion

American higher education has changed dramatically in recent years. A college education is now available to a much broader portion of the socioeconomic spectrum than in years past. The university's role in producing useful knowledge and useful people and in preparing the way for social reform is now universally acknowledged. The fragmentation of scholarly fields into narrower specialties has accelerated, undermining the assumed coherence of broadly conceptual fields like the humanities. The rationale and efficacy of the traditional liberal arts core in undergraduate education have been called increasingly into question. This transformation—now of nearly four decades' duration—continues, and Afro-American studies will necessarily be affected as the American university continues to adapt to changing social, political, economic, and academic conditions and circumstances.

The postwar assumption that the university is an agent of democratic change and an instrument of social reform is now well established and is not likely to be reversed. Demographic changes—specifically those resulting from the ebbing of the tide of applicants produced by the coming-of-age of the postwar "baby boom" generation—are already having effects on college admissions policies, which will in turn have significant consequences on the social mix of future college classes. Many private colleges, competing for their share of shrinking numbers of applicants, are beginning to question (and to modify) the principle of "need-based" financial aid. High tuitions and other college costs have made the greatest impact on middle-class parents and students, and some college administrators have been tempted to shift scholarship funds to merit-based criteria so as to attract the most gifted student applicants. This shift has not been entirely unwelcome to Black students and their parents. The great majority of Black students now attending private institutions are considered "middle-class," but often only because both parents work full-time to make ends meet. Need-based financial aid formulas place a heavy burden on many parents and force students into considerable debt for their college education. Some among them would benefit from scholarships based on achievement rather than on need.

In any case, rising college costs, reduced federal and state assistance, and smaller numbers of students will make a difference in the number of Black students in college, in the socioeconomic background of those who attend, and in the attitude of those students toward their education and the institutions they choose. In the next decade, many Black students who might once have attended private colleges will choose state and city institutions instead; many will settle for community or other two-year colleges; many others will be unable to go to college at all. The result is already being felt in all colleges and universities: the return of de facto middle-class higher education. For many scholars and administrators, especially those with unpleasant memories of the tumultuous sixties and seventies, this will be a welcome development.

The earlier crises have passed. Administrators, faculty, and students no longer hear or make demands comparable to those of the 1960s and 1970s. There have been costs, however, particularly to the traditional concept of the liberal arts. The extraordinarily high costs of higher education (especially in the private institutions) have provoked parental and student demands for a clear and immediate payoff. As a result, many colleges have drifted into a preprofessionalism that undermines the traditional concept of general and liberal education. Black parents and students, no less than White, now search for the most direct route to the professional schools. Students may want to study the fine arts, philosophy, music, or literature, but they are quick to give them up in favor of what they think is "good for them" professionally, economics, political science, biology, and so forth. In this sense, Afro-American studies is just one more field perceived by many undergraduates as being of marginal utility. The assumption is, in fact, faulty: most professional schools are indifferent to a student's undergraduate field of concentration; in most instances, a major in Afro-American studies has been considered an asset by admissions officers. But combined parental pressure, personal ambivalence, and overly cautious academic advising tend to push students into the conventional and well-worn paths.

There will, of course, be those students who see their professional careers (in law, government, business, or medicine) as being enriched by a knowledge about Blacks in America, and there will be those who follow their tastes and intellectual interests despite the trends. With the political motive no longer compelling, it will be from among this minority of Black and White undergraduates that Afro-American studies will draw its students and its future scholars. And programs and departments of Afro-American studies will become more attractive as they bring the most sophisticated methodologies of the social sciences to bear on contemporary Black issues and as they enliven discourse in the humanities by the broadening of perspective.

In small Afro-American studies departments and programs, high quality of faculty and teaching will be even more essential to success than it is in larger departments and programs. Great care must be given—more than in conventional and larger departments—to faculty appointments and questions of promotion and tenure. Needless to say, even one tenured professor who is mediocre or worse can seriously damage or even kill a program. But even poor choices of junior (untenured) faculty may have woeful consequences. Great patience, sustained attention to scholarship and teaching, and a willingness to dismiss marginal faculty even in the face of emotional and political opposition are thus called for. Black and White faculty and administrators must also resist the temptation to make Afro-American studies appointments a substitute for meeting affirmative action goals.

After an increase in the sixties and seventies in the number of Blacks entering graduate schools, there has been a sharp drop in the eighties. The increased numbers of Blacks pursuing academic careers was an anomaly of the past decade. Earlier, the chances of a Black scholar being appointed to the faculty of a northern university were extremely slight—so much so that very few Blacks chose to pursue scholarly careers. Projections of the academic job market for the next fifteen or twenty years are not promising for most fields in the humanities and social sciences. High costs and relatively lengthy periods of training for the Ph.D. (seven years on average as opposed to three years for law and two years for business) will push many of the best and brightest Black undergraduates into nonacademic fields. The number of Blacks enrolled in doctoral programs has been declining and very few Blacks are coming forth to fill faculty vacancies. If this trend continues, affirmative action in faculty hiring will be moot as far as Blacks are concerned.

Of course, the field of Afro-American studies need not depend on Black scholars alone, nor should it. It is desirable, furthermore, that Blacks, like other academics, should choose their fields of study on the basis of personal interest and intellectual commitment, not of race. It is nevertheless natural to assume that consequential gains in our knowledge of Afro-American life, history, and culture depend in large part on the presence of significant numbers of Black scholars in the humanities and social sciences. The prospect of declining numbers of Black scholars thus portends more serious problems for the field than small class enrollments do.

Given the still uncertain status of Afro-American studies departments and programs throughout the country, probably the best institutional support for the development and extension of the field of study will come from one or two centers or institutes of advanced study devoted to the subject. It seems to me that the movement to make academically legitimate the study of a wide range of issues and questions having to do with the Black experience in America has been the most valuable outcome of the struggles during the last decade. Afro-American studies will achieve greater impact and influence the more it is permitted to resonate in the conventional disciplines. Standard offerings in history, American literature, economics, political science, and so on should be informed and enriched by scholarship in Afro-American studies.

Notes

[1] Archibald MacLeish, *The Next Harvard,* Cambridge, MA: Harvard University Press, 1941.

[2] Clark Kerr, *The Uses of the University,* Cambridge, MA: Harvard University Press, 1963.

[3] C. H. Arce, "Historical, Institutional, and Contextual Determinants of Black Enrollment," unpublished doctoral dissertation, University of Michigan, 1976. Cited in Gail E. Thomas, ed., *Black Students in Higher Education: Conditions and Experiences in the 1970s.* Westport, CT: Greenwood Press, 1981, pp. 21–23 and passim.

[4] Ibid., p. 21; cites 1978 Census Bureau data.

[5] James A. Perkins, *The University in Transition,* Princeton, NJ: Princeton University Press, 1966. The book is composed of lectures delivered at Princeton in 1965.

[6] A provocative recent discussion of the plight of the humanities is Walter Jackson Bates, "Crisis of English Studies," *Harvard Magazine* LXXXV (September/October 1982), pp. 46–53.

[7] Perkins, op. cit., p. 22.

[8] The assumption was (and is) by no means restricted to predominantly White institutions. If anything, southern Black schools have been more insistent on the centrality of the classical and Renaissance tradition of humane letters than northern White schools.

[9] Daniel P. Moynihan, *The Negro Family: The Case for National Action,* Washington, DC: U.S. Department of Labor, Government Printing Office, 1965.

[10] The significance to Blacks of these killings cannot be overstated. In subsequent years, Black students bitterly compared the great public outcry at the killing of White students at Kent State to the apparent White indifference to the killing of Blacks at Orangeburg.

[11] Kenneth B. Clark and Lawrence Plotkin, *The Negro Student at Integrated Colleges,* New York: National Scholarship Service and Fund for Negro Students, 1963.

[12] In terms of adaptability to the institutions and expectations concerning higher education, these class differences are important to note. The sense of class alienation may have been as important in many instances as the sense of racial alienation.

[13] See Cleveland Donald, Jr., "Cornell: Confrontation in Black and White," in Cushing Strout and David Grossvogel, eds., *Divided We Stand: Reflections on the Crisis at Cornell,* New York: Doubleday, 1970, pp. 151–204. This essay provides a rare insight into the workings of Black student politics at a time of university conflict.

[14] It is probable that four-year liberal arts colleges avoided disruptions over Black Studies for several reasons. Even with active recruitment, the number of Black students remained small. Much student protest, White and Black, was against the gigantic, seemingly insensitive and unresponsive university bureaucracy. The smaller four-year college provided an experience on a human scale and encouraged the impression that grievances were listened to and taken into account.

[15] *New York Times,* various articles from roughly September 29, 1968, to March 3, 1970. Nathan Hare left San Francisco State in 1970.

[16] "Report of the Committee Appointed to Review the Department of Ethnic Studies," 1973. Unpublished. University of California, Berkeley. The history department was quite strong, consisting of Leon Litwack, Lawrence Levine, Winthrop Jordan, and others.

[17] Armstead L. Robinson et al., *Black Studies in the University,* New Haven: Yale University Press, 1969, p. viii. Robinson was at the time a senior at Yale College. After earning his Ph.D. in history, he went on to become one of the most respected young Black scholars. He currently heads the Afro-American Studies Program and the Carter G. Woodson Institute at the University of Virginia.

[18] In addition to Friedel, Social Sciences 5 was taught by Peter Wood, Martin Kilson, and Daniel Fox, with guest lecturers.

[19] Henry Rosovsky subsequently served as Dean of the Faculty of Arts and Sciences, from 1974 to 1984.

[20] Henry Rosovsky, "What Happened at Harvard," *The American Scholar* XXXVIII (Autumn 1969), pp. 562–572.

[21] Reported in *Trans-Action* VII (May 1970), p. 14.

[22] Vincent Harding, "Achieving Educational Equality: Stemming the Black Brain Drain," *Current* CV (March 1969), pp. 37–40.

[23] Clarke and Plotkin, op. cit., pp. 28–39. This study does reveal, however, that the small number of dropouts in this survey voiced complaints anticipating (mildly and without political intent) Black student complaints of the sixties. This may suggest that objective conditions were the same but expectations differed.

[24] M. L. Dillon, "White Faces in Black Studies," *Commonweal* XCI (January 30, 1970), pp. 476–479.

[25] John Blassingame, ed., *New Perspectives on Black Studies,* Champaign, IL: University of Illinois Press, 1971.

[26] This crisis of identity is by no means unique to Black people; witness the upsurge of "ethnicity" in the sixties and seventies.

[27] This became a general criticism raised by Black and White scholars; for instance, by John Blassingame, op. cit., pp. 75–168; by C. Vann Woodward, in "Flight from History," *Nation* CCI (September 20, 1969), pp. 142–146; and by Benjamin Quarles.

[28] Consider, for instance, the general treatment of W. E. B. Du Bois's *Black Reconstruction,* a work that eventually brought about a general revision of the history of that period.

[29] Carter G. Woodson, *The Mis-Education of the Negro,* Washington, DC: AMS Press, 1933; W. E. B. Du Bois, "The Field and Function of the Negro College;" in Herbert Aptheker, ed., *The Education of Black People: Ten Critiques 1906–1960,* Amherst, MA: University of Massachusetts Press, 1973, pp. 83–92.

[30] Wilson Record, "Can Black Studies and Sociology Find Common Ground?" *Journal of Negro Education* CLIV (Winter 1975), pp. 63–81; Morris Janowitz and James Blackwell, eds., *The Black Sociologists,* Chicago, IL: Chicago Center for Afro-American Studies and Research, 1973; Joyce A. Ladner, ed., *The Death of White Sociology,* New York: Random House, 1973; other divisions are in psychology, political science, and African studies.

[31] Harry Edwards, *Black Students,* New York: Free Press, 1970. The quotes are from the dust jacket, which contains proposed curricula for Black Studies. See also Nathan Hare, "The Sociological Study of Racial Conflict," *Phylon* XXXIII (Spring 1972), pp. 27–31.

[32] The strengths in history had to do with the fact that Afro-American history was a lively and developing area in American history. Black scholars, of course, and many Whites—Leon Litwack, Winthrop Jordan, Eugene Genovese, Herbert Gutman, August Meier, Lawrence Levine, etc.—were building reputations in the field.

[33] Maulana Ron Karenga, "The Black Community and the University: A Community Organizer's Perspective," in Robinson, op. cit., pp. 37–54.

[34] Wesleyan appointed a new chairman/director in 1981: Robert O'Meally, a fine scholar with strong academic interests. He plans to establish a strong program with interdepartmental cooperation. The center remains quasi-independent, however, and it has withstood, because of student loyalty, past attempts at reform.

[35] The Afro-American Studies program at UCLA, for instance, is a quasi-institute. It offers no instructional courses but provides means for research for graduate students and postdoctoral scholars.

[36] My information about IBW comes from the pamphlet "About the Institute of the Black World" and from manuscript reports, copies of which are in my possession.

[37] National Council for Black Studies, *Black Studies Core Curriculum*, Bloomington, IN: National Council for Black Studies, 1982, pp. 4–7.

[38] Undergraduates also report considerable parental pressure to follow courses of study with a "payoff." Black students, often able to attend college only as a result of great sacrifice by their parents, are especially susceptible to parental pressure to make their education "practical."

[39] Blassingame, op. cit., "Black Studies, an Intellectual Crisis," pp. 149–168. See also his "Model of an AfroAmerican Studies Program," ibid., pp. 229–239.

[40] In the winter of 1984, the dean of the faculty at the University of California at Riverside recommended the disestablishment of the Black Studies department, Chicano studies) as well as some other small departments. The justification was both economic and academic. UC Riverside has been an economically marginal unit of the UC system. It is as yet unclear whether the recommendation to disestablish will be approved.

[41] Cleveland State University requires, for the A.B., four semester courses in Afro-American studies. The courses are well attended and the students (White and Black) seem to accept the requirement without undue complaint.

[42] By this I mean enrollment for academic rather than political reasons. In the mid-seventies, many Black students took courses to "support the program," voting with their feet, as it were. That phase is past.

[43] The claim is made by White conservatives at Harvard despite the fact that all Black students fall well within the range of all those admitted to the college.

[44] Community action programs and all such practical work are not much valued by traditional academics, who tend to regard them as activities of questionable merit for undergraduate training. On this question of community work and Black Studies, see Kenneth B. Clark, "A Charade of Power," *Antioch Review* XXIX (Summer 1969), pp. 145–148, and Stephen Lythcott's rejoinder, ibid., pp. 149–154.

PART TWO

African American Studies from Implementation to Institutionalization: The Harris, Hine, McKay Report

An Introduction to the Harris, Hine, McKay Report
Farah Jasmine Griffin

Three Essays: Black Studies in the United States
Robert L, Harris, Jr., Darlene Clark Hine, Nellie McKay
Preface by Franklin A. Thomas, President, Ford Foundation

African American Studies from Implementation to Institutionalization

Introduction to the Harris, Hine, McKay Report

In 1987, "recognizing the rapid growth of the field and the emergence of a new generation of scholars,"[1] the program officer Sheila Biddle commissioned the foundation's second report on African American Studies. Completed in 1989, Three *Essays: Black Studies in the United States* was published in 1990. As intellectual and administrative leaders in the field and within the larger profession, as evidenced by the reception accorded their research and scholarship, the three authors—Robert L. Harris, Darlene Clark Hine, and Nellie Y. McKay—had contributed greatly to the field's development and institutionalization.

It is significant that Dr. Harris's essay opens the report. In his study, Huggins had referred to Cornell University as "one of the most separatist and militant in the country" at its founding. At the time of the report's publication, Dr. Harris served as director of the Africana Studies and Research Center at Cornell; he is currently vice provost of Diversity and Faculty Development at the same institution and also serves on the Executive Council of the Association for the Study of African American Life and History.

Dr. Hine was then John A. Hannah Professor of History at Michigan State; she is now interim chair of the department and director of the Center for African American Studies at Northwestern University. The late Dr. McKay was professor of American and Afro-American Literature at the University of Wisconsin, Madison, and former Director of African American Studies.[2] Hine and McKay have been central to the emergence of Black Women's Studies, especially in the fields of history and American literature. Hine has served as president both of the Organization of American Historians and of the Southern Historical Association.

Three Essays: Black Studies in the United States differs from the Huggins report in important ways. Its three authors represent the interdisciplinary nature of the field as well as its regional and geographical diversity. It compiles three points of view: an historical essay, an overview of the field, and an evaluation of a specific region and its institutions.

Although Harris, Hine, and McKay set out to evaluate diverse centers, departments, and institutions with the intention of keeping the report confidential (as would be necessary if it were to contain an honest assessment), many within the field expressed interest in the findings, and the foundation decided to publish a general report.

Robert Harris's essay "The Intellectual and Institutional Development of Africana Studies" continues to be one of the most extensive statements about the history of the field; it ought to be more widely known and accessible. The essay makes two important contributions:

1. Harris opens with a comprehensive definition of Africana Studies as a field that stretches beyond African, African American, and Black Studies, outlining the key themes with which the field has been concerned.
2. Where Huggins provides the postwar historical and political context for the emergence of Black Studies on White campuses, Harris takes the long view, offering an intellectual genealogy of the field. He identifies four stages in the development of the field from the last

decade of the 19th century when African Americans founded a number of organizations that sought to preserve and publicize the legacy of the African diaspora through the theoretical refinement and more sophisticated analysis and interpretation of the mid 1980s.

Harris's stages of development set the parameters for an evaluation process and are enormously helpful in mapping and assessing the growth and current state of the field.

In her "Black Studies: An Overview," Darlene Clark Hine explores the nomenclature of the field: African American, Afro-American, Africana, Black Studies—titles evidencing the diversity of the field. Hine found, however, that although many programs sought to broaden geographical and disciplinary reach—that is, to fully explore the lives and experiences of peoples of African descent wherever they are on the globe—few possessed the resources or faculty to be truly *Africana* Studies programs. She cites the need to address such topics as curriculum, identity, mission, structure, graduate programs, faculty recruitment and retention, accreditation, and professionalization. Yet, by 1987, when Hine began her study, she found that White college administrators enthusiastically supported African American Studies as the site that had racially diversified the university population and curriculum—notably, the study of Black women was then the new frontier of African American Studies.

By contrast, Nellie McKay, in her "Black Studies in the Midwest" acknowledges a commitment among predominantly White institutions to strengthen African American Studies but questions the extent to which the field has been accepted in the scholarly community. She notes the backlash against African American Studies, Black faculty, and Black students on a number of campuses throughout the country. In addition, she identifies the special difficulty of recruiting Black scholars to the Midwest because of the lack of racial diversity within the region. (Here I assume she is not speaking of such major Midwestern cities as Chicago, Cleveland, Detroit, or Cincinnati.) McKay is the first to take note of the impact of the "star system" on African American Studies, noting that few public institutions in the Midwest can afford academic superstars. To McKay, this system is good for individual scholars and has some positive implications for the field even as it increases the burden on those who continue to engage students over time through teaching, counseling, research, and administrative leadership. But what McKay does not point out is that this burden often falls upon women scholars. Finally, as do those whose essays precede hers, she encourages foundation attention be directed to the pipeline. But McKay also recommends regional collaboration to share resources and address scholars' feelings of isolation in the Midwest. This recommendation led to the creation of the Midwest Consortium of African American Studies in the opening years of the 21st century—a successful model of institutional cooperation that could well be replicated at other universities in different regions.

Farah Jasmine Griffin
(2006)

Notes

[1] Franklin A. Thomas, Preface to "Three Essays: Black Studies in the United States" (1990).

[2] The Midwest consortium for African American Studies included the University of Wisconsin, University of Michigan, Carnegie Mellon University, and Michigan State University.

Three Essays:
Black Studies in the United States,
Report to the Ford Foundation
(1990)

Robert L. Harris, Jr.
Darlene Clark Hine
Nellie McKay

The Harris, Hine, McKay Report
Contents

Preface to the Harris, Hine, McKay Report

The Ford Foundation has supported Black Studies since the first programs were established on American college and university campuses in the late 1960s. Since 1969 the foundation has granted some $19 million to assist the development of both graduate and undergraduate programs and, more recently, to strengthen scholarship and research at selected centers of Afro-American and Africana Studies. Another $1 million has supported editing, archival, and oral history projects documenting the Black experience. Given the size of the foundation's commitment and the growing impact of Afro-American scholarship on traditional disciplines, in 1982 the foundation asked Nathan Huggins, then the director of the W. E. B. Du Bois Institute for Afro-American Research at Harvard University, to review the evolution of Black Studies and its future prospects. His report was published by the foundation in 1985.[1]

Recognizing the rapid growth of the field and the emergence of a new generation of scholars in the 1980's, the foundation commissioned a series of consultancies in 1987–88 intended to provide a sense of the current state of Black Studies in the United States. Three distinguished scholars were invited to survey selected Black Studies departments, programs, institutes, and centers judged to be representative of the structural diversity and programmatic scope of Afro-American and Africana Studies across the country; to evaluate their present capacities and strengths; and to assess their future needs. From their reports, we hoped to gain a fuller understanding of the resources in the Black Studies field and its intellectual and institutional priorities over the next decade. Thus informed, the foundation would be better able to design the next phase of its continuing support for Black Studies in a way that responded to the concerns of scholar/teachers in the field.

From the outset, it was recognized that the survey could not be comprehensive. Further, it was understood that the consultants' reports would be confidential. But as the consultants traveled around the country visiting various Black Studies enterprises, word of the survey spread, and interest in their findings grew. The foundation received numerous inquiries asking if the reports would be released in some form. Since both the consultants and the individuals they interviewed had understood that these conversations, and the observations resulting from them, were confidential, we could not release the reports in full. Nevertheless, the reports contained a substantial amount of general information about the Black Studies field, and it seemed to us and to our consultants that these observations and assessments should be made public.

The three essays that follow have been edited to delete all references to individuals and institutions except those cited to illustrate a general point. The essays vary in length and character partly because of the order in which the consultancies were undertaken and also because, apart from specific information requested on each site visited, we did not ask the consultants to adhere to a single format. Our first consultant, Darlene Clark Hine, John Hannah Professor of History at Michigan State University, surveyed a substantial number of institutions, but time constraints prevented her from visiting the Midwestern universities she had hoped to include in the extensive report she submitted to the foundation. Nellie McKay, professor of American and Afro-American Literature at the University of Wisconsin, agreed to cover Black Studies in the Midwest. Believing it unnecessary to restate at any length the general points Professor Hine had made about the state of Black Studies nationwide, Professor McKay concentrated on the distinguishing aspects of the field in the Midwest and on the sites she visited. Robert L Harris, Jr., director of the Africana Studies and

Research Center at Cornell University, prefaced his survey of Black Studies in the City University of New York and the State University of New York with a discussion of the development of Black Studies as an area of scholarly inquiry. His preface serves as a useful introduction to the two essays that follow.

The foundation is pleased to publish these essays. We are grateful to the three scholars who served as our consultants for the intelligence and commitment they brought to the project. We believe they have made a significant contribution to Black Studies and to all who have an interest in promoting the health and continuing growth of the field.

Franklin A. Thomas
President, Ford Foundation

The Intellectual and Institutional Development of Africana Studies

Robert L. Harris, Jr.

Africana Studies[*2] is the multidisciplinary analysis of the lives and thought of people of African ancestry on the African continent and throughout the World. It embraces Africa, Afro-America, and the Caribbean, but does not confine itself to those three geographical areas. Africana Studies examines people of African ancestry wherever they may be found—for example, in Central and South America, Asia, and the Pacific Islands. Its primary means of organization are racial and cultural. Many of the themes of Africana Studies are derived from the historical position of African peoples in relation to Western societies and in the dynamics of slavery, oppression, colonization, imperialism, emancipation, self-determination, liberation, and socioeconomic and political development.

There have been four stages in the intellectual and institutional development of Africana Studies as an area of scholarly inquiry. The first stage began in the 1890s and lasted until the Second World War. During this first stage, numerous organizations emerged to document, record, and analyze the history, culture, and status of African peoples. For example, the Bethel Literary and Historical Association of Washington, D.C., formed in 1881, sponsored lectures on numerous topics, such as the Egyptians, the Zulus, and various aspects of African culture, in addition to contemporary issues affecting African Americans. Other organizations functioned in a similar manner—for example, Philadelphia's American Negro Historical Society, established in 1897; Washington, D.C.'s American Negro Academy, also started in 1897; and New York's Negro Society for Historical Research, organized in 1911.

These early Black literary and historical associations sought to preserve and to publicize the legacy of African peoples. They were superseded in 1915, when Carter G. Woodson formed the Association for the Study of Afro-American (formerly Negro) Life and History (ASALH), which still survives today. Woodson laid the groundwork for systematic study of African peoples through the association's annual meetings; the Journal of Negro History, launched in 1916; the national observance of Negro History Week (now Black History Month), started in 1926; publication of the Negro History Bulletin, begun in 1933; and the formation of Associated Publishers to print books on the Black experience in America and throughout the world. ASALH has been the premier organization in promoting historical consciousness and in generating greater understanding of African heritage in the United States.

In 1897 W. E. B. Du Bois initiated an ambitious program at Atlanta University to examine various categories of African-American life in ten-year cycles. He proposed that such studies be continued for at least 100 years to provide knowledge and understanding of the Black family, church, social organizations, education, and economic development in the United States. From 1898 to 1914, the Atlanta University Studies produced sixteen monographs, which consisted of more than 2,100 pages of research. Du Bois, Woodson, Lorenzo J. Greene, Charles H. Wesley, E. Franklin Frazier, Ralph J. Bunche, Charles S. Johnson, Abram Harris, Sterling Brown, and other pioneering Black scholars produced an impressive body of scholarship to correct the errors, omissions, and distortions of Black life and history that prevailed among white academics and the American public.

The second stage for Africana Studies began with the study of Black America by Gunnar Myrdal. This stage was in some respects a setback. Myrdal, who began his project for the Carnegie Corporation in 1939, confined his analysis to the American social, political, and economic order. There was growing concern about the role and place of the Black population during the Second World War, as a majority of African Americans became urban. Black migration northward, which had begun in large numbers during the 1890s, had accelerated during World War I, and had slowed during the Depression of the 1930s, mushroomed during World War II, making the Black presence in America more a national than a regional or primarily southern concern. Believing that Black people in the United States were fundamentally Americans who had no significant African cultural background or identity, Myrdal accepted the formulation of the University of Chicago School of Sociology that ethnic and racial contact led not only to conflict but also to inevitable assimilation and absorption into the dominant society. His two-volume study, *An American Dilemma: The Negro Problem and Modern Democracy,* published in 1944, had an important influence on scholarship, especially the work of white academics during this second stage.

White scholars, by and large, had ignored Black people. The Columbia University historian John W. Burgess had boldly stated: "[A] Black skin means membership in a race of men which has never itself succeeded in subjecting passion to reason; has never, therefore, created any civilization of any kind." After World War II, as the Black population in the United States became predominantly urban and as scholarship in general shed notions of inherent racial inferiority and superiority with the Nazi debacle, white scholars devoted increasing attention to African Americans' status in the United States. They sought environmental rather than biogenetic explanations for African Americans' inferior status.

In *Mark of Oppression* (1951), Abram Kardiner and Lionel Ovesey hypothesized that African Americans emerged from slavery without a culture, with "no intra-psychic defenses—no pride, no group solidarity, no tradition." They argued: "The marks of his previous status were still upon him—socially, psychologically, and emotionally—and from these he has never since freed himself." Stanley Elkins in his book *Slavery* (1959) concluded that African Americans were not genetically inferior but were made inferior by the process of enslavement, which they internalized and passed on to succeeding generations. In *Beyond the Melting Pot: The Negroes, Puerto Ricans, Jews, Italians, and Irish of New York City* (1963), Nathan Glazer and Daniel P. Moynihan attributed African-American status to the absence of middle-class values and norms among the Black population in general. Two years later, in *The Negro Family: The Case for National Action,* Moynihan wrote: "Three centuries of injustice have brought about deep-seated structural distortions in the life of the Negro American." He concluded that "the present tangle of pathology is capable of perpetuating itself without assistance from the white world."

Whereas Burgess had implied that Africans had never created anything of worth and therefore African Americans were descended from an inferior people, post–World War II white scholars, in the main, identified African-American status not with an inglorious African past but with deficiencies occasioned by slavery, segregation, and discrimination. It is important to note that these scholars believed that the end of racial oppression would not immediately produce racial equality, not because of lack of social opportunity but because of the accumulated pathological behavior of Black people. In other words, Black people were not divinely created inferior but were made inferior over time. The sum of racial oppression and its alleged internalization by Black people dramatically affected their lives across generations.

Another significant post–World War II development was the creation of African Studies programs that had no real link to Black people in the New World. Although Melville Herskovits, a white anthropologist and proponent of African Studies, tried to join the study of Africa with the lives of Black people in the New World, African Studies became wedded to a modernization theory that measured African societies by Western standards. African history, culture, and politics were explored more within the context of the colonial powers than with any attention to African cultural continuities in the Western hemisphere. This compartmentalization of knowledge regarding Black people departed significantly from the scholarship of individuals such as Du Bois and Woodson during the first stage in the development of Africana Studies.

The civil rights revolution, the Black power drive, and the Black consciousness movement initiated a third stage of Africana Studies. During this era, larger numbers of Black students entered predominantly white colleges and universities. Most of these students were the first generation of their families to attend college. They encountered faculties that were almost entirely white and a curriculum that was primarily Eurocentric in perspective. The "melting pot" thesis prevailed as the paradigm of American society in which all groups, regardless of background, assimilated to an ideal that was primarily white, Anglo-Saxon, and Protestant. Ironically, at a time when African nations were achieving independence from colonial rule, Africa seemed unrelated to Black people in the United States. If Africa was discussed in classes, it was generally as an adjunct to European imperialism. In large measure, Black people were seen as pawns rather than as actors, as victims more than as victors.

Together with many Black scholars from the first stage of Africana Studies, Black college students challenged the prevailing orthodoxies on predominantly white campuses. They demanded the employment of Black professors and the establishment of Africana Studies departments and programs. They pressed for the inclusion of African Studies in the newly formed Africana Studies programs. The inclusion of African Studies was important for several reasons. First, African Americans have historically linked their destiny with the future of Africa. Second, the image of Africa has had significant consequences for the status of African Americans. Third, African ancestry has informed the cultural heritage of African Americans as much as their presence in the United States. Fourth, the history, politics, and culture of Africa could stand as a counterweight to the dominance of Western culture in American education.

The Eurocentric focus of the college curriculum basically excluded people of African ancestry or studied them through a European filter. Eurocentrist scholars ignored the growth of civilization in Africa, especially in Egypt, or co-opted Egyptian civilization as part of a European rather than an African continuum. They also ignored the African heritage of African Americans, characterizing them as having begun their existence in North America as tabulae rasae—blank slates to be imprinted with Euro-American culture.

Although some colleges and universities were willing to establish Africana Studies programs, they were less willing to organize Africana Studies departments. Faculty within the traditional departments were reluctant to give up their prerogative of determining what constituted a course in history, literature, or government; who would take such courses; and how the professors teaching them would be evaluated for employment, promotion, and tenure. Advocates of Africana Studies departments questioned how members of traditional departments that had not offered courses on the Black experience or hired Black faculty could sit in judgment on the nature and quality of work being done in this newly emerging field of study.

The third stage of Africana Studies, from about the mid-1960s to the mid-1980s, was a period of legitimization and institutionalization. Few scholars were prepared to teach Africana Studies courses. The shift in perspective from Eurocentrism to Afrocentrism required the recovery, organization, and accessibility of research materials that made Black people, their lives, and their thoughts the center of analysis and interpretation. Many white scholars in particular had assumed that there was not sufficient documentation on which to base sound judgments about the personal and collective experiences of Black people in the United States. However, with the new interest in Black life and culture, federal, state, and local archivists combed their collections for materials on the African-American experience and published several useful guides. Major projects began assembling and publishing the papers of Black leaders, writers, and organizations. It is now clear that there are abundant materials (print, visual, and sound) to reconstruct and to interpret the African-American past.

The prodigious research of Black and white scholars has dramatically changed the manner in which we now view African Americans. Most scholars today acknowledge the persistence of African culture in the United States. They no longer accept the idea that African Americans passively acquiesced to oppression, recognizing that, on the contrary, they actively resisted oppression in a variety of ways. In large measure, scholars have come to accept the United States as a pluralistic society with multiple viable cultures, rather than as a "melting pot." We think more of acculturation, with give-and-take, than of assimilation—particularly in the form of total absorption into the dominant culture, which itself is now being redefined.

Africana Studies has achieved legitimacy and has become institutionalized within higher education. It now has moved into a fourth stage of theoretical refinement and more sophisticated analysis and interpretation. The fundamental research tools have been developed, although there will certainly be a need to update and to supplement them as new materials become available. In general, the field is in fairly good condition, but there are some problems, or perhaps opportunities to improve it.

Because the formats for multidisciplinary programs vary from campus to campus, there will probably not be a single method of organization for Africana Studies. The ideal format is the department structure, which allows for selection of faculty and development of curriculum. Programs with faculty in traditional departments can also be successful, provided that they have some control of faculty lines. The program, however, becomes a more complex arrangement, especially in decisions for hiring, promotion, and tenure. Joint appointments carry similar problems, especially for junior faculty. They are less burdensome for senior faculty, whose tenure has already been established. Cross-listing of courses is one means by which departments and programs can take greater advantage of faculty resources on their campuses. However, before such cross-listing can be effective, there must first be a strong core faculty within the department or program. Otherwise, the Africana Studies curriculum becomes too dependent on the priorities of other departments.

One goal for the fourth stage of Africana Studies should be to broaden and deepen the field of inquiry. This prospect becomes somewhat difficult for those departments and programs with limited numbers of faculty. Small faculties are stretched thin when they attempt to offer a major and to cover Africa, Afro-America, and the Caribbean. Offering a comprehensive program in Africana Studies has meant that some departments and programs play primarily service roles in providing introductory courses that are used to fulfill one or more distribution requirements for graduation. These efforts have little opportunity to supply depth in the field of study.

Faculty become very much occupied with servicing large introductory courses and have little time for research and writing in an area of specialization. There is a tendency for faculty to become generalists familiar with a broad range of knowledge rather than specialists who advance the frontiers of specific areas of knowledge.

As Africana Studies moves into its fourth stage, as well as its third decade on predominantly white campuses, there is a need to reexamine the curriculum on many campuses. Some departments and programs offer a hodgepodge of courses that have evolved over time in response to student interest and faculty availability. Many departments and programs, particularly those with small faculties, need to determine what they can do best with their resources. Some have specific strengths upon which to build; others need to reconsider where they want to concentrate their resources. Unless they have the faculty and the administrative support, many departments and programs cannot offer successful comprehensive Africana Studies courses. In a 1986 report on the "Status of Afro-American Studies in the State University of New York," Dr. Kenneth Hall showed that the preponderance of students are attracted by courses on Afro-American history, the civil rights movement, film, music, and contemporary Africa. Courses on history and culture (literature, music, film, drama, and dance) seem to appeal most to a cross-section of students (Black and white), with politics close behind.

In many respects, Africana Studies faculty need to return to the basic question: Africana Studies for what? There was much discussion and debate on this question during the early days of organizing, when the focus was on the quest for legitimacy and institutionalization. On many campuses, Africana Studies was to provide the Black presence, to supply role models for students, to have an active advising and counseling function, to organize film series, lectures, and symposia, and to influence traditional departments in the composition of their faculty and curriculum. This was a tall order that exhausted many Africana Studies faculty. Having expended their energy on getting the new field off the ground, many faculty had not devoted sufficient time to research and publication and thus were caught short when evaluated for promotion and tenure.

Today, there is some debate about whether Africana Studies faculty should play their former roles of counselors and mentors or give more time to research. Some of this tension would be eased if administrators supported campus-life specialists who would organize cultural activities for Black students in particular and for all students in general. Faculty development is an important element within the university, and it is especially important for Africana Studies faculty, many of whom need to reorient themselves toward greater scholarship.

Public colleges that are clustered in metropolitan areas have a unique opportunity to foster scholarship in Africana Studies by establishing master's degree programs and research institutes. Such projects might encourage Africana Studies departments and programs to develop strengths in specific areas. These strengths could be drawn upon for graduate programs and research institutes to promote greater scholarship by identifying areas of investigation and by bringing together scholars with similar interests. Research institutes might also be a means to influence more students to pursue advanced degrees and expand the number of minority scholars.

Answers to the question of "Africana Studies for what?" will have a significant effect on the shape and content of the curriculum. To address these issues, the National Council for Black Studies has already embarked on a program of summer institutes for college teachers. Such responses will also influence the role of Africana Studies on different campuses. Africana Studies will continue to vary from college to college. Ultimately, however, there is a need for greater clarification and understanding through more dialogue about its specific function on various campuses.

Black Studies: An Overview

Darlene Clark Hine

During the late 1960s and early 1970s, unique historical circumstances propelled the development of Afro-American and Africana Studies in colleges and universities. Few of these early endeavors were the result of careful and deliberate planning and analysis. Typically, they were established in response to political exigencies rather than intellectual and academic imperatives. These and other factors contributed to ongoing structural and organizational diversity. Today it seems that no two Black Studies programs are alike. Their diversity is evidenced in faculty size and composition, relations with university administrators and more traditional departments, curriculum, degrees offered, budgets, spatial resources, range of special programs, and the nature of their community outreach.

An important objective of this investigation was to examine the present status of these programs: How well have they been supported by their institutions? To what degree have they been able to secure productive faculty? Have they provided their faculties with the requisite resources and nurturing that encourage the quality teaching, research, and service required for success in the academy?

The ongoing debate over nomenclature is a graphic illustration of residual problems growing out of the turbulent times in which these programs burst upon the academic scene. The term "Black Studies" has become a generic designation, vociferously opposed by some who view the phrase as less than illuminating. Critics argue that this designation suggests that only Black students and Black faculty should be interested in this area of intellectual inquiry. Most institutions appear to prefer the titles "Afro-American," "African and Afro-American," or "Africana" Studies. On the one hand, those who insist on the term "Africana Studies" maintain that "Afro-American Studies" implies that the primary focus of teaching and research is the historical, cultural, and political development of Afro-Americans living within the boundaries of North America. Moreover, "African and Afro-American Studies" neglect the Caribbean and other parts of the Americas. On the other hand, "Africana Studies" encompasses a broader geographical, if not disciplinary, reach, spanning both North and South America, the Caribbean, and the African continent—in short, the African Diaspora. Of course, few of the current programs possess the requisite institutional resources, faculty positions, or budget lines to be truly "Africana." But the intent points in the right direction and therefore is certainly praiseworthy.

The attempt to identify and assess Black Studies endeavors accurately is further complicated by the differences in structure and mission between "departments," "programs," "centers," and "institutes." Black Studies "departments" are best characterized as separate, autonomous units possessing an exclusive right and privilege to hire and grant tenure to their faculty, certify students, confer degrees, and administer a budget. Black Studies "programs" may offer majors and minors but rarely confer degrees. And perhaps more importantly, all faculty appointments in programs are of the "joint," "adjunct," or "associate" variety. These professors are in the unenviable position of having to please two masters to secure appointment and tenure.

"Centers" and "institutes" defy easy categorization. As a rule, they tend to be administrative units more concerned with the production and dissemination of scholarship and with the professional development of teachers and scholars in the field than with undergraduate teaching. Unfortunately, considerable confusion surrounds the name "center." Many people view centers as merely cultural or social facilities designed to ease the adjustment of Black students to predominantly white campus life. Thus, centers are often denigrated and dismissed as having little or no relevance to Black Studies, which is imagined to be purely an academic or intellectual endeavor, albeit with political-advocacy overtones. However, the good work being done at centers like those at the University of California at Los Angeles (UCLA) and the University of Michigan certainly should correct these misconceptions.

University Administrators

It was encouraging and refreshing to encounter so many white university administrators who sang the praises of their Black Studies departments, programs, centers, and institutes. In fact, there was scarcely a discordant note. From the perspectives of the more positively inclined administrators on predominantly white campuses, it appears that Black Studies not only has come of age but also has been making important contributions to the academy. Although it is heartening to witness this attitudinal transformation, given the initial vehement objections to the creation of Black Studies units, it is nonetheless necessary to probe beyond the surface to assess fully the contemporary status of Black Studies.

Twenty years ago, when Black students first demanded the establishment of Black Studies departments, programs, and centers, few of the beleaguered white administrators would have predicted a long life for these enterprises. Many undoubtedly wished that Black Studies would go away; others tried to thwart growth and development. Most of those who opposed the creation of Black Studies units claimed that these units would lower academic standards because they believed such endeavors lacked intellectual substance.

It is not surprising that at some institutions Black Studies units offered little intellectual challenge. Undertrained people were brought in to head programs hastily contrived to preserve campus peace. Unfortunately, the early development and subsequent evolution of Black Studies were further tainted by the media's sensationalized coverage of the armed Black students at Cornell University and the 1969 shoot-out at UCLA, which left two students dead. In the minds of many, Black Studies would forever remain nothing more than a new kind of academic ghetto. University administrators who valued "peace" and "campus rest" had little inclination, courage, or will to insist on quality. Thus, Black Studies units seldom were held to the traditional modes of evaluation and scrutiny observed elsewhere in the academy.

By 1987, however, the tide had turned. There has been a discernible shift among college administrators from amused contempt or indifference to enthusiastic support of Black Studies. Now administrators are eager to improve the quality of their programs and departments. One potent factor has been the availability of a larger pool of productive, well-trained Black scholars willing, indeed anxious, to head and/or work in Black Studies. No longer do administrators have to rely on the local minister or community activist to oversee and teach Black Studies. If they are willing to put up the money, administrators can recruit productive Black scholars.

Another motivation fueling the change in attitude toward Black Studies is institutional expediency. Faced with the specter of declining Black student enrollments, university administrators are increasingly using strong Black Studies departments, programs, centers, and institutes as recruitment devices. Moreover, as is often the case, the only critical mass of Black faculty working at many of these institutions is housed in Black Studies divisions. It is sad but true that without Black Studies, Chicano Studies, women's Studies, or Native American Studies departments or programs, few colleges and universities could boast of having an integrated or pluralistic faculty.

Institutional expediency and a larger pool of Black scholars notwithstanding, one fact deserves underscoring. Black Studies departments and their faculties have proven to be a continuing source of intellectual stimulation on many American campuses. Black Studies has opened up vast and exciting new areas of scholarship, especially in American history and literature, and has spurred intellectual inquiry into diverse social problems affecting the lives of significant portions of the total population. Lectures, seminars, and conferences sponsored by Black Studies units provide a threefold benefit: Students introduced to authorities from outside of the academy are impressed with the fact that there are many ways of expressing and knowing. Faculty, Black and white, have the opportunity to share their expertise, test assumptions, and receive immediate feedback on work in progress. Finally, Black community residents are encouraged to perceive universities as more accessible and less foreign. As members of these communities begin to identify with universities, they develop a greater appreciation for learning, and a respect for the scholarship of Black professors.

Black Studies Curriculum

Despite its contributions and successes over the past twenty years, Black Studies still has to contend with and resolve rampant confusion, conflict, and creative tensions. The issues being debated include nomenclature; curriculum; identity, mission, and structure; graduate programs; faculty recruitment, retention, and development; accreditation; and professionalization. There is an ongoing debate, with no signs of immediate resolution, over whether Black Studies is a field or a discipline. The problems surrounding curriculum are worthy of special attention. Even within the same departments, faculties often find it impossible to agree upon a standard or core for all sections of the same introductory course in Afro-American Studies. It is regrettable that there is no special summer institute or training program where Black Studies administrators and faculty could discuss and perhaps map an appropriate and effective curriculum.

The curriculum—whether it is called Black Studies, Africana Studies, or Afro-American and African Studies—should reflect an ordered arrangement of courses progressing from the introductory through the intermediate to advanced levels. In terms of content, a sound Black Studies curriculum must include courses in Afro-American history and in Afro-American literature and literary criticism. There should be a complement of courses in sociology, political science, psychology, and economics. A cluster of courses in art, music, and language and/or linguistics should also be made available to students. Finally, depending on resources and the number of faculty, a well-rounded Studies effort should offer courses on other geographical areas of the Black Diaspora—the Caribbean and/or Africa. African and Afro-American and Africana Studies programs and departments should, as their names imply, offer a variety of courses on Black societies in the New World as well as on Africa.

Although deciding what to name a unit and developing a sound and coherent curriculum are challenging, a more daunting task is acquiring resources to recruit and retain an appropriate faculty, one that includes assistant, associate, and full professors. In the late 1960s and early 1970s, Black Studies units simply drew into their domain whoever happened to be available and willing to join them. Thus, little uniformity in curriculum could be achieved across the country. With the economic difficulties and retrenchment of the late 1970s, many Black Studies faculties declined in size, producing an even more fragmented curriculum. To ensure that existing courses were offered on a reasonable and routine basis, Black Studies administrators had to rely heavily on part-time, visiting, or temporary appointees. Most often those available to accept such positions were in the creative arts: musicians, dancers, poets, and fiction writers.

More recently, Black Studies departments have increasingly relied on cross-listing courses to augment curriculum. The cross-listing of courses is both reasonable and advantageous because it builds bridges between Black Studies and the more traditional departments within the university, thus decreasing somewhat tendencies toward isolation and marginality. To be sure, there are pitfalls, and cautious administrators must be ever vigilant. Adaptive "survival" measures may encourage some university administrators to reduce further the resources allocated to Black Studies. After all, if Black Studies is consistently able to "make do" with less, one could logically conclude that it needed fewer resources in the first place. This is a special concern for departments and programs with small numbers of majors and minors and with low course enrollments.

All of these factors—lack of a critical mass of well-trained faculty, excessive reliance on temporary hires, absence of a coherent curriculum and of content consensus for even introductory courses, and the increasing use of cross-listing of courses—bespeak the difficulties confronting and perhaps threatening the autonomy of many Black Studies departments. These are certainly among the concerns of the leadership of the National Council for Black Studies (NCBS). I suspect that the officers of NCBS will experience considerable frustration as the organization attempts to design a standardized curriculum. Although it is perhaps perverse to see anything positive in this disarray, the major strength of the Black Studies enterprise may well be its ever-changing and evolving nature. The rapid proliferation of knowledge in the field is a strong argument in support of institutional flexibility. Faculty in this area need to be free to develop new courses, to experiment with different methodologies, and to adopt nontraditional texts, just as quickly as new knowledge is produced.

Undergraduate and Graduate Degree Programs in Black Studies

One of the characteristics of a viable discipline is the authority to confer degrees and certificates to students who have mastered a particular body of knowledge. Black Studies faculty and administrators have been quite concerned with this issue. The majority of the more autonomous departments of Black Studies do, in fact, award B.A degrees. Programs in Black Studies vary. Some offer majors while most offer at least minors to students receiving a degree from the more traditional academic disciplines. In other words, the student may receive a B.A. degree in history, sociology, political science, or biology, chemistry, business administration, or education—with a concentration in Afro-American Studies.

Few Black Studies units offer master's degrees. Of the half dozen or so that do, the departments at Cornell and UCLA and the program at Yale are the most visible and are highly respected. Most of the M.A. degree students at Cornell and Yale go on to pursue Ph.D. degrees in traditional disciplines at some of the better institutions in the country. Others enter the labor force, working in social service agencies, businesses, or state and local governments. Cornell's Master of Professional Studies degree is specially designed to prepare students to work in community settings.

As with many other issues in Black Studies, there is no consensus about the wisdom of developing graduate degree programs in Afro-American

Studies. Certainly, at this stage in the evolution of Black Studies, there is a need for a creditable Ph.D. degree program. As I traveled around the country, Black Studies scholars expressed enthusiasm about the prospects of making a Ph.D. degree program available to students.[3]

Black Scholars and the Modern Black Studies Movement

At present, there are a number of top-flight Black scholars, more than at any time in history. They are producing first-rate, indeed award winning, books and articles in areas of Black Studies. By far the most exhilarating part of the entire project involved meeting these scholars and becoming familiar with their work. No assessment of the overall status and impact of Black Studies would be complete without noting the research activities of this latest generation of Black professors and administrators. Because the absolute numbers of Black professors is small and declining, it is easy to lose sight of the quality and breadth of their research and to minimize the impact that they have had on scholarship in all branches of knowledge.

The collective scholarship of Black professors provides a sound foundation for the future development of Black Studies as a discipline. To a great extent, this scholarship will ensure the eventual institutionalization of Black Studies within the academy. As long as Black scholars remain productive and competitive, and devote considerable attention to recruiting and training the next generation of scholars, Black Studies will enjoy a presence on America's campuses. It is, however, precisely the need to recruit, retain, and educate young Black men and women in the humanistic and social science disciplines that casts a cloud over the joy and exuberance accompanying any serious examination of the quality of Black scholarship in the last two decades. For a variety of reasons, fewer Black students are entering graduate school with plans for academic careers. At every stop on my tour of Black Studies units, faculty members and administrators, Black and white, broached the topic and admitted that this problem was of critical importance to the future of Black Studies.

The numerous monographs, articles, and manuscript editing projects produced by Black scholars have fueled the movement to reclaim the forgotten or obscured dimensions of the Black past. Their new interpretations of past and present conditions affecting all aspects of Black life have wrought a veritable revolution, albeit a still largely unheralded one, in the ways in which even traditional historians, literature theorists, sociologists, anthropologists, philosophers, psychologists, and political scientists approach their work whenever it touches upon the experience of Black people.

There is reason to be excited and pleased with the record of intellectual accomplishment evident in scattered institutions around the country. Regrettably, most of these Black scholars have little contact with each other. Nevertheless, because there are so many recognizably productive and accomplished scholars the future of Black Studies appears bright in spite of all of the structural complexities and creative tensions. In the remainder of this paper, I will address several factors concerning Black scholars: the role of philanthropic foundations in their development, the perspectives reflected in some of their works, and the relationship between their scholarship and Black Studies as an organized unit within universities and colleges.

Any perusal of the acknowledgments and prefaces of some of the refreshingly original recent works of Black scholars demonstrates the critical importance of the scholarships and fellowships made available by foundations and other organizations, including those specifically set aside for minority group scholars. Without these special fellowships, I dare say the record of productivity in Black Studies would not be so impressive.

To illustrate this point, I shall discuss three recently published and widely praised (within Black Studies circles, that is) volumes authored by Black women scholars, the most recent group to establish a viable presence in the academy. Gloria T. Hull, professor of English at the University of Delaware, co-editor of *All the Women Are White, All the Blacks Are Men, But Some of Us Are Brave: Black Women's Studies* (Old Westbury, NY: The Feminist Press, 1982) and editor of *Give Us Each Day: The Diary of Alice Dunbar-Nelson* (New York: Norton, 1984), has recently published a provocative and icon-shattering book, *Color, Sex, and Poetry: Three Women Writers of the Harlem Renaissance* (Bloomington: Indiana University Press, 1987). No one who reads it will ever again be able to think of the Harlem Renaissance in quite the same way. Hull effectively unveils the rampant sexism and chauvinism of the Black male leaders of the Renaissance. In her preface, Hull wrote that in addition to a faculty research grant from the University of Delaware and a summer stipend from the National Endowment for the Humanities, a Rockefeller Foundation fellowship enabled her "to do the requisite, remaining travel and research" (p. ix).

E. Frances White, MacArthur Professor of History and Black Studies at Hampshire College, Amherst, Massachusetts, and author of *Sierra Leone's Settler Women Traders: Women on the Afro-European Frontier* (Ann Arbor: University of Michigan Press, 1987), observed in her preface: "I received funding from the African American Scholars Council, the Danforth Foundation (Kent Fellowship) and the Roothbert Fund to aid me in my initial research. An A. W. Mellon Faculty Development Grant and a Fulbright Senior Research Scholar Fellowship helped me to return to Sierra Leone to collect further material" (p. x). White's brilliant study contributes a feminist perspective to the continuing debate over the impact of colonial rule on women in Africa.

I first learned of Sylvia Ardyn Boone's *Radiance from the Waters: Concepts of Feminine Beauty in Mende Art* (New Haven: Yale University Press, 1986) from Black historian Nell Irvin Painter of the University of North Carolina. Painter commented, "It's a wonderful book that takes real Black beauty, African beauty, seriously, in an academic not a commercial way."[4] The volume is indeed dazzling. Boone noted in her acknowledgment, "The Foreign Area Fellowship Program of the Social Science Research Council funded the first part of my work in England and later in Sierra Leone. A Dissertation Year Fellowship from the American Association of University Women and a grant from the Ford Foundation National Fellowship Fund financed additional research and then the write-up" (p. ix). Boone is an associate professor of the history of art and African and Afro-American Studies at Yale University.

I have highlighted these outstanding examples of Black scholarship because the study of Black women is the current frontier in Black Studies. Combined with the historical Studies of professors Jacqueline Jones of

Wellesley College (*Song of Sorrow, Song of Love: Black Women, Work and the Family in Slavery and Freedom*, New York: Basic Books, 1985) and Deborah G. White at Rutgers University (*Ar'n't I a Woman: Female Slaves in the Plantation South*, New York: Norton, 1985), the novels of Toni Morrison, Alice Walker, and Paule Marshall, the literary criticism of Prof. Barbara Christian at the University of California, Berkeley (*Black Women Novelists: The Development of a Tradition*, Westport, CT: Greenwood, 1980), and the Black feminist theory of Prof. bell hooks of Yale University, the three examples of Black scholarship mentioned above would make for a dynamic course. Because the curriculum in Black Studies is so flexible and fluid, unfettered by disciplinary constraints, such a course would be introduced and taught with elan. Moreover, it should be noted that quite a few of the directors and chairs of Black Studies—for example, at Cornell and at the University of Mississippi—have established working ties with women's Studies.

In addition to fellowship support, foundations have provided major funding for a host of Black editing projects. A few of the notable projects are the Frederick Douglass Papers, John Blassingame, editor; the Booker T. Washington Papers, Louis Harlan, editor; and the Freedmen and Southern Society Project, Ira Berlin, editor. These projects have made accessible to scholars invaluable documents and primary sources. Their significance to Black Studies scholarship cannot be exaggerated.

The massive Black Periodical Literature Project edited by Prof. Henry Louis Gates, Jr., of Cornell University, who is also author of *Figures in Black: Words, Signs, and the "Racial" Self* (New York: Oxford University Press, 1987), is a particularly important venture. His monographs continue to break new ground in literary theory and are indeed changing the way theorists evaluate and interpret Black literature. The fiction project, on the other hand, reclaims the literary efforts of past generations of Black writers. Gates's efforts are well-funded and deservedly so.

An especially encouraging sign of the vitality of Black Studies is the rising number of Black scholars who are contemplating and/or engaging in collaborative research projects. This progression from individual research to collaborative efforts involving many people from different disciplines is a natural one. A typical first book or major publication is usually a revised dissertation. Now that many Black scholars are working on second and third books and, most importantly, have acquired tenure, they are eager to develop collaborative Studies. This impulse should be encouraged, as it bodes well for the development of Black Studies as a discipline.

In the early years, Black Studies units justified their intellectual existence on the grounds that they shattered the confining and restrictive boundaries of traditional disciplines. Actually, as far as I have been able to discern, most of the individual scholars in these programs and departments have published works that are very much in keeping with the methodological canons of the disciplines in which they were formally trained. It was naive and unrealistic to expect the young historian or sociologist of the Afro-American experience to retool, master a new, still inadequately defined Afrocentric methodology, and then prepare publishable manuscripts and win tenure—all within a six-year period.

In sum, I am optimistic about the future of Black Studies because of the energy, creativity, industry, and achievements of Black scholars. The dream that Black Studies can be in the forefront of interdisciplinary research and writing deserves all available nourishment. The contemporary Black Studies movement will be considerably enhanced and sustained by serious professional scholars engaged in research and writing of the Black experience. The creative potential of Black Studies, however, will become a reality only to the extent that foundations and universities provide full support.

Black Studies in the Midwest

Nellie McKay

In the Midwest, as elsewhere, Black Studies cannot be reduced to a simple or single formula that explains it. At present, the field is defined and practiced in many ways, which vary from institution to institution. There are those whose mission is essentially the pursuit of knowledge inside the academy, so that this knowledge may be applied broadly to the world outside. For others, the primary goal is full identification with the Black community outside the walls of white academia. The common reference point is the validity of the African Diaspora experience: the creation of an active consciousness that a rich culture springs from Africa, which her children, scattered across the face of the globe, share and celebrate for its uniqueness, power, and strength.

Beyond that, as the Hine report noted, among no combination of programs is there even an agreement on curriculum. This, of course, need not reflect negatively on the field of Black Studies. On the contrary, the diversity of approaches is healthy, offering a breadth and scope of expression that emphasize possibilities not yet discovered. In surveying Black Studies in the Midwest, I discovered that as Black Studies reaches the end of its second decade of existence, there is a new surge of energy and a renewed commitment among many people, white and Black, to make this new field a permanent part of our Western knowledge base.

I also perceived a renewed commitment among predominantly white institutions to strengthen Black Studies and to increase the number of Black faculty on their campuses. This comes at a time when at least one group of Black scholars inside of these universities—those who completed graduate work between the mid and late 1970s and who have proved themselves good citizens of the intellectual world have achieved a level of maturity that enables them to know exactly what they want for Black Studies, as well as how to deal with academic politics in more sophisticated ways. Without doubt, the new institutional commitment is good for Black Studies and for Black scholars.

Nevertheless, my optimism about the general picture also comes with qualifications. One wonders whether there is a direct relationship between the positive activity of white administrators and "the ugly racial incidents" at the University of Michigan, the University of Massachusetts at Amherst, and the University of Wisconsin at Madison, among other institutions, over the past few years. Such incidents reflect deep-seated problems that have negative implications for Black students and for Black Studies. In the Midwest, as in other parts of the country, Black faculty and Black Studies (including the work of white scholars in Black Studies) are still engaged in a constant struggle to validate their existence. I agree fully with Hine that, as a whole, the scholarly community has come a long way in its general attitudes toward Black Studies, and that the field has undergone a dramatic change of status inside the academy. Black Studies, however, has still not achieved full acceptance in the scholarly community, despite the fact that it has been one of the prime movers in revolutionizing the nature of accepted knowledge in the 1980s.

We have only to look at developments in Western literature as an example. A little more than a decade ago, few could have imagined the revisions that women and minorities, especially Blacks, are currently making to the "sacred" canon. Still, Black Studies has a long way to go to achieve full dignity and acceptance in the academic community much further, for instance, than women's Studies. This gap is keenly felt in the Midwest, where some of the largest public institutions of higher education and strongest Black Studies programs in the country are located.

But the battle is not lost, and there is also reason to feel positive about the achievements and future of Black Studies. On the campuses that I visited, I heard high praise for Black Studies personnel from administrators, none of whom seemed to fear for the future of the field at their institutions. Black Studies programs are aware of this administration support. Department and program chairs to whom I spoke unanimously agreed on that point, even as they spoke of other problems that impede their development—problems created by the unavailability of sufficient faculty to teach courses in various areas of the field, or by fiscal difficulties in the institutions.

Despite these difficulties, all Black Studies programs in the Midwest (weak and strong) were seriously recruiting faculty during the 1988–89 school year, and were engaged in searches for multiple old and new positions—not simply replacing faculty who have left. There is keen rivalry among the strongest programs, as each institution attempts to fill a number of positions.

The difficulty in securing adequate faculty is a common problem for all Black Studies units in the Midwest. Geography plays an important role in this. Both established and younger Black faculty—even those trained in the Midwest—are less likely to settle in the area. They seek appointments on the East or West coasts, usually in or near large urban centers with diverse populations. The problem is that many of the most academically attractive institutions of higher education in the Midwest—for example, the universities at Madison, Iowa City, and Evanston—are located in communities with very little ethnic and/or cultural diversity, and are therefore less appealing to minority faculty. The difficulty in attracting sufficient Black Studies faculty to these institutions results in certain courses not being taught regularly, which leads to a falling off of student interest and a loss of enthusiasm for the program among students who should support it most. This is a serious problem that needs to be addressed.

Attracting faculty to the Midwest is part of an even more serious problem facing Black Studies across the country: the extremely small pool of scholars in the field on both the junior and senior levels. On the junior level, we must convince more bright undergraduates to choose college and university teaching for a career. We have the opportunity to train them and to make sure that the work we began goes on when we can no longer do it. On the senior level, many of the Black scholars who entered the job market a decade ago did not survive the stresses, and their loss leaves the small group of those who remained bearing a heavier load today. In addition, some who remained have been unable to pursue research and writing to advance themselves professionally. That has made the pool even smaller.

Many of those who are now successful mid-career scholars are being offered appointments in the nation's most prestigious institutions of higher education, with phenomenal salaries, minimal teaching loads, and generous research budgets. Black scholars have begun to join the ranks of academic luminaries, and their position is richly deserved. It is clearly in their best interests to take advantage of such opportunities.

On the other hand, only a few scholars remain to engage in the day-to-day struggles of full-time teaching, research, counseling, and other duties. They have to cope with less talented undergraduates and the frustrations of overwork. In the Midwest, this issue is more serious than in some other parts of the country. Few institutions (especially state institutions) in this region can afford "stars." For those that can, the value of a single star is dubious in light of the resentment such a scholar can inspire among colleagues.

Although I can personally offer no swift or easy solution to this difficulty, it seems to me that Black Studies scholars in the Midwest might address the problem collectively, to the advantage of all concerned. For one thing, the strong Black Studies programs in these states are sufficiently different to create a productive dialogue and allow room for more cooperation than has existed so far. At Michigan and Ohio State, I floated the idea of a regional Black Studies conference in 1990—an academic conference— to celebrate the twentieth anniversary of the field. This conference would be somewhat like the American history conference held at Purdue a few years ago, but on a broader scale. Such a conference not only would give us a chance to enumerate our gains and to applaud ourselves, but also would allow us to think and plan seriously together for more consolidated and unified success over the next twenty years.

Black Studies is very much alive in the Midwest. Many programs are doing well, others are experiencing difficulties, and there are miles to go before any among us will be allowed to sleep. But Black Studies has survived its infancy and early childhood, and it is now moving ahead into what might well be a troubled adolescence. Nevertheless, the signs point to effective growth toward maturity. One measure of health is the number of students who take Black Studies courses, not as majors but for educational enrichment. Most people with whom I spoke noted the popularity of Black Studies classes, especially among white students seeking to learn something about the Black experience. There is still a long road ahead, but Black scholars, and white scholars in the field, are convinced that they must travel the hard path they have chosen so that when the "great books" on our civilization are opened, the history, literature, music, and culture of Africa's scattered children will have been prominently recorded, and the Mother can never again be denied.

Notes

[1] Nathan Huggins, *Afro-American Studies. A Report to the Ford Foundation* (1985); reprinted in present volume, pp. 10–92.

[2] For a discussion of nomenclature in Black Studies, see pp. 15–16.

[3] In 1988 Temple University established the first Ph.D. program in African American Studies.

[4] Painter to Hine, June 22, 1987.

PART THREE

Funding Change: The O'Meally, Smith Report

An Introduction to the O'Meally, Smith Report
Farah Jasmine Griffin

Evaluation of Ford-Funded African American Studies Departments, Centers, and Institutes
Robert G. O'Meally and Valerie Smith

Funding Change:

Introduction to the O'Meally, Smith Report

In 1993, eleven years after Huggins's *Afro-American Studies: A Report to the Ford Foundation* and three years after Harris-Hine-McKay's *Three Essays: Black Studies in the United States,* program officer Sheila Biddle commissioned a new report that would be conducted by two scholars of African American literature—Drs. Robert O'Meally, Zora Neale Hurston Professor of English and Comparative Literature, and Valerie Smith, then professor of English at UCLA.

The very title of this third report—*Evaluation of Ford-Funded African American Studies Departments, Centers and Institutes* (1994)—says much about the field's evolution since Huggins. There is an implicit recognition that Ford funding, though central to the field, does not constitute it. The title tells us that there are a number of programs not funded by the Ford Foundation. And, of the three reports, O'Meally-Smith is the first to assess the impact of Ford funding on specific programs.

In 1988, in addition to its other African American Studies program grants, the foundation began awarding three-year grants of approximately

$300,000. For this study, O'Meally and Smith followed up on the recipients of these large-scale grants to "leading departments, programs and centers." The goal of the grants had been to encourage the next generation of scholars, support research projects, and disseminate the best new scholarship.[1] Four Ivy League and six state schools were the recipients of these grants. Ford monies helped to support graduate students and, in one instance, provided grounding for the establishment of the Ph.D. program. The Ford funds also provided needed resources, reduced by fiscal crises, to the state institutions.

All in all, Ford Foundation funding gave prestige to individual programs and their campuses and allowed the development of new structures: advanced degree programs, summer institutes, courses, and conferences. The authors acknowledge the impact of the field on traditional disciplines, its creation of newer interdisciplinary methodologies, and the leadership provided by the field to Ethnic Studies.

Following an evaluation of the uses to which specific programs put Ford funds, O'Meally and Smith generate a valuable list of best practices gathered from the most successful programs, including:

1. Committed partnership from schools' top administrators.
2. Programmatic leadership that perceives the mission and culture of the institution as a whole and designs courses of study and other structures accordingly.
3. Flexible and expansive broad-based leadership that initiates dialogues regionally, nationally, and internationally.

Indeed, O'Meally and Smith recommended broadening the scope of funding that encourages connections across a city or region through seminars or floating conferences—especially in places like New York and Washington, D.C.—noting that this model would also help scholars in institutions where there are no African American Studies programs or departments. The authors further recommended support for large research projects that help create the necessary tools for the discipline.

Envisioning future concerns about the relationship between Ethnic Studies and African American Studies, O'Meally and Smith caution that

African Americanist scholars seem more willing to pursue Diaspora models than interethnic configurations. Does the tension arise from a feeling that "ethnic does not often mean Black"? To address this issue, the authors recommend that the two programs be funded separately so that each can bring its own resources to collaborative projects.

In sum, O'Meally and Smith conclude that "despite well-publicized examples of racial romanticism and defensive rigidity at the periphery of the field, African American Studies has established itself as a vibrant and expansive area of scholarly work within liberal arts and sciences." Implicit in this statement is an understanding of the assaults on African American Studies launched by segments of the academy and the media. Most notably, these critiques have been directed at more Afrocentric programs. Indeed, on the heels of the O'Meally-Smith report, in 1995, Dr. Cornel West—a widely recognized African American Studies "star"—was the object of highly negative publicity.[2]

In the midst of this politically charged atmosphere, it must be noted, the foundation supported production of Stanley Nelson's award-winning film documentary, *Shattering the Silence: The Case for Minority Faculty* (1997). The film explores faculty diversity by focusing on eight minority scholars in the humanities and social sciences—among them Darlene Clark Hine, co-author of the second Ford report: *Three Essays: Black Studies in the United States.* The film examines teaching, research, and the impact of this work on students, universities, and disciplines. Countering the mainstream media coverage, it follows these scholars in both their professional and personal lives to draw a more complex and multidimensional portrait of African American intellectuals.

Farah Jasmine Griffin
(2006)

Notes

[1] While grants prior to this period also sought to support research projects and disseminate the best new scholarship, the amounts of individual grants were much smaller.

[2] The March 6, 1995, issue of the *New Republic* received a great deal of media attention when it published Leon Wieseltier's critique of Cornel West as its cover story. In bold white letters against a Black background, the cover headline read "The Decline of the Black Intellectual." Although Wieseltier's article focused on Professor West, the bold headline conflated the most well-known contemporary Black intellectual with the status of Black intellectuals broadly. In addition, controversial comments made by Leonard Jeffries, former chair of African American Studies at City College of New York, also led conservative critics to unfairly label all forms of Afrocentricity anti-Semitic.

Evaluation of Ford-Funded African American Studies Departments, Centers, and Institutes (1994)

Robert G. O'Meally
Valerie Smith

The O'Meally, Smith Report
Contents

The Report
Introduction
General Assessments
Site Visits and Observations
      Cornell University
      Harvard University
      Indiana University
      Michigan State University
      University of California, Berkeley
      University of California, Los Angeles
      University of Michigan
      University of Pennsylvania
      University of Wisconsin
      Yale University
Summary and Recommendations
Notes

Introduction

Beginning in fiscal year 1988, the Education and Culture Program of the Ford Foundation awarded three-year grants to leading departments, programs, and centers of African American Studies. Ford's stated goals were to encourage the next generation of scholars, to support research projects, and to disseminate the field's best new scholarship. From January until June 1993, we visited the institutions that received these grants—UC Berkeley, Cornell, Harvard, Indiana, Michigan, Michigan State, Pennsylvania, UCLA, Wisconsin, and Yale—to assess the uses to which Ford funding had been put.

In each instance, we were favorably impressed by the ways in which the academic units[1] had developed programming that suited the needs and strengths of their institutions and communities. The range of initiatives that Ford funding has supported testifies to the vibrancy and diversity of African American pedagogy and research at this point in history, clearly justifying future funding in the area. With the enterprises of scholarship, teaching and outreach deeply linked, the comments that follow describe the highlights of each unit.

At such public institutions as Indiana, UCLA, and Wisconsin, funds helped to offset shrinking resources during a time of economic crisis. At each of these schools, some of the grant money was earmarked to enhance the professional development of graduate students and nontenured faculty by supporting research travel, faculty-student mentorships, and conferences. At Wisconsin, Ford funds were used to support a major national conference on

"Afro-American Studies in the 21st Century" that explored the various intellectual, ideological, and cultural meanings of African American Studies.

At Michigan, funds were used similarly, with particular emphasis on disseminating the most groundbreaking work in the field. The centerpieces of the initiative there were lecture series and a major conference featuring leading African Americanists. Reviewing the history of the field, conferees addressed the topic: "Reflections and Revisions: Twenty Years of Afro-American and African Studies."

At Michigan State, the concern to establish a context for new research led to the development of the first Ph.D. in Comparative Black History—a program that evolved with Ford support. And at Berkeley, the Ford initiative has strengthened the department's emphasis on diasporic, interdisciplinary research through course development, collaborative research projects, and partnerships with secondary and community college teachers.

Pennsylvania, Harvard, and Yale have been especially concerned with outreach to faculty at other institutions, sponsoring summer institutes, visiting professorships, and conferences, respectively. The success of this first funding cycle warrants the renewal of grants to these institutions and to clusters of schools (e.g., in Washington, D.C., and New York City) to enhance the possibilities for intellectual exchange among scholars. Within this broad network, we would encourage the Foundation once again to allow the institutions to articulate the best uses to which such awards might be put, given the particular needs of their constituencies.

General Assessments

Beginning in fiscal year 1988, the Education and Culture Program of the Ford Foundation awarded three-year grants of approximately $300,000 each to leading departments, programs, and centers in the field of African American Studies. These grants went to Cornell, Harvard, Indiana, Michigan, Michigan State, Pennsylvania, UC Berkeley, UCLA, Wisconsin, and Yale.

These awards were quite timely. During the current economic crisis (one often compared with the Great Depression), cutbacks and freezes in the academic sphere have been the difficult order of the day. The American academy has been a scene of shrinking public funds and private donations, layoffs, and increases in tuition, alongside reductions in faculty salaries and stipends to needy students. Of course, the impact of the current crisis has been harder on schools in some parts of the country than others; but no institution of higher education has been unshaken. As a comparatively new field of study on most college and university campuses, African American Studies and its various components—curricula, faculty, administrative staff, and student service systems—all are vulnerable in such an unstable economic climate. At virtually every institution we visited, the Ford grant helped to brace African American Studies against upending times.

Grants from the Ford Foundation enabled African American Studies at Michigan State not just to stay afloat but to develop its path-breaking Ph.D. program in Comparative Black History. Likewise, Ford money permitted the

Black Studies departments at Berkeley, Indiana, Michigan, and Wisconsin to support graduate student and junior faculty research and to generate nationally acclaimed meetings. Ford enabled these schools to nurture their fledgling intellectual communities in African American Studies and, in fact, to operate as national centers of inquiry in a way that has had the effect of democratizing the field: ensuring that more than a handful of institutions could be counted as top leaders.

Coming at a key moment in the field's evolution, these Ford grants contributed in a very significant way to the growth and development of African American Studies as a scholarly/pedagogical enterprise. We agree with Robert L. Harris, Jr., who, in *Three Essays: Black Studies in the United States*,[2] observed that in the mid-1980s Afro-American Studies entered the second stage of its recent manifestation in the U.S. This stage has moved through a time of "legitimization and institutionalization," to the present period of "theoretical refinement and more sophisticated analysis and interpretation."

By the mid-1980s, African American Studies on many campuses was engaged in a struggle between what appeared to be conflicting agendas. On one hand, faculty at a wide range of schools felt themselves compelled to solidify and extend the intellectual bases of the field. On the other hand, many African American students felt this emphasis on the strictly scholarly component of Black Studies came at the expense of the field's keystone social and/or activist functions, thus betraying its origins on predominately White campuses in the forthright political struggles of the 1960s.

In its current phase (Harris's fourth stage), African American Studies appears to have emerged substantially intact from these struggles. Many institutions have succeeded in establishing African American cultural centers, and other such structures where students, diverse in ethnicity, may find support. Thus freed from the complex of extracurricular duties that marked the first years of Black Studies, many retooled academic programs and departments have been able to function as places where students and faculty could concentrate their best attention on the exigencies of research and study. In some cases, African American Studies has addressed the old 1960s to 1980s (and 1990s) socio-political action versus the "strictly academic" split by creating theories and structures that make clear that the

Black Studies scholar can pursue research which has a vital impact on public policy. (Note that the new Institute for African American Studies at Columbia University has declared its intention to emphasize questions of public policy, and to some degree, the role of the Black Studies scholar as an activist or public intellectual.)

Despite all economic difficulties, the 1980s and 1990s have been a time of rapid intellectual evolution within the academy as a whole. Spurred to a significant degree by what might be termed the Black Studies Movement (as well as by the hard realities of America's shifting demographic cartography), colleges and universities in the United States have felt the pressure to revise their curricula to reflect more fully the range of American "ethnic" groups. In the midst of these national mandates and discussions, African American Studies has been uniquely positioned for leadership.

Having sought, since its beginnings, to address problems of inclusiveness, exclusiveness, and the meaning of "racial" and ethnic difference in America, African American Studies has often played a vanguard role in this season of scholarly and curricular change. Its scholars have been actively involved in theorizing and consolidating African American Studies within the traditional fields (i.e., History, Literature, Psychology, and Anthropology); expanding it into other established fields (Natural and Physical Sciences, Philosophy, and Linguistics); and establishing such newer interdisciplinary methodologies as those of gender and cultural studies.

To be sure, this questioning of the agenda in Black Studies—both as an independent area of study (some would say a discipline) and as part of an interdependent community of scholarly units—has been good for the field. Even when issues have not been definitively resolved, spirited debates and the far reach of their implications signal the field's vitality and importance. No longer can African American Studies easily be pressed to the margins as an off-beat province "for Blacks only" or dismissed as a sop to Black student pressure. Serving many students (majors and nonmajors, Blacks and non-Blacks; often doing so in required "core" or "distributional" courses, African American Studies classes have come into their own.

Having become more self-consciously theoretical about its project as an interdisciplinary field of inquiry, African American Studies is often presented as suggesting new directions for the university of the future. It is often lifted up, for example, as a model for new programs in such fields as Women's Studies, Ethnic Studies, American Studies, and even in such distant fields as Medieval Studies. The present round of Ford grants to African American Studies has helped immeasurably in this time of self-scrutiny and new direction.

To cite but a few examples of Ford's impact on these processes of redefinition and growth: At Yale, Ford money has helped to establish a film collection in African American Studies that expands the department's definition as a site of significant pedagogical and research possibilities in visual culture. At Indiana, Ford funds enabled faculty to develop an archive of African American Music, History, and Culture that would complement the holdings of the Film Center Archive and enhance the departmental emphasis on African American cultural life. And at Berkeley, Ford funds have been used to encourage collaborative projects between faculty members and graduate students that would enable participants to explore the interdisciplinary implications of their joint projects. Very important, too, is the increasing emphasis at Berkeley, and at several of the schools we observed, on African American Studies as a field that encompasses not only the experience of U.S. Blacks but of peoples and cultures of African lineage throughout the Americas and indeed throughout the world.

Ford funds provided support for undergraduates, graduate students, and junior faculty at a time when it has been necessary to ensure the existence of a coterie of intellectuals to carry the work forward into the next generation. As colleges and universities acknowledge the importance of African American Studies and other Ethnic Studies areas to their curricula (in some cases establishing a new "diversity" requirement); as new areas in African American Studies develop, increased numbers of African Americanists are needed to fill the available positions. Moreover, as the field gains in visibility and as the research continues to address timely and engaging topics, growing numbers of students have been inspired to enter Ph.D. programs in the area. In order for the leading universities to nurture undergraduate and graduate students alike, they have needed to provide financial and intellectual support. Several of the institutions we visited have found creative ways to address this situation.

At Harvard, for example, the Visiting Scholars Program now calls for such scholars to not only pursue their own research, but teach one course per year. In this way, students are exposed to areas that otherwise are not taught there while visiting faculty receive much needed time to complete their research projects. Visiting scholars at Cornell are likewise able to take advantage of superior research facilities and contribute to the ongoing life of the University. And at Penn, the Center for the Study of Black Life and Culture (CSBLAC) has sponsored summer seminars in Black Studies for professors in the northeast region. This program has had an impact on the work of scholars at Penn and those at nearby colleges, universities, and secondary schools.

Graduate students at Wisconsin repeatedly express the impact that various Ford-sponsored conferences have had on their development; the students report their delight at having heard the conferees' broad range of perspectives, to have met prominent scholars, to have participated in public debates and in some instances, to have presented papers. Their counterparts at Berkeley, Indiana, UCLA, Yale, and elsewhere were similarly enthusiastic about the opportunities extended them to meet and exchange ideas in such settings. So the broad goal of bringing new scholars into the field, of keeping the pipeline moving, has been addressed by the present round of grants with very positive results.

What is clearer than ever is that however successful may be the efforts to enhance "'the pipeline drama"—that vibrant process of inviting new scholars into the field and of supporting them as they advance toward and beyond tenure—other Black Studies scenarios must also be enhanced. Several scholars we visited made the point that, if "phase one" of the contemporary Black Studies struggle has been to assist the pipeline, then "phase two" might very well focus on the need to give special support to scholars involved in long-term projects designed to create the tools of research: the tools that make the tools. Here the point is that African Americanists often lack such building blocks of research as encyclopedias, concordances, critical editions, special dictionaries, electronic databases, and other fundamental reference materials. Lacking tools in such categories, too often our scholars find themselves starting a project as if no one else ever worked on anything like it before: reinventing wheels.

To meet this problem of research tool-making, several schools in the present review were funded specifically to establish or to enhance existing research components of their African American studies units. UCLA's grant was targeted specifically for its Center for Afro-American Studies, the research component of that school's operation. Berkeley, Cornell, Harvard, Indiana, Wisconsin, and Yale all used their grants to improve their research sites and tools, notably their holdings in film and videotape. At Michigan State, Darlene Clark Hine edited *Black Women in America,* a two-volume encyclopedia that provides an extremely useful source-book for scholars. Though not funded by this grant specifically, that encyclopedia project stands as a rich research tool, a model enterprise that will suggest thesis and book projects for years to come.

Likewise, Harvard's Black Fiction Project, through its publication programs and consultations with inquiring scholars, has assisted students of Black literary history in very substantial ways. Building the tools to do research in Black Studies is an idea that already is working and that may suggest funding goals for the future. Don't let us be misunderstood here. We speak not of a complete change of direction but a nuanced change, a shifting of the weight in favor of scholars who are building large research tools. This is not to recommend that Ford purchase research hardware or other such "tools" in that sense of the term; rather that Ford give more support to those whose projects are to make such new tools as encyclopedias and concordances themselves.

One very positive effect of this round of Ford grants to African American Studies departments, programs, and centers has been to address the field's general problem of isolation. Scholars in this field often feel cut off, as if they were going it entirely alone. Of course, this is an issue for all members of the contemporary university, with its wide spread of tight specializations. But it is particularly a concern for African Americanists, so often marginalized, to put it bluntly, along the color line. To combat this problem in its myriad guises—including the group's own temptations in the directions of provincialism, defensiveness, and romanticism—African Americanists at the schools we visited discussed how Ford grants helped in the forging of links: scholar to scholar, department to department, school to school, school to larger community.

At Cornell, one professor met this problem of intellectual isolation by rewriting his syllabus to encompass not just one or two "data points" but three or more. According to this strategy, his students were reading about Blacks throughout the Diaspora. They also read about other groups with similar concerns relating to cultural expression and political position.

At Cornell and elsewhere, this issue of intellectual isolation was structurally addressed by team-taught courses and jointly appointed faculty members. In both instances these collaborations sometimes involved work between Africana Studies and other academic units. In this same spirit of university-wide collaboration, certain Africana courses serve the needs of programs in agriculture and development, as well as in the liberal arts college as a whole. Such ventures at schools we visited have helped to make Multicultural Studies more than just a slogan.

Clearly, the Ford-sponsored conferences also addressed this issue of isolation. Graduate students at Yale who said they sometimes feared that their highly specialized scholarly "discourse" was spoken only in New Haven were delighted to have visitors come to town speaking the same language. Ford money sent such students from Yale (and elsewhere) to conferences where they met their counterparts and future colleagues. Faculty benefited from monies to plan and run conferences or just to attend them. Indiana's conferences on "Joe Louis and the American Press" and "Black Religious and Musical Expression in American Cinema" were models of interdisciplinary work under the aegis of African American Studies. Both represented collaborative work on a very high level. At Wisconsin and at other schools we visited we heard about joint projects, conferences, and other evidences of useful partnerships with departments and institutes studying issues of gender and sexuality.

Just as significant a model for collaboration on the faculty level is Harvard University's "working group." Set up to involve faculty from a dozen or so institutions across the nation in quarterly conferences, Harvard working groups have explored such cross-disciplinary topics as "History and Memory in African American Culture" and "The Role of the Black Intellectual." In many cases, these sessions permitted first hearings of works-in-progress, with responses from colleagues across a range of disciplines. Two such groups have climaxed in international meetings that included African Americanists beyond the United States. Collections of the finished papers are to be issued in book form by Oxford and Harvard University Presses. Again, what is clear from these collections, as well as from many other important signs, is that the field has become increasingly diasporic; engaging scholars concerned with blacks in Africa, Europe, and Asia, as well as in the Americas.

This impulse to reach out beyond immediate boundaries takes other significant forms sponsored by Ford. Cornell has established programs encompassing other local colleges and high schools. Penn's summer program for college teachers in the Eastern Atlantic region made for collaborative research, study, and conversation; it also meant that the impact of the seminar extended to major and not-so-major schools from many states. Many of last summer's participants expressed their elation at being in touch with colleagues who similarly suffered the sense of working with a minimum of intellectual support.

In certain instances, Ford grants assisted the subtle process of making or remaking connections within the structures of the Black Studies programs themselves. At Harvard, where the Department of Afro-American Studies had dwindled nearly to nothing while the Du Bois Institute for Afro-American Research had done distinctly better, the Ford grant played a decisive linking role. As mentioned, Institute fellows were required to teach in the Department. In addition, however, in formal consultations and informally, they made themselves available to students and regular colleagues. Formal presentations by Ford Fellows were well attended by those affiliated with the Department and Institute; indeed they often attracted the participation of students and professors campus-wide.

At Yale, the beginning of the current grant cycle coincided with the arrival of Gerald Jaynes as Chair of the African American Studies department. Having some money to dream with, Jaynes worked hard to draw his colleagues into the circle of decision makers and planners. So the grant made for a new, collaborative spirit that has launched an era of reinvigorated activity and sense of purpose. As Yale puts into place its new Ph.D. program in African American Studies, it does so with a spirit that pervades the field:

one of collaborative leadership within the department itself and of vigorous partnership with other departments, too.

What makes the winning teams we surveyed work? There are no secrets here. The programs that have prevailed have done so because of familiar ingredients: smart programmatic leadership; solid funding, particularly from within the school itself; fine staff support; and committed partnership from the school's top administrators. Crucially, the successful program leader(s) perceived with creative insight the peculiar mission and culture of the institution as a whole, and they designed courses of study and other structures accordingly. So at Cornell, where the university's mission encompasses agricultural studies on an international scale, it made good sense for Africana Studies to offer courses to complement this broad institution-wide goal. With this idea in mind, Africana's courses in African languages and cultures (taken by students preparing to work in the context of Africa's agricultural projects) have a context that is central to things Cornellian.

Similarly, Harvard has dropped its plan to establish an M.A. program; the M.A. is not generally regarded as a terminal degree at Harvard. Instead it is working to set up the more typically Harvardian Ph.D. program.

The other obvious characteristic of the most enduring programs is that they are flexible and expansive in scope. They are seizing the current moment, which is distinctly favorable to African American Studies. They are doing so by sponsoring cross-cultural, interdisciplinary courses and professional meetings that encompass issues of race, gender, nationality and social status—current campus-wide concerns which have been debated in Black Studies since its inception. Each one of the schools we reviewed was planning in terms of broad-based leadership in the academy, not just regionally and nationally but in some cases also internationally.

These Ford grants yielded a number of significant unforeseen benefits. Black Studies leaders at every school we visited felt the boon of having extra money during our era of general financial tightening. The extra money allowed for reassessment and planning. Through the grants, African Americanists had the chance to meet together when, instead of a crisis, there was an agenda for intellectual comradeship and challenge. This boon made way for expanding and crisscrossing networks. It also made for higher quality conversation. When asked about the hidden benefits of the Ford grant, Randall Burkett at Harvard answered right away that it made for more magnanimous exchanges among the scholars involved: it made for "more good talk," he said.

The success of winning the grants led to other successes. These awards gave African American Studies departments new prestige on their home campuses that translated into material gains. Suddenly, for example, other departments were coming to African American Studies for possible co-sponsorships, etc. Inevitably, this meant that other academic units were influenced to consider guest speakers and conference topics that might attract the co-sponsorship of African American Studies: African American Studies was not a suffered poor relation but a partner with money of its own.

Being able to bring in new people—junior level faculty or senior scholars—also produced benefits that were unforeseen and far-reaching. Holes in curricula could be filled. Introductory courses in particular could be enriched and enlivened. Having the visiting scholars as students in the Penn summer program (along with the senior visiting presenters) even kept seminar leaders on their toes. And generally speaking, the visitors, whether at Penn or elsewhere, made for intellectual stimulation and cross-fertilization that benefited the hosts in immeasurable ways.

How does one to measure the impact of the grant-sponsored activity on students, particularly graduate students, the field's leaders of tomorrow? In many instances, conferences were designed with direct involvement from graduate students who were instrumental in running things in ways that will help shape their careers. They had practice doing the administrative work involved in conference-making, for example. And, whether as chauffeurs, dinner guests, tour guides, or as special assistants, graduate students were able to confer with leading scholars on an informal basis and to observe them in their various roles onstage and behind-the-scenes.

Out of the general fermentation, new structures are emerging: new advanced degree programs, summer institutes, courses, conferences, etc., and also new structures of feeling; new ways of thinking. All this activity has helped win new and stronger students to the field. And it has changed the map of academia writ large. When we call the schools named here major schools, more than ever what we mean is that they support African American Studies programs that are genuinely vital and comprehensive.

Everyone we asked about where best to target the next round of grants said to keep funding the programs that already were working well. (Here of course they meant to keep funding themselves.) On the question of how to broaden the circle of grantees, we often heard of ideas to build connections across a city or, a region—partnerships that would help in the process of sharing limited resources. In this way, schools not automatically on the list of strong Black Studies centers—but which are not without some important strengths—could be brought under Ford's sponsorship.

For example, a metropolitan Washington, D.C., grant might join the University of Maryland's excellent Black Studies structures with the resources of American, Catholic, George Mason, George Washington, Howard, and UDC. Perhaps the Smithsonian, the Library of Congress, or the National Gallery—just to mention a few obvious possibilities—would be interested in such a consortial partnership. Similarly, Los Angeles, the Bay Area, Boston, New York, or Philadelphia consortia could spread the Black Studies wealth in a way that is creative and broadly enriching. In this way, too, historically Black colleges and universities—some of which have been singularly unenthusiastic about the Black Studies revolution and some that have nurtured significant Black Studies scholars and special library holdings in the field—could be brought into the picture as participants and potential leaders.

Projects could choose such year-long themes as "Black Modernism," "Black Music and Its Impact on the American Culture," "From Critical Discourse to Course Design in Black Studies," "Black Expression and the Public Sphere," or "New World Africanism: Looking at the Audience." On the D.C. scene, a subject like "Home Rule and the Politics of Race in Washington" would be most appropriate. With someone like Mary Helen Washington (at Maryland) as the leader, a city-wide planning session could be devised. Black Studies faculty—convened at Professor Washington's invitation—could iron out a precise topic and share responsibilities.

One or two scholars specializing in the topic could be invited to spend a year in Washington; perhaps each visitor could be housed at Maryland (with no teaching duties) and could give a lecture series (two lectures per term), each at a different school. One can easily imagine someone like Deborah McDowell or Manthia Diawara giving such a lecture series. Each lecture could be preceded by an introductory note on the host school's resources in Black Studies and followed up by discussions with faculty and students. Each session could be set up as a sort of mini-conference, with papers and responses given by scholars at the host school. Some students could attend all lectures; perhaps Maryland and the other schools might be able to set up the series of meetings or conferences as a course. Perhaps the series would culminate in a large, special conference and/or a book. There are other ways to work out such collaborations. But the point would be to share resources in Black Studies and to bring together the community of African Americanists.

Of course, the plan outlined so far would work best in a metropolitan area like Washington, New York, or Atlanta, or in a setting like Amherst, Chapel Hill, or Claremont where consortial arrangements already are in place. At other places, where the lines of communication are not so direct, or where distance is an added problem (one thinks of the state university systems, for example), we are not sure what to suggest. If a "floating conference" model would not work in the way outlined above, perhaps a statewide topic could be fixed; seminars led by visitors could be conducted at home campuses culminating in a statewide conference at year's end. Transportation to this gathering for students and faculty could be provided and a volume of the year's findings made available.

At some schools where there is no significant department or program in Black Studies, serious African Americanists nonetheless go about their business with significant success as scholars and as teachers. How could Ford help such people? Perhaps by setting up individual teaching and/or research awards, the field could still be enriched in a very profound way. Scholar X who is struggling to teach a truly interdisciplinary course could be given a grant to invite five or six visitors to address the class. This approach might be particularly helpful in an introductory Black Studies course, but not only there. According to this same sort of model, individual Scholar Y could get a grant to attend four conferences over a two-year period or to set up a conference at his or her home institution. What we found is that sometimes African Americanists operate almost as departments unto themselves and could be much better participants in the field if their efforts were supported without the usual departmental aegis. In other words, perhaps at times Ford could support Black Studies not just as a program but as a set of individuals who function outside Black Studies units.

Ford might also find ways to sponsor ongoing research projects aimed at producing tools of future research. In this way, Ford could cover multiple bases: assisting vital "pipeline" projects not just by pushing and pulling scholars and scholars-in-training through the system; assuring that they have the tools they needed once they find themselves, at last, with the time and space to do their scholarly work; offering grants for graduate researchers to work on such projects; and then requiring that they do some teaching.

Finally, what we observe is that African Americanists are still run rather ragged by the multiple demands besetting them. Often what they need more than anything is a semester or a year off to pursue their own work free of all encumbrances. Next time around, perhaps there will be individual grants to some of our field's leaders that place them at a clear desk with no phone on top –just a computer and a pass to the stacks.

In the coming years, the question of where African American Studies will stand in relation to "Ethnic Studies" and revamped American Studies programs will be prominent and difficult. What is at stake in these struggles is nothing less than the picture of reality that will take us into the future. Our sense is that many African Americanists have been very cautious about embracing the model of an Ethnic Studies Department within which Black Studies would function because, as one Black Studies scholar at Queens put it, "When people say 'ethnic' they don't usually mean Blacks." The fear is that an Ethnic Studies program can come along that capitalizes on the Black Studies Movement to sponsor efforts in fields that do not include Black Studies in a central role. On the other hand, there have been collaborations that have worked. Our best advice here is to look very, very closely at Ethnic Studies proposals that specifically include Black Studies. We recommend that Ford check with the Black Studies scholars on the given scene to be sure that they are true partners in the proposal and not just listed for legitimacy's sake.

We know we are guessing here, but our best guess is that while Ethnic Studies (in one of its various forms) will be bidding for legitimacy in the coming years, Black Studies will continue to need funding under its own banner. Perhaps the best partnership between Black Studies and Ethnic Studies will come about with both camps having their own pots of cash to affect their own programs—and to collaborate if they wish. Some grants could be set aside specifically for programs sponsored by both camps; certainly both Ethnic Studies and Black Studies have much in common and could have much to share.

We have to ask: where did the grants or the grantees go wrong? Where was there waste or misdirection? These questions are hard to address not because we flinch from them but because we frankly found so little to dislike on our tours. Yale would appear to be the easiest to target in this complaints department. The Chair, Gerald Jaynes, is not a superbly organized bookkeeper, it appears. But then again it was Jaynes who stepped into an impossible briar patch of problems—the recent history of departmental drift, lingering in-house squabbles, sinking faculty and student morale. Jaynes put the Department back on its feet. Finding the Ford grant a real boon—but one that he inherited with funds allocated in what struck him as the wrong categories—Jaynes brought the Department together to decide how to approach Ford with a new plan of action to meet real needs.

Here's where there is room for complaint: at times Ford wondered what Yale was doing with the money. But, as evaluators, we felt strongly that finally Jaynes and company spent the money with great care, and that he did his best to consult with Ford about changes in the grant's specific purposes. Above all, he and the departmental leaders acted responsibly to serve the grant's largest goals. In the end, the proof is that the Department is growing again; morale has undergone a sea-change. Once again, Yale is a key player in the national effort to consolidate the gains in Black Studies and to chart its new directions.

This is as close as we can come to a real complaint to register. And even here, obviously, we think Yale colleagues are to be praised, on the whole, not reprimanded. They and the Ford representatives showed the flexibility and resiliency to look at a plan that did not suit the new Department's needs and to improvise one that worked extraordinarily well.

Again, our lack of negative commentary is not because we wish to perpetrate a whitewash; that would serve no one's purposes. Rather, our general assessment is that these grants represented very careful advance thinking and excellent execution by truly outstanding professionals. In other words, as hard as we looked for trouble, we found virtually nothing worth reporting. These grants worked.

Site Visits and Observations

Cornell University

Ford's grant to Cornell was to bring visiting scholars to the Africana Studies and Research Center, three visitors a year over a three-year period. Over the span of the grant, and for two years beyond it, Cornell would undertake to hire three new faculty members in Africana Studies. Cornell's larger motive vis-à-vis Black Studies has been to assist an academic program and research center in the process of reinvigoration. These three goals stand out:

1. To strengthen the quality of the faculty;
2. To increase the emphasis on research and writing in the field; and
3. To help Africana studies establish and nurture linkages to other academic units within the university community and beyond the university's walls.

Simply put, Cornell's program has suffered from its isolation from the rest of the campus and from its failure to attract and retain research scholars at the highest levels. Ford's grant was designed to help Cornell confront these difficult problems as it prepared for a new decade and a new century.

Cornell's Ford programs were conspicuously successful. The professors we met—Professors Rae Banks and N'Dri Thérèse Assie-Lumumba—are both excellent scholars who have served the Center's missions exceedingly well. Banks and Assie-Lumumba sounded chords heard throughout our travels: the grant rescued them from the drudgery of day-in/day-out teaching, gave them time to write, and provided access to superb research facilities and services. Both of these women came to Cornell from schools with very limited resources (the University of the Virgin Islands and the University of Lome, Togo, respectively) and felt tremendously fortunate to be able to work at Cornell. "At Lome," Assie-Lumumba told us, "I was the library." Particularly in the case of Assie-Lumumba, the more senior of the two scholars, the Ford Fellows lent prestige to the Cornell program as a faculty of researchers.

The key to Cornell's renewed success is Professor Robert Harris who embodies the goals and values of the Center; and, in his quiet but forceful way, has guided it to its new position as a full partner in the greater Cornell mission. Working with colleagues across the campus, Harris has made Cornell's historic emphasis on the Africanness of Africana Studies work in a way that suits Cornell's particular academic culture. He has forged links with David Lewis, director of Cornell's Institute for African Development to co-sponsor (in the truly collaborative sense of that term) programs for specialists both in African culture and political/economic development. Such a partnership takes advantage of Cornell's identity as a public institution (though, in fact, a private university) concerned with practical issues of policy-making in such areas as Agriculture and Business. Scholars coming to campus to study problems of drought relief are, therefore, well served by the Center's programs in African Languages, History, and Art, as well as in the sciences and social sciences.

Cornell is a real "teaching school." The graduate students we met are very serious and enthusiastic about the Africana Studies Program. They are thrilled by the availability of new faculty, thanks to Ford; and they are connected with programs that take them into local schools—spreading the word of Black Studies.

This is a program excitingly on the rise. As indicators, the team-taught courses (one in Black/Jewish relations, for example), campus-wide lectures and exhibits and the growing roster of Black and White students, all speak well for the "new Cornell."

Harvard University

Harvard's grant from Ford was designed to fund its ongoing Visiting Scholars Program and faculty "working groups." Harvard's proposal made clear that African American Studies is in the process of revitalization and that the University views the grant as part of this new growth. Specifically, the grant was meant to shore up the Du Bois Institute in ways that would positively impact the Department of Afro-American Studies as a teaching force and locus of intellectual activity. Accordingly, the Harvard proposal aimed "to reshape the visiting scholars program so that it would serve the needs of the Department as well as the Institute." In addition to pursuing individual research projects and teaching one course per year, fellows were to participate in the weekly colloquium series and deliver one public lecture. Thus, Ford's support of scholarly "working groups" also supported a program creating linkage with the Department and the students.

The program worked. Visiting scholars fulfilled their duties to the Department, and did significantly more than the minimum. Professors George Frederickson and Fawzia Afzal-Khan became informal advisors to graduate and undergraduate students not necessarily enrolled in their specific courses. The colloquium series has become a true intellectual center of the Institute and the Department—indeed of the University. These working sessions presenting new research by top scholars have helped shape African American Studies (both the Department and the Institute) as one of those key places on campus to find out what new wood is being cut in the academy.

Harvard's program works because of several key strengths:

1. Unequivocal support from the central administration;
2. Henry Louis Gates, Jr. is not just a star but a man of enormous energy who has taken pains to learn how Harvard ticks and to build African American Studies (Institute and Department) in ways that complement the overall Harvard mission; and
3. Randall Burkett, the keystone administrator/scholar.

The Ford-funded projects here include *Transition*, a scholarly magazine of the Black Fiction Project, and a thrust to hire new faculty members in a program that is rebuilding. Each effort complements the others. Visiting scholars are considered as possible new faculty appointees. The Black Fiction Project supports the research of fellows, regular faculty, and students.

Transition broadcasts the questions raised in working groups and colloquia to a broader community.

There are still problems at Harvard. Student majors complain that there are too few courses, and that those offered are so diverse as to feel diffused. Some worry that too much of the program that works well is riding on the coattails of one key scholar (Professor Gates). The students wonder, if he leaves, what would remain?

Despite such questions, the visitor leaves Harvard very impressed with its high purposes and strengths. The visit makes clear that, by supporting Harvard, Ford has assisted in the "pipeline drama." Visitors—junior and senior—are helped in their efforts at research (and thus in the thrust for promotion and tenure); while those in "permanent" residence—faculty and students—are also supported. What's most striking here is that, in addition to assisting with the pipeline, Ford's other grants have helped in the equally vital project of producing concordances, encyclopedias, annotated editions, ongoing research projects (like the Black Fiction Project) which at last provide the basic materials for a field that is coming-of-age.

Indiana University

The Department of Afro-American Studies at Indiana University confronts many of the same challenges as other schools we visited. It is a large public institution in the Midwest, located in a state with a small African American population. The Department at Indiana has been able to use Ford resources to enhance its strengths, to heighten its visibility on campus and nationwide, to support especially graduate students and junior faculty members, and to alleviate the problem of student isolation. We were impressed here too by the extraordinary feeling of enthusiasm, productivity and collegiality.

Given the limited level of university funds available for faculty and graduate student research support, significant portions of the Ford grant have been reserved each year for conferences, research travel and graduate assistantships. Everyone we spoke to truly valued the opportunities made available under the Ford grant. Students who had traveled to archives and delivered papers at conferences benefited from the feedback they received and were able to publish their work. Such student beneficiaries reported feeling that they had gained a deeper understanding of what it meant to be a scholar. Faculty, too, felt that their re-search was greatly enhanced by their ability to travel and initiate research. Pro-fessor Valerie Grim's work on Black rural workers provides but one example of the impressive, original research underwritten by the Ford grant. A new junior professor, she has already completed several articles and a book manuscript.

We were especially impressed by the various ways in which the de-partment drew upon its considerable strengths to heighten its visibility on campus, in the city of Bloomington, across the state, and nationwide. The University is well known for its Black Film Center Archives directed by Pro-fessor Phyllis Klotman, for the vision of former director Portia K. Maultsby, and for her accomplishments and that of Mellonee Burnim, the current di-rector, in Black music. These constitute the strongest suits of the depart-ment and perhaps explain the particular emphasis on African American cultural life. Thus, Ford funds were earmarked to develop an archive of African American Music, History, and Culture that would complement and enhance the holdings of the Film Center Archive. We were impressed by the comprehensiveness of the archive and by the sophisticated level of online cataloging that facilitated access. We also felt that these acquisitions seemed to have enormous impact on the quality of teaching at Indiana. Since African American Studies, by definition, is interdisciplinary, these archives enabled professors and students to explore easily and in depth the links be-tween print, visual, oral, and music culture within the field.

Conferences were a less central component of the Indiana initiative than they were at other institutions we visited. However, two conferences in 1991–92 did attract national attention and again capitalized on depart-mental strength. Professor William Wiggins's ongoing work on Joe Louis provided the inspiration for a conference entitled "Joe Louis and the Amer-ican Press." Interdisciplinary in concept, the conference featured lectures, films, an exhibition, and musical presentations.

The second conference of that year, "In Touch with the Spirit: Black Re-ligious and Musical Expression in American Cinema," was held in conjunc-tion with the Indiana Black Expo and drew over one thousand attendees. The conference showcased interdisciplinary work in African American Studies, bringing together film makers and scholars whose work draw from a wide range of sources.

Faculty members at Indiana were deeply committed to guaranteeing the future of African American Studies as a discipline in general and as a department at Indiana in particular. This commitment was evident in the attention paid to nurturing each other's work and that of their students. Their cultural and intellectual involvements in the surrounding community were impressive, as were their pedagogical innovations.

Michigan State University

Ford's grant to Michigan State is designed to support an evolving Ph.D. program in Comparative Black History—that is, Black History on several continents. This innovative program, the first of its kind in the United States (or anyplace else, it appears) offers courses to burgeoning historians specializing in the Black experience in two or more cultures. Ford gave the program a running start by providing a visiting professorship for David Barry Gaspar, who (in Fall 1992) gave a course in "Slavery in Maroon Societies." He has also participated in the planning the program and expediting its growth and development. Other scholars visited, not for a whole term but for a full day of serious talk and collaboration.

Michigan State is excellently positioned for this type of program because it already has several historians of the Black experience. Still more faculty was needed with so many areas of study involved in a true comparative approach. To fill extant gaps, experts conducted seminars on comparative slavery and comparative experiences of emancipation.

Currently, eight graduate students are training as specialists in African American history at Michigan State. Of these, two are committed to the comparative approach. But each of these new seminars has involved fifteen to twenty students; and some of the visiting presenters attract faculty and graduate student participants from all over campus. Students not formally enrolled in this program are also undertaking work directly stemming from participation in these seminars.

The new course of study has changed the conversation campus-wide. Darlene Clark Hine, the program's designer and leader, says, "The rippling effect is quite something. The teaching in ordinary courses has had to change as students come into them asking new questions." After a day-long session with a visiting comparatist, one grad student emerged to say to Professor Hine: "This program makes you smarter. Just sitting there I could feel my I.Q. going up!"

The formula for success is the same here as elsewhere: brilliant, inspired faculty leadership (Hine), excellent partnership with the central administration, fine staff help, and—always a significant factor—money.

University of California, Berkeley

Of the programs we visited, the Ford initiative at Berkeley was the least advanced. With the period of their award being July 1, 1991, to June 30, 1994, they were just completing the project for which they had been funded. As with all of the institutions we visited, Berkeley, as a state school, was struggling with budget cutbacks resulting from state and national financial crises. However, since the economy of the state of California was particularly hard hit, and the Berkeley campus especially so within the system, we were struck by how timely this award has been and how much it has contributed to the intellectual life and vigor of students and faculty alike.

The thrust of the Berkeley proposal has been to strengthen the department's emphasis on interdisciplinary research on the African Diaspora. This initiative is designed to improve undergraduate courses and to provide the foundation for the department's proposed graduate program. Until now, courses have tended to focus on one approach or methodology and a single national context. Much of the Ford grant has been earmarked to encourage collaborative projects between faculty members and graduate students that would enable all participants to explore the interdisciplinary and diasporic implications of their joint projects. These projects have simultaneously impacted pedagogical practice and research. From them, more innovative and interrelated courses ensue. They are meant to reinforce close links between junior and senior faculty, and to heighten the degree of mentoring that students receive; thereby enhancing the sophistication of theses and dissertations. Without Ford money during this financial crisis, none of these initiatives could have been undertaken.

Ford funds have been earmarked to develop film and video resources, to provide support for the Poetry Center founded by Professor June Jordan, to strengthen links between Berkeley and other scholars and institutions through publications and lecture series, and to enable the department to be a resource for teachers of community college and secondary school students.

Of all the institutions we visited, Berkeley seemed most involved in community outreach projects. "Partnerships in Education" is an ongoing faculty/staff program that disseminates research and teaching ideas to local parents, teachers, and administrators. During the summer and again in the fall, most of the AAS faculty members make presentations and direct workshops in these areas, encouraging undergraduate and graduate recruitment and making concrete their commitment to the broader community—a concept to which most African American Studies units do little more than pay lip service.

Ford funds have also provided some release time for Professor VeVe Clark to develop a brilliant writing intensive course that orients students to the University from a diasporic perspective. This course is designed to counteract the high attrition rates of Black Berkeley students by introducing them to the wide range of resources both within and outside the university. Participants study films and readings, diverse in cultural context, that encourage thinking and writing on the idea of "the university."

The atmosphere at Berkeley was extraordinarily rich and exciting. The economic crisis notwithstanding, faculty, staff and students alike had all thought—in strikingly original ways—about how intellectual and institutional connections could be enhanced and reconceived.

University of California, Los Angeles

At UCLA, the Center for Afro-American Studies (CAAS) is a research (rather than a teaching) component of the University. Here, the Ford initiative facilitated interdisciplinary innovation and synthesis in the field, thereby enhancing the Center's vitality and productivity. UCLA's Ford initiative, ASPIR—an acronym for Afro-American Studies Program for Interdisciplinary Research—sought to accomplish these goals by providing faculty release time, graduate student apprenticeships (sometimes called "mentorships"), and travel grants.

ASPIR produced many positive results. Faculty and graduate students found that their research and writing were greatly enhanced by the challenge to explore the interdisciplinary implications of their projects. Graduate students were especially gratified to be able to work with faculty members who challenged them to think beyond national and disciplinary boundaries. All felt that the project prevented them from feeling isolated, intellectually and culturally, and provided them with valuable training to pursue sophisticated research goals. They especially felt that their professional development was helped immeasurably by the funding they received to attend conferences, deliver papers, and benefit from the responses of other intellectuals.

Ford funding underwrote several conferences that attracted large audiences and showcased the strength of CAAS in the social science and public policy areas: the "Decline in Marriage Conference" (1989); "Back to the Basics: Black to the Future" (1990), held at the Audubon Junior High School in Los Angeles; "A War on Drugs or a War Against the African-American Community?" (1990). Ford-underwritten graduate student workshops on funding, research, and cross-cultural studies, assisted graduate students in ways that had typically eluded them in their home departments.

Because of the size of the University and the complex structure of CAAS, an academic coordinator (Jim Turner) and an administrative coordinator (Sandra Sealy) were hired to supervise the ASPIR program. Everyone to whom we spoke praised the professionalism with which the program was run, and they all felt that much of its effectiveness, especially for the graduate students, was due to the fact that Turner and Sealy worked hard to ensure that participants shared their research and capitalized on the possibility for community that ASPIR offers.

University of Michigan

A significant portion of the Ford grant at Michigan was earmarked to support undergraduate and graduate research, although the proposal primarily centered on research that "defines and advances the field." Michigan has a long-standing tradition of recruiting clusters of African American Studies faculty in traditional departments. However, during the mid- to late 1980s, several members of the Center for Afro-American Studies (CAAS) faculty were recruited by other institutions. The University successfully recruited new faculty, but these personnel changes created some feeling of discontinuity. The Ford initiative provided an important means for CAAS to reconstitute itself as a cohesive intellectual center.

Ford funds were used to provide release time for faculty to develop CAAS curriculum and research resources, including a study abroad program in Barbados. Individual awards went to faculty and students for travel and research. In addition, the Ford grant underwrote "Reflections and Revisions: Twenty Years of Afro-American and African Studies" (1991), a major conference; a series of graduate student conferences; and "Race, Culture, and the Politics of Intellectual Inquiry," a colloquium series.

We were impressed by the fact that although Michigan is a large campus, CAAS programming succeeded in maintaining a sizeable audience from diverse campus constituencies. By all accounts, the conferences and colloquia contributed to the establishment of ongoing debates and discussions that still enliven CAAS intellectual activity. Moreover, the graduate students with whom we met were an exceptionally gifted group. All felt that CAAS faculty, plus the programs and opportunities offered, enabled them to explore the interdisciplinary implications of their work in ways that their home departments would not have allowed.

One of the major strengths of the Afro-American Studies faculty at Michigan is its interest in diasporic studies. As a result, the graduate student projects, lectures, and travel-abroad components of the undergraduate program mutually reinforce that priority. CAAS is to be commended for its leadership in conceptualizing new directions in African American Studies.

University Of Pennsylvania

Of all the programs we have reviewed, Penn's is the most straightforward in design and motive. Ford's grant was joined with other monies to fund a summer seminar in Black Studies for professors in the northeast region. The idea was to invite people from a wide range of disciplines to spend an intensive six-week period reading about the history of and approaches to Black Studies, discussing key questions in the expanding field with leading scholars in the field from Penn and beyond.

The challenge of this program was to "re-tool" scholars who want to catch up with a quickly changing field by providing opportunities to see interdisciplinary work in action: writing and teaching by veterans who do what they do with great expertise. The participants tested their own papers against the criticisms of one another and heard presentations by the likes of Marcellus Blount, Manthia Diawara, and Evelyn Brooks Higginbotham. In all cases auxiliary readings were assigned to provide each session with as rich a context as possible.

The program has had its ups and downs. The first summer's stunning success was followed by a summer of division and discontent. This past summer—with the topic back to the first year's broad "History, Content and Method in Afro-American Studies," the group seems very solid and serious; the group's leadership is vigorous and committed.

Penn's success with this program was both local and regional. The Ford imprimatur has helped the Center for the Study of Black Literature and Culture in its relations with the University as a whole and with other granting agencies. One success has led to another. Ford's sponsorship has helped the seminar's faculty leaders and graduate student assistants in their ongoing efforts to stay abreast of the field's new work. Graduate student affiliates have been especially rewarded by their association with the seminar. Not only do they hear and read some of the field's best new work, they gain administrative experience in helping to run a major conference with many parts and many special needs.

Of course the formal participants are the sessions' greatest beneficiaries. The summer work changes them. They return to their home schools with new agendas, new senses of their roles as members of a community of African Americanists. In some cases they have had to shift to new schools where the sort of innovative, progressive research they witnessed at Penn could be more highly appreciated.

What makes this one work is:

1. Houston Baker's steady, experienced leadership;[3]
2. Good sponsorship and spirited guidance by the central administration; and
3. John Roberts and the Center's staff of hard workers.

University of Wisconsin

The Department of Afro-American Studies at the University of Wisconsin, Madison, was established in 1970. Located in a university, a city, and a state comprised of a racially homogeneous population, the faculty and the students in this department risked intellectual isolation. However, the university's commitment to faculty recruitment, and the strong sense of departmental and institutional loyalty on the part of such faculty members such as Sandra Adell, Stanlie James, Nellie McKay, Freida Tesfagiorgis, Michael Thornton, William Van Deburg, and Craig Werner have created a challenging, cohesive, and productive environment.

African American Studies at the University of Wisconsin used the grant from the Ford Foundation in a variety of ways with two related goals: first, to contribute to the career development of students and junior faculty members, and second, to deepen the connections between the Department and the outside world. In all years, some portion of the money was allocated to administrative support so that the department could successfully coordinate the various initiatives the grant allowed.

As a public institution, Wisconsin lacked sufficient funding to adequately support most of its M.A. students and risked the possibility of losing some of its top students to institutions that could offer them more lucrative financial aid packages. The Ford grant allowed them to offer research assistantships to more graduate and undergraduate students. Not only did these assistantships provide financial support, they allowed the students to develop more sophisticated research skills that, in turn, improved the quality of their own papers and theses. Ford monies allowed graduate students and faculty to travel to academic conferences for which there would otherwise have been little (if any) financial support. The Ford grant was also used to provide junior faculty with some release time, given the disproportionate amounts of time they spent advising students and serving on university committees.

During 1989–90, a significant portion of the Ford grant was used to fund a Black Feminist Working Symposium organized by Stanlie James. The forum brought twenty participants from throughout the African Diaspora for a three-day period to network, share papers, and rigorously critique each other's work. In addition, under the direction of Sandra Adell, several graduate students were invited to share their work before the participants. The meeting was repeatedly praised for providing a context within which Black feminists from a range of disciplinary and cultural perspectives might productively share insights; for allowing graduate students to benefit from the group process; and for showcasing the cluster of Black feminist scholars at Wisconsin (specifically James, Adell, and McKay). From these meetings, a book entitled *Theorizing Black Feminisms*[4] was published.

During the second year, Ford funds were used to support a major national conference on "Afro-American Studies in the 21st Century." Featured speakers included Molefi Kete Asante, Houston Baker, Hazel Carby, Henry Louis Gates, Paula Giddings, Darlene Clark Hine, Manning Marable, Nell Painter, Arnold Rampersad, Bernice Johnson Reagon, and Cornel West. The conference explored the various intellectual, ideological, and cultural meanings that attach to the notion of African American Studies. The conference achieved national coverage. Several of the papers were published in a special issue of *The Black Scholar;* there are plans to anthologize the essays. Once again, undergraduate and graduate students were encouraged to attend the conference. The students to whom we spoke were uniformly delighted by the opportunity to be exposed to so many points of view, to meet scholars whose work they had read, to watch African Americanists disagree, and to learn how to ask questions and participate in debates in a public academic forum.

In the third year, Ford funds were used to develop a collection of African American music for research and pedagogical purposes, and to prepare *The*

Black Scholar volume. In this year, the outreach component was defined more narrowly, though no less valuably. A portion of the Ford grant was used to co-sponsor a series of colloquia with the University's Havens Center for the Study of Social Change. This series brought together faculty and graduate students from various disciplines to discuss seminal texts in the debate over multicul-turalism and diversity in intellectual life. In the wake of such highly success-ful and visible projects as the Black Feminist Symposium and the African American Studies conference, this colloquium series had the effect of consol-idating the power and visibility of the African American Studies department as an intellectual center on campus.

A university as large as Wisconsin runs the risk of seeming impersonal with students left to fend for themselves. We were very impressed by the ex-tent to which the faculty in African American Studies at Wisconsin dis-played its commitment to each other and to its students. The Ford grant contributed substantially to the construction of an atmosphere in which students felt intellectually, financially, and emotionally supported. It also helped center African American Studies on campus and across the nation as a key player in the production of ideas across disciplines.

Yale University

Yale's Department of Afro-American Studies and its uses of the Ford Foun-dation grant require the special attention of evaluators. This is because the proposal was designed in a period of transition by Professor Edmund Gor-don, who left the University just as the Foundation funds became available. The program's fine new leadership (with Professor Gerald Jaynes as Chair and with the faculty drawn more than ever into the circle of decision mak-ers) found that the grant had not been set up to suit the program's newly evolving needs.

As the new Chair, Jaynes set up a review panel, headed by the late Pro-fessor Sylvia Boone, to screen requests for grant money. In collaboration with the faculty (and to some degree with Sheila Biddle at Ford), Jaynes began to redesign the budget of Yale's grant. The same essential categories were kept intact:

1. Visiting scholars;
2. Research funds for faculty and students;
3. Student travel;
4. Conferences and colloquia;
5. Cataloging and collecting conference papers and unpublished research; and
6. Purchase of works for the Charles T. Davis Reading Room.

Using these broad categories as guidelines, the Department then used Ford money primarily to support faculty and student research projects; to put on national conferences on film and Postcolonialism; to establish a film collection; to redesign the curriculum in preparation for the new Ph.D. program; and to bring in guest teachers and lecturers, particularly to build and sharpen the undergraduate introductory course.

Generally speaking, Jaynes's plan was to use the money to reinvigorate a program that had endured several long years of drift and disaffection. Ford's grant was invaluable in this process of bringing the faculty together to think about the program's directions for the coming years. During a time of budgetary scarcity, it provided the money needed to dream and to plan. The results are frankly quite dramatic and impressive. Under the new leadership, Yale has a newly strengthened sense of comradeship and possibility. The first payoff is quantifiable in the increased number and quality of M.A. applications.

The conferences were booming successes. The film conference served to establish African American Studies at Yale as a place for cultural studies on the world of Blacks in film. With important new "hires" in the offing, with a new Ph.D. plan on the verge of acceptance, and with a new center for interdisciplinary research ready to be launched, Yale seems well placed to again assume a position of very strong leadership in this field.

The "secret weaponry" in this new impetus at Yale is the teamwork and brilliant leadership of Professors Hazel Carby and Vera Kutzinski. They are outstanding scholars, teachers, and leaders in the Department. A large part of what has been working at Yale comes from these two getting together and making something new happen in an old place.

Summary and Recommendations

This report embodies our findings as evaluators of those African American Studies programs awarded grants in the period from 1988 to 1991. Ford's goals for this cluster of grants were very clear: to offer substantive assistance to the nation's top programs (and by extension to the entire field) by encouraging younger scholars making their way through the pipeline, by funding solid research, and by spreading the good word of the field's newest scholarship. Projects that promoted collaborative work and broadened the community of participants in the Black Studies enterprise were viewed with special favor.

We wish to underscore our unambiguous finding that—despite well-publicized examples of racial romanticism and defensive rigidity at the periphery of this field—African American Studies has established itself as a vibrant, expansive area of scholarly work within the liberal arts and sciences. In our travels across the nation, we saw African American Studies courses that were fully enrolled at the undergraduate and graduate levels. Black and non-Black students competed for spaces in these courses taught by Black and non-Black experts in the field.

What is encouraging, too, is that at the schools with top programs (and elsewhere) students are selecting African American Studies as a field in which to major or concentrate. And, in significant numbers, these undergraduate scholars-in-training go on to graduate programs in the field—quite often at the schools funded by Ford to support or even to help establish such programs—and then they begin to make their way as specialists. At a time of drastic fiscal shrinkages, Ford has provided this new, rising generation of African Americanists with money to travel to conferences and sites of field research, as well as to engage in study and teaching. Significantly, these newcomers do finish their dissertations; they do get jobs in academia; they complete their research projects and against a treacherous market, they earn tenure. The proof is in the journals, in the bookstores, and on the mastheads of African American Studies programs at the schools we visited. The next generation is coming on.

Beyond any question of sheer numbers, whether in classes or moving through the pipeline, the quality of the African American Studies enterprise as a whole is higher than ever before. This field attracts excellent students at all levels: some who are serious about understanding their own cultural inheritances and many who want to gain the perspectives of a growing area of study that has had a profound impact throughout the academy. Effective teaching over the years has made for this success. So, of course, have events in the news that make clear the importance of multi-ethnic societies learning to cope with their various cultures. African American Studies has been uniquely well placed to offer insight into the meanings of "race" and "difference" and, moreover, into the meanings of contemporary life in our global community.

A major ingredient in the field's broad success has been the quality of research and writing in African American Studies. Every school we visited had on its faculty two or more scholars whose work has been important well beyond the reaches of the African American Studies field itself. Required reading across the disciplines in colleges and universities these days includes the work of such well-known figures as Henry Louis Gates, Jr., Arnold Rampersad, Cornel West, and Nobel Laureate for Literature Toni Morrison; literary theorists Houston Baker, Hazel Carby, and Hortense Spillers; and historians Darlene Clark Hine, David Levering Lewis, and Nell Painter. Such assigned readings as these are making a difference in what it means to be literate as we approach the new century. Ford's support of new research by the pathfinders of African American Studies, their junior colleagues and students, has helped to change the face of American higher education.

To spread the Black Studies wealth, Ford has sponsored faculty seminars (sometimes involving several schools) along with regional and national conferences some of which have led to important publication projects. Some of these grants also helped to forge collaboration between research institutes and teaching units—even between universities and secondary schools. One major victory of the grants has been to promote a sense of a moving, growing community of African Americanists whose work is important to the nation. In a phrase, the past round of grants was tremendously successful.

Ford has had enormous impact in African American Studies. We applaud the resounding success of the current cycle of grants. We anticipate more growth and strength in this new field which Ford has helped to nurture and whose fruits the country and the world are starting to see in abundance.

Notes

[1] In the O'Meally-Smith report, the authors collectively refer to African American Studies programs, departments, institutes, etc., as "units."

[2] Harris argues that Africana Studies as a field has actually passed through four stages since its inception in the 1890s. See his essay "The Intellectual and Institutional Development of Africana Studies," in *Three Essays: Black Studies in the United States,* Robert L. Harris, Jr., Darlene Clark Hine, Nellie McKay (New York: The Ford Foundation, 1990), pp. 7–14 (also included in this volume, see pp. 141–148).

[3] Houston Baker is currently a Distinguished University Professor in the English Department at Vanderbilt University.

[4] *Theorizing Black Feminisms: The Visionary Pragmatism of Black Women,* Stanlie James and Abena Busia editors, London: Routledge, 1993.

PART FOUR

A Changing Political Context: The Pinderhughes, Yarborough Report (2000)

An Introduction to the Pinderhughes, Yarborough Report
Farah Jasmine Griffin

A Review of African American Studies Programs for the Ford Foundation
Dianne M. Pinderhughes and Richard Yarborough

A Changing Political Context: Introduction to the Pinderhughes, Yarborough Report

As with the Supreme Court's Bakke decision of 1978[1] that prohibited "taking race into account as a factor in . . . admissions decisions" on the grounds that "quotas" had denied entrance to a White male, November 1996 ushered in another major shift in public policy. California passed Proposition 209 which constricted attempts to reverse years of segregation through affirmative action. "Prop 209," as it was called, prohibited "state, local governments, districts, public universities, colleges, and schools and other government instrumentalities from discriminating against or giving preferential treatment to any individual or group in public employment, public education or public contracting on the basis of race, sex, color, ethnicity, or national origin."[2] That same year the Fifth District Federal Court in Texas handed down the *Hopwood* decision banning the affirmative action program at the University of Texas Law School (which did not admit Black students until 1950). The next year Black enrollment dropped more than 90 percent. Mexican American enrollment dropped approximately 60 percent.[3]

It is in the context of these times that, in 1998, program officer Janice Petrovich commissioned the foundation's fourth report on African American Studies. Political scientist Dianne Pinderhughes of the University of Illinois, Urbana Champaign, and literary scholar Richard Yarborough of the

University of California, Los Angeles, were chosen to conduct a further site study of Ford-funded programs.

In tandem with the field it surveyed, the Pinderhughes-Yarborough report is more in-depth and visionary than its predecessors. It warns of serious challenges threatening the stability of the field itself, documents the results of site visits to Ford-funded programs, provides a broad-based overview of the health of the field, and attempts to inform an agenda for the future. These are daunting tasks for any one document.

As the authors note, the late 1990s witnessed "a whole-scale brutal assault both on the goal of increasing educational access through such mechanisms as affirmative action and also on the most obvious institutional signs of that hard won access, Ethnic Studies." For this reason, by 2000 when Drs. Pinderhughes and Yarborough completed their study, structural stability remained of utmost importance to the field; on most campuses institutional stability had not been accomplished. The authors also note that the healthy presence of African American Studies institutional structures on campus did not necessarily guarantee the presence of Black scholars on campus. Thus, despite such gains as more students than ever encountering Black-authored texts and the heightened professional profile of individual scholars, "the institutional stability of the majority of African American Studies units ha[d] not significantly increased over the past decade." Consequently the growth of the professoriate—especially in a climate that, even today, threatens affirmative action—remains crucial.

This problem is not just felt on individual campuses. By 2000, there still was no national professional meeting regularly attended by administrative heads of major African American Studies units. Given the growth in Ph.D. programs, the mechanism by which to evaluate these programs remained a necessity. "For a range of reasons," Pinderhughes and Yarborough concluded, "the National Council for Black Studies has not been able to fill that role; yet there is little indication that any other organization is better suited to do so."

The Pinderhughes-Yarborough report offers a series of suggestions for future actions that remain relevant. First and foremost they called for a meeting of the heads of Ford-funded programs or a meeting of a larger group of administrators of African American Studies programs to be convened by the Ford Foundation and they encourage the foundation to continue the following approaches:

1. Nurture African American Studies as a field of scholarship.
2. Build African American Studies institutionally.
3. Stimulate the pipeline supplying African Americans to the academic profession.
4. Educate administrators and development officers regarding the needs and institutional value of African American Studies by convening a meeting of university development officers with major African American Studies units to discuss fundraising. Such a gathering would assist the universities in locating funding sources that would help the programs become more self-sustaining.

Finally, Pinderhughes and Yarborough concede the future of African American Studies as "hazy except for the most highly publicized" programs. They cite a need for leadership development and a need to relieve Black faculty of their inordinate nonscholarly responsibilities. But most important, they continue:

> What appears to be desperately needed at both the national and local levels is sustained and open conversation regarding the growing number of advanced degree programs in African American Studies. At present there has been no real attempt to keep track of such programs and more importantly there is no clearing house of information such as course syllabi, curriculum design, and program proposals through which schools might learn from each other's experiences.

The authors called upon the foundation to convene a meeting of the heads of African American Studies graduate programs for a discussion of goals and strategies for dealing with student financial aid, collaboration with other departments on campus, curricula, introductory courses, job placement, and research planning.

Indeed, on June 16, 2000, program officer Margaret Wilkerson did convene a meeting of African American Studies program and department directors. Participants discussed a range of issues including the challenges of departmentalization and of establishing Ph.D. programs, the role of national African American Studies organizations, the importance of technology to the development of the field, the continued need for gender analysis in African American Studies scholarship, and the need for gender balance in African American Studies leadership—a theme that would lead to publication of a book on the subject by Johnnetta B. Cole, president of Bennett College, and Beverly Guy-Sheftall, Anna Julia Cooper professor of Women's Studies and English at Spelman College (see *Epilogue*).

Farah Jasmine Griffin
(2006)

Notes

[1] U.S. Supreme Court, *Regents of the University of California v. Bakke,* 438 U.S. 265 (1978).

[2] http://vote96.ss.ca.gov/Vote96/html/BP209.htm.

[3] http:/tarlton.law.utexas.edu/hopwood/effects.html.

A Review of Ford Foundation-Funded African American Studies Programs (2000)

Dianne M. Pinderhughes
Richard Yarborough

The Pinderhughes, Yarborough Report
Contents

The Report

Introduction

The end of the twentieth century marks roughly thirty years of existence for the oldest formally established African American Studies units[1] at U.S. colleges and universities. It also marks the close of another round of funding initiatives in the field by the Ford Foundation, an organization that has played a key role in the growth and stabilizing of the field in institutions of higher education for some time. Accordingly, the time is right for an assessment not only of the effectiveness of the most recent Ford-funded programs, but of the state of the field itself.

As one head of a Black Studies unit recently observed with no little bitterness: what other fields have been subjected to so many evaluations, reviews, and reconsiderations? Indeed, he suggested, such public scrutiny might ironically serve to contribute to some of the perceived institutional instability that plagues academic units in the field. Furthermore, because such evaluations have almost inevitably focused on certain universities and not on others, there may have been a tendency to reinforce a hierarchy of privilege among both Black Studies scholars and institutions that ultimately works against the overall health of the field. That some of these projects involved consortia of universities and colleges is, however, a sign that there are, in fact, some structured attempts to "share the wealth," so to speak.

However, while we are sensitive to the thrust of hierarchical concerns, given the way the Ford projects were structured, we will first review particular institutions and then address collective concerns in our recommendations for possible future Ford initiatives. In addition, it cannot be stressed enough that any review of the field, no matter how extensive, can only scratch the surface in terms of the myriad African American Studies units that one finds at U.S. universities and colleges and of the many scholars working in the field, often in relative obscurity and with scant resources.

In his portion of *Three Essays: Black Studies in the United States,* the Ford Foundation report published in 1990, Robert L. Harris, Jr. breaks the development of the field down into four distinct phases. The first runs from the late nineteenth century until the 1940s and is marked by the rise of "early Black literary and historical associations." Harris dates the second phase from the appearance of Gunner Myrdal's study of African America in 1944, and contends that it was characterized by an ultimately unfortunate overemphasis on assimilationist models of racial interaction and on alleged Black "pathology" resulting from slavery and subsequent oppression. He suggests that the third stage, "from about the mid-1960s to the mid-1980s, was a period of legitimization and institutionalization." The fourth, which Black Studies is just entering at the beginning of the final decade of the century, is one of "theoretical refinement and more sophisticated analysis and interpretation."[2]

Although this scheme might imply a linear development of inevitable progress, Harris is quick to note the extent to which this last stage will depend upon institutional stability and growth in curricula and faculty resources. While the "theoretical sophistication" that Harris anticipated continues apace through the excellent and diverse work of a broad base of scholars, it is also clear that the structural stability requisite for institutionalization of this work has, at many institutions, not been achieved. This problem has resulted, in part, from the reluctance of some universities and colleges to develop a strategy for moving Black Studies units into the mainstream of the institutional structure. Some of these units occupy the same, often unique status as when they were created—this, often as a result of political pressure outside the normal academic structures of the school. Few of the units that started out as interdepartmental programs have achieved departmental status and, with that, the power and stability of departments. The units created as departments from the beginning are often still struggling for a solid resource base, even after three decades of existence. Finally, one would not have predicted in the late 1960s and early 1970s, when many of these units were born, that we would see in the 1990s a wholesale, brutal assault both on the goal of increasing educational access through such mechanisms as affirmative action and also on the most obvious institutional signs of that hard-won access—Ethnic Studies programs and departments.

Indeed, as the findings of this report relate, the undermining of affirmative action in particular and the accompanying backing away from the commitment to increase diversity among undergraduate student bodies, graduate programs, and faculties may have a devastating impact on the institutional status of African American Studies at many universities and colleges. That the number of graduate students of all races who are interested in African American Studies is, at the same time, growing may also portend a future presence of African American Studies courses independent of the presence of African American faculty on that campus. This last issue—that is, the relationship between the growth of the field of African American Studies and the growth of the African American professorate—is a complex and politically vexing one that must be faced directly.

Any such report as this one must at some point address the issue of terminology and the related topic of just how the field is defined. In the aforementioned 1990 Ford report, Darlene Clark Hine provides an excellent discussion of the range of ways in which Black Studies units characterize their missions and thus the parameters of the field in each case.[3] This issue is no closer to reaching resolution through consensus in 1999 than it was at the end of the 1980s. Although one can argue that diversity in this regard is a strength or at least a reality that must be acknowledged, it is increasingly clear that such distinctions often entail a divergence in ideological or philosophical thrust which merits serious attention. That is, units that incorporate both African American Studies and African Studies confront radically different challenges in the area of curriculum development, for example, than do those that focus exclusively on the experience of people of African descent in the United States or the Western Hemisphere. Furthermore, the rise of Postcolonial and Diaspora Studies in the 1990s has put new pressure on scholars and administrators to clarify just how the field is to be configured at their schools. This issue might superficially appear to be narrowly theoretical in nature and of relevance primarily to scholars. However, the ways in which the field is defined can lead to real tension and instability in units faced with making difficult curricular and hiring choices.[4]

Coming to terms with this issue of field definition will likely become even more pressing as the number of Black Studies doctoral programs increases. At present, in 2000, such programs exist at Temple, UC Berkeley, and the University of Massachusetts, Amherst. Harvard and Cornell are but two schools that may soon start them. Morgan State and Michigan State both grant doctorates in History with a special focus on Black Diaspora Studies. Meanwhile, masters programs at such schools as UCLA, Wisconsin, Cornell, and Yale continue to produce students, and a program has been implemented at Indiana and at the University of South Florida.[5]

The establishment of advanced degree programs in the field is certainly one dramatic sign of its increased institutional presence and status. However, this trend also raises a number of concerns. Among them is the untested viability of the Black Studies Ph.D. in what is already a tight academic marketplace. Also, at what point will there need to be a mechanism in place for the evaluation of such programs and perhaps even for some regularizing of curricula? For a range of reasons, the National Council for Black Studies has not been able to fill that role. Yet, there is little indication that any other organization is better situated to do so. Indeed, in any overview of the current growth of advanced degree programs in Black Studies, one cannot help but be struck by how little contact the various degree-granting units actually have with each other. At present, for instance, there is no professional meeting that is regularly attended by the administrative heads of the major Black Studies units in the country.

This situation is not a healthful one. In gauging the progress made in the field over the past ten years, one notes a number of significant advances. Among them is the growth in the professional profile of a sizable number of individual Black Studies faculty members. More scholars in the field now hold endowed chairs and positions of distinction at major universities than at any time previously. College curricula are more integrated than ever before, in terms of the inclusion of materials related to African Americans. This latter development, in turn, means that countless more students are encountering Black-authored texts and considering issues related to Blacks in their course work than in the past.

However, one of the sobering ironies of the 1990s has been that, despite these gains, the institutional stability of the majority of Black Studies units has not significantly increased over the past decade. Furthermore, the dwindling number of Black students at many colleges means that the production of future Black academics, scant even in the most flush of times, will likely decrease in the near future. The dire consequences of this cannot be overstated. Even if solutions are found that can reverse this trend, we are already confronting a generation of administrators of Black Studies units who may not have successors when they retire. This is not to overlook the considerable administrative and scholarly contributions made by non-Black faculty members in the field. Rather, one must simply acknowledge the extent to which the careers of many Black scholars have been intimately linked to the evolution of Black Studies at many schools. Finally, African American Studies generally still provides a ready target for right-wing ideologues looking for scapegoats in their assaults on the "sorry state of American higher education." This serves to remind us that the field that was spawned—both intellectually and institutionally—out of political struggle must keep alive that tradition of struggle if, as we enter the new century, it is not only to grow, but to survive.

Organization of the Report

This report was commissioned by Ford Foundation Program Director Janice Petrovich in the spring of 1998 and overseen to completion by Program Officer Margaret Wilkerson. The reviewers were given a list of key topics and questions by Petrovich and Wilkerson, which we used to guide our research. The reviewers also asked each program to provide relevant documentation in a number of areas. In terms of structure, the report provides individual commentaries on the universities evaluated, arranged in alphabetical order.

The review of each school includes summary comments on the Ford-funded project, followed by a description of the department, interdepartmental program, or research center, and its institutional context.

Cornell University

The Project

The Ford-funded project administered by the Africana Studies and Research Center (ASRC) at Cornell University involved the mounting of a series of three graduate seminars that drew upon faculty and students from four universities: New York's Cornell, SUNY Binghamton, Syracuse, and Maryland's Morgan State. The three New York schools had already established collaborative linkages in a number of areas; key goals of the project were the strengthening of these connections and the inclusion of an HBCU, Morgan State.

For the first year (1996–97), the seminar schedule included both concurrent meetings at each school and joint sessions, for which all of the students would travel to one of the three New York campuses. To facilitate their participation in the seminar, up to five Morgan State graduate students were to be in residence at Cornell for the entire semester. The topic for the course in that first year was "Black Intellectual Traditions: Humanistic and Social Scientific Approaches." Twenty-four students from the four campuses participated. Based upon the syllabus from the Cornell seminar (coordinated by Professor Don Ohadike) and the wide range of faculty members invited to lead seminar meetings, it appears that the focus of the course was truly interdisciplinary and cross-cultural in nature. It is also worth noting that the "common seminar," as it was termed, received significant press coverage in the last months of 1996.

As a follow-up to the seminar, a workshop on African Studies was convened in May 1997, involving twenty-five faculty and graduate students. The topics of discussion ranged from pedagogical strategies and syllabi to specific research projects being conducted by professors and students in attendance. Also in this first year of Ford funding, a number of faculty members received research grants; students from the participating schools were given travel grants that enabled them to attend scholarly conferences in the field.

In the second year of the grant, the format of the seminar was much the same as it was in the first. Professor Anne Adams served as the 1997–98 Coordinator. The title of this course was "Movement, Exile, and (Re)Making Identities in Africa and the Diaspora." In the third year, distance-learning technology played a key role in the organization of the course. This shift was largely due to the fact that family, financial, and other considerations made it difficult to recruit Morgan State students able to move to Cornell's Ithaca campus for four months. Accordingly, the seminar participants from Cornell, Syracuse, and Binghamton met as a group three times on each campus; then three times during the semester (once at each campus), an audio-video hookup was established with Morgan State. Via teleconferencing, this enabled students to participate in the common seminar in real time. The Morgan State students then traveled once during the semester to each of the three New York campuses for the common seminar meeting.

This model for distance-learning holds considerable promise for other, similarly constructed multi-institution courses. The key, of course, is the presence of the requisite hardware and support staff at each site. The facilities at Cornell, for example, appeared to be state-of-the-art, and one can imagine that competition over access to them might become fierce in the near future. Should the problem of disparate resources be solved, however, such electronic links could facilitate not just courses but also research workshops, conferences, and other scholarly meetings.

In sum, the common seminars appeared relatively successful in strengthening institutional ties among the four universities involved. In addition, the syllabi generated for the three courses (by a committee of faculty from each campus) could serve as useful models for interdisciplinary offerings on the African Diaspora elsewhere. The very breadth of the focus of these courses necessarily entailed some gaps noted by the students who were enrolled. One student felt that the experience of Hispanic Blacks had been shortchanged; others noted the relative lack of attention paid to gender issues. This latter observation appears to have contributed to a highlighting of gender in the final year's seminar coordinated at Cornell by Professor N'Dri Assie-Lumumba, "Knowledge, Freedom, and African Renewal." Indeed, formal steps were taken from the outset to obtain feedback from the participants of the seminars and workshops; and it is clear that the resultant comments and suggestions received serious attention.

A problem noted by one of the faculty coordinators involved the extent to which the student participants in the seminars brought widely varying levels of expertise in African/African American Studies. This problem is, of course, hardly unique to this common seminar; it often arises in cross-listed Black Studies graduate courses in which the students enrolled come from different departments within the same university. This pedagogical challenge is one not often encountered to the same degree in graduate seminars that are limited to students within a single discipline. Accordingly, it would merit some serious attention in the context of a broad-based consideration of the teaching of Black Studies. Finally, two of the faculty coordinators from Cornell expressed regret that they had not been able to receive teaching assistant or research assistant support in their work on the common seminars. Although it might involve the same amount of lecturing as a conventional offering, overseeing a seminar such as the ones mounted at Cornell can be extremely demanding logistically; budgeting for adequate staff support could ease the load on the faculty coordinator considerably.

Africana Studies at Cornell University

In terms of longevity and influence, the Africana Studies and Research Center (ASRC) at Cornell has to be considered one of the leading such units in the country. The ASRC was founded in 1969; two years later it began offering B.A. and M.A. degrees. Since 1973, it has granted 64 master's degrees, making it surely among the nation's leading programs in that category. That ASRC occupies its own building on campus is but one literal indication of its institutional independence; another is the fact that ASRC reports directly to the Provost, not through an intermediate administrator.

Perhaps the distinguishing characteristic of Africana Studies at Cornell is the fact that it has, from the outset, represented a curricular and ideological fusion of African Studies and African American Studies—two related disciplinary areas that have separate institutional identities at many schools. This arrangement brings with it a number of advantages. Conceptually, it enables the inevitable and necessary links joining Black cultures in the African Diaspora to be smoothly and logically maintained without crossing departmental or programmatic boundaries. In terms of curriculum, it encourages a comparative approach to Black Studies. And practically speaking, it allows for centralized support of Black Studies on the campus. For instance, ASRC has received Ford Foundation grants designed to target initiatives both African American Studies and African Studies units as well as Title VI[6] funding. Finally, that ASRC controls its own FTE (full-time equivalent) allocations means that it can hire and promote faculty according to its own needs and maintain a relatively stable curriculum.

As in the case of other similarly structured programs (the Department of African American Studies at UC Berkeley comes to mind), ASRC's very independence has come at a price. There is some concern regarding the administration's willingness to provide the new faculty resources that ASRC would need should it start a doctoral program. And while the possibility of making joint appointments might provide a means of justifying such requests by pointing up the multiple units that would benefit from such lures, a joint faculty appointment with another interdisciplinary unit has already proven problematic.

Other challenges confronting ASRC have little directly to do with its particular institutional character and, in fact, are evident at a number of universities and colleges across the country. First, there is the impending generational shift in leadership. Like some other Black Studies units, ASRC has had relatively few directors over its three decades of existence. With inevitable faculty retirements, a new leader will have to emerge administratively within such departments, centers, and programs. Second, some faculty at Cornell also commented on the changes in the Black student population at the university. Not only do Latino students now constitute a larger presence on campus than do Black students, but there appears to be less diversity among the Black students themselves (especially in terms of class) than in previous years. Third, as is occurring at other schools, an increasing emphasis at Cornell is being placed on development. It is clear that

ASRC needs to be given a more central place in the university's fundraising agenda.

In closing, several important projects that can be viewed, to varying degrees, under the broad umbrella of ASRC at Cornell deserve mention. One is the ongoing collection development in the John Henrik Clarke Library,[7] a branch of the Cornell University library system, is housed in the ASRC building. In addition to its collection of roughly 14,000 volumes, the Clarke maintains a Web site that is home to a number of promising research and archival initiatives. Perhaps the most ambitious of these focuses on African written languages and is directed by Visiting Professor Ayele Bekerie. In another notable collaboration, ASRC Assistant Professor Salah Hassan has been instrumental in the mounting exhibitions and developing Cornell's Herbert F. Johnson Museum of Art collection. Largely as a result of Professor Hassan's leadership, the Johnson Museum has made a major commitment to the work of modern African artists. Professor Hassan is also one of the editors of *NKA: Journal of Contemporary African Art,* a publication now produced in conjunction with ASRC. Finally, ASRC currently offers a Swahili course in New York City through Cornell's School of Continuing Education and Summer Sessions. At least one faculty member has expressed interest in ASRC's establishing a greater presence in New York City as part of what is clearly an ongoing and ambitious institutional commitment to outreach.

Harvard University

The Project

The goal of Ford-funded Du Bois Institute for Afro-American Research[8] project at Harvard University had as its goal to strengthen the Du Bois Institute's linkages with the Department of Afro-American Studies and the Committee on African Studies. Specifically, Ford funds were used to support fellowships for one senior and one junior Africanist scholar for each of three years. Each scholar would teach one course for the Afro-American Studies department, lead one of the noncredit faculty and graduate student seminars sponsored by the Committee on African Studies, and present a paper in the Du Bois Institute's colloquia series.

Ford funds were also designated to "support the expansion of an existing Internet listserv group for scholars and students conducting research on African and African American-Studies." This listserv—AFROAM-L—has been located at the Du Bois Institute since 1992 and has been moderated by Lee Baker, a former predoctoral fellow at the Institute. The Ford grant was intended to facilitate the growth of this listserv through supporting outreach efforts designed to encourage more scholars to subscribe.

The approach taken in conceptualizing and executing the Harvard grant centered on exploiting programs already in place, most notably, by both expanding the well-established Du Bois Institute postdoctoral fellows program and taking advantage of the strength of the Afro-American Studies department. Although there exists a Committee on African Studies at Harvard, the Afro-American Studies department provides the bulk of the "African-related event" at the university. (Note that Kwame Anthony Appiah, head of the African Studies Committee, is on the Afro-American Studies faculty.) Much of this situation results from the fact that, at Harvard, departments constitute the dominant institutional entities. As explained in the Du Bois Institute's proposal, "The Committee is a multidisciplinary group of scholars appointed to coordinate teaching and research on Africa within Harvard's departments and faculties." Practically speaking, the committees appear to be units with little power or budgetary authority and no control of the tenuring and promotion of faculty, and the low organizational standing of committees at Harvard reveals a great deal about the status of African Studies there. (As one faculty member noted, Harvard did not offer its first class in an African language until 1998.)

Given that this distribution of institutional power is not likely to change in the near future, it indeed makes sense to strengthen African Studies on campus by providing additional resources to an already relatively resource-rich unit, the Afro-American Studies department.

Although the review team was able to interview only one of the Africanist scholars who have received these fellowships, the project appears to have achieved its somewhat modest goals. The individuals brought to campus strengthened the African Studies presence on campus, particularly through their contributions to the curriculum; in turn, the fellowships gave the recipients the chance to make significant progress in their own research.

African American Studies at Harvard University

African American Studies at Harvard has been institutionalized through the creation of two related units—the Department of Afro-American Studies and the W. E. B. Du Bois Institute for Afro-American Research. Although the units are not identical, the same individual, Henry Louis Gates, currently heads them, and they draw upon the same core of faculty. The key distinction appears to be that the Du Bois Institute provides the umbrella for the major research projects in Afro-American Studies on campus while the department mounts the curriculum and provides the institutional home for the faculty. Both units sponsor programming in the discipline on campus.

Founded in 1975, the Du Bois Institute may currently be the best-known African American Studies unit in the country. Having received considerable public notice in recent years for its high-profile recruitment of unusually talented and extraordinarily well-published and well-networked scholars, the roster includes Gates as Chair, Cornel West, and William Julius Wilson. The growth in the field at Harvard is also evident in the development of the Afro-American Studies degree program. In 1987–88, there were 11 concentrators, and the department's courses drew a total enrollment of 119 students. In 1996–97 those figures were 47 and 952. However, the path taken by the Afro-American Studies department and the Du Bois Institute to its current success has been an extremely uneven one. At a low point roughly a decade ago, Afro-American Studies had one full-time tenured faculty member; the department also went through a period in receivership. By the end of 1997, however, Afro-American Studies had a core faculty of seven. In addition, the Advisory Board of the Du Bois Institute now consists of 21 faculty members drawn from across the entire campus.

A number of factors have been offered to explain this dramatic turnaround. One that has occasionally been overlooked is the role played by Nathan Huggins, who headed the department and the Institute in the 1980s and who brought considerable stability to these units' relationship to the rest of the university. His leadership was marked by several important initiatives. First, he solidified Ford Foundation support for the Du Bois fellows program and, furthermore, expanded it to include not just doctoral but predoctoral fellowships. (There are now more than 200 former Du Bois Fellows.) Second, he sought the involvement of a number of distinguished senior African Americanists in the Du Bois Institute. Third, by bringing to Harvard foreign scholars working in the field, he acknowledged the importance of international perspectives in African American Studies.

The next dramatic development was, of course, the arrival of Henry Louis Gates at Harvard in 1991. Building on initiatives put in motion by Huggins, Gates has overseen the development of Afro-American Studies into one of the more dominant units on campus. His tenure as Chair of the department and Director of the Du Bois Institute has been marked by a number of notable achievements. First, one cannot help but attend to the remarkable effectiveness of his development efforts. Winning support from both foundations and individual donors, Gates established Afro-American Studies as one of the most successful fundraising units on campus. (At Harvard, every unit raises its own money.) Indeed, as of late 1998, Afro-American Studies had raised roughly $17 million in the decade, including a $2 million endowment. In addition, the Alphonse Fletcher Chair was established and used to recruit Cornel West from Princeton; and the Du Bois Institute library was named for Harvard alumnus, Franklin Raines, director of Fannie Mae, and director and former director of the U.S. OMB (Office of Management and Budget), who had contributed money to the unit.

Ironically, despite the distinction and public notoriety of the faculty and the financial wherewithal of alumni and others who seek affiliation with Harvard, development efforts by Afro-American Studies and other high profile units must actually be restrained on occasion. As Associate Dean Carol Thompson put it, "Institutionally, our goal is to keep fundraising down." Second, there is the oft-discussed group of well-known scholars (sometimes described as "The Dream Team") whom Professor Gates and Harvard have brought to the university. Faculty hiring in the Harvard department was thus based on attracting scholars who were already well established in their disciplines at institutions such as Chicago, Duke, and Princeton. A less-noted aspect of these recruitments is the fact that almost all of these faculty members have joint appointments, which gives the field a critical presence in departments other than Afro-American Studies. (Two members of the Afro-American Studies faculty, Professors Wilson and West, actually hold endowed chairs as university professors.)

Also noteworthy in this context is the number of extremely ambitious and significant projects that the Du Bois Institute has sponsored over the past decade. Among them are the *African Art Database*, the *Harvard Guide to African American History*, the *Trans-Atlantic Slave Trade Database*, and the *Image of the Black in Western Art Photo Archive*. Moreover, not only do Professors Gates and Appiah (Afro-American Studies and Philosophy) edit the important international journal Transition out of Harvard but they also oversaw the production of the *Encarta Africana CD-ROM* in collaboration with Microsoft, perhaps the most notable application of new computer and media technology to African American Studies in recent years. Finally, the Du Bois Institute provides an academic home for the Institute on the Arts and Civic Dialogue, a Ford-funded project headed by playwright, actress, and Stanford professor Anna Deveare Smith.

In addition to the energetic and ambitious leadership of Professor Gates, the strong support of the Harvard administration has been indispensable to the growth of African American Studies at the university. (President Neil Rudenstine and former Dean of Harvard College Henry Rosovsky deserve special mention here.) A perhaps less central, but still relevant, factor has been the unique status of the Afro-American units at Harvard. That is, there appears to be little support among the current faculty and administration for creating new freestanding Ethnic Studies departments and programs. (Similarly, Harvard has a comparatively small number of student groups defined along racial or ethnic lines.) One might even venture to say that had not the Afro-American Studies department and the Du Bois Institute been founded when they were, they might not even exist today.

The growth of African American Studies at Harvard shows scant indication of slowing anytime soon. The rapid building of an endowment in the Du Bois Institute (supported by a Ford grant in 1997) and the ongoing support from foundations such as Ford, Rockefeller, Kellogg, and others should ensure the fiscal well-being of the unit generally and of the fellows programs specifically. The curriculum continues to expand as well. Indeed, a proposal for a Ph.D. in the field has been generated and might soon lead to a new degree program in the department.

Reviewers' Recommendations

There is cause for concern on a number of fronts. Should the aforementioned proposal for a degree program be approved, the already strained faculty resources in Afro-American Studies would be burdened even further. Given the relatively small size of the department, the departure of one or two faculty members could have a disproportionately negative impact. In terms of junior faculty, the recent tenuring of Professor J. Lorand "Randy" Matory, an anthropologist, is a positive development. However, the pattern for building departments at Harvard continues to involve primarily hiring at the top. This strategy has apparently worked thus far in the case of Afro-American Studies; however, only time will prove the long-term viability of this approach. What is clear is that few other universities in the country can afford to follow Harvard's lead in this regard.

As to the representation of women among the senior faculty of Afro-American Studies (as among the faculty at Harvard generally), with historian Evelyn Brooks Higginbotham the only African American female, the matter deserves aggressive attention. Afro-American Studies had sought to make Lani Guinier's appointment to the Law School a joint one; however, the Law School policy of maintaining full control over this FTE blocked this attempt. Guinier does serve, however, on the Advisory Board of the Du Bois Institute.

Finally, as is the case at most of the other institutions under review, one confronts the inevitable dilemma of leadership. When Professor Gates steps down from one or both of his administrative positions with Afro-American Studies and the Du Bois Institute, will there be faculty members ready to come forward and carry on the ambitious program that he and his colleagues have put into motion? In sum, regardless of the direction that African American Studies as a field takes at Harvard, the current status and visibility of the department and the Du Bois Institute are unquestioned.

Indiana University

The Project

For its Ford-funded project the Department of Afro-American Studies at Indiana University (Bloomington) proposed an undergraduate seminar in 1995: "An Invitation to the Ford Foundation to Make a Grant in Support of Indiana University's Afro-American Studies Summer Seminar Program (1996–1998)." The three-year Black Atlantic Seminar (1996, 1997, and 1998, with a theme for each year) was funded by the Foundation. The Seminar focused on the arts in 1996, followed by "Population Movement and Migrations" in 1997 and "Black Atlantic: Religion and Political Systems" in 1998. The department had previously been awarded a grant for thirty-eight months beginning in May 1990 for faculty and course development.

The department designed the seminars "to expand the discussion of issues facing African American Studies units beyond local boundaries . . . and to focus on the concept of the African Diaspora as a dynamic network of associations and expressions."[9] The seminars were staffed by faculty from the Department of Afro-American Studies, African Studies, and Latin American and Caribbean Studies.

The Seminars

A careful review of the teaching samplers for each year of the seminar showed distinct progression from 1996 through 1998. One cautionary point must be made: because each Teaching Sampler was completed after the seminar was finished, it is difficult to know exactly what the students received as a syllabus. The samplers vary considerably, in volume and content: thirty-four pages in 1996, thirty-seven in 1997, and twenty in 1998. The sampler for the first summer (1996) is somewhat idiosyncratic without consistent types of material for each lecturer. The second summer sampler's content is also somewhat varied, but each presenter includes commentary on his/her lecture topic; most include assigned readings, and some specify writing requirements. The third is most consistent in format with topics, commentary, and readings for each of the lecturers. In the latter two years, the substantive integration of the seminar's themes—on "Population Movement and Migrations" (1997) and "Religion and Political Movements" (1998)—addressed topical issues that repeat fairly consistently in the materials included. These supporting documents—more detailed and considerably richer than the first year's—suggest that greater communication and discussion occurred between the director and the prospective faculty as they prepared for the seminar.

The seminars operated for approximately six weeks each of the summers and met daily for three hours with thirteen students from ten Midwestern and three HBCUs enrolled in 1997. In 1997 the seminar used a resident tutor as liaison among the directors, teaching faculty and students; and to carry out activities in support of the seminar such as copying, book orders, library reserve, films, and equipment. The department contracted with the university's conference bureau to handle financial arrangements, travel, and housing. In November 1997, the faculty who participated in the seminar also participated in a university "Forum on Migrations and Population Movements." In January 1998, the students returned for a mini-conference during which they presented their completed research papers and participated in discussions with faculty and graduate students.[10] This summer seminar was used as a model to develop an interdisciplinary course, "The Black Atlantic." The department had proposed and secured approval for the course through the University's curriculum process by fall 1998. The seminar has been designed as an undergraduate or graduate-only, interdisciplinary, team-taught seminar. Presumably, Indiana University will offer minority fellowships to graduates of the 1998 Black Atlantic Seminar, if they are admitted to the graduate program.

This three-year seminar was truly distinctive when compared with the other programs the consultants reviewed. It was aimed at undergraduates at other institutions; it focused, in a relatively limited way, on creating a single interdisciplinary course. Indeed, the department had managed—and manages—several other external and internal programs. The Telluride Association based at Cornell University funds a sophomore Seminar, which has been offered for nine years for high school sophomores who are then offered scholarships to Indiana University. The department also offered the Wells Scholars Program for college students. But, the "Black Atlantic Seminar" was seen as "moving up a step," setting up a stream of students for admission to the University who would eventually enter a graduate program in Afro-American Studies. This gateway course was designed, therefore, to attract students into Indiana University graduate programs and to establish a stream for the department's master's program that began in fall 1999. This was implied rather than explicitly framed by departmental planning documents.

Historical and Contemporary Status of the Department of Afro-American Studies

Afro-American Studies was created in 1970 as a program under the direction of Herman Hudson, Associate Professor of Applied Linguistics and the first Vice Chancellor of Afro-American Affairs. Hudson immediately pushed for the development of the program into a department, which was approved in April 1971. In 1970, the departmental faculty included three tenure track faculty and five associate instructors. But, by 1990, there were four full professors, five associates, and five assistant professors, along with thirteen associate instructors and five graduate assistants. *The College Incentive Plan (CIP) Humanities Study Group Report* noted that between 1996–97 the department had lost six faculty through four retirements, one departure, and one tenure denial, but it had hired four—three at the assistant and one at the associate level. In contrast to units such as those at Ohio State and UCLA, where William Nelson and Claudia Mitchell-Kernan led the department and Center, respectively, for long periods in the 1970s and 1980s, Indiana's department has been chaired by a series of faculty: Herman Hudson 1970–72, 1981–85; Joseph Russell 1972–81; Portia Maultsby 1985–1991; Mellonee Burnim 1992–95; and John McCluskey 1995–1999.

The department's mission is to introduce students "to a wide range of current research and scholarly opinion on the history, culture and social status of Black Americans and their African heritage. As an intellectual enterprise, the department provides an eclectic analysis of the Afro-American experience and trains students in many skills essential for later success in life."[11] The department's original concentration on arts and humanities has continued throughout its existence. Although the departmental core faculty includes an historian, an historical specialist in Education, and a criminologist, 75 percent of the faculty concentrates on research in the arts and humanities. These fields include three faculty members in Ethnomusicology, two in Afro-American Folklore, two in Creative Writing and African American Literature, and one in Dance Composition.

Moreover, the department also founded and controls several humanities archives. The Black Film Center Archive, founded in 1981, "holds a collection of [6,000] films and related materials by and about Blacks," the Archives of African American Music and Culture, founded in 1991 and directed by Portia Maultsby, includes audio and video recording, photographs, original scores and oral histories, etc.[12] These archives are unique and very important, but the information revolution generated by computers and the World Wide Web pose interesting questions regarding whether and how the department may want to consider making these materials more easily accessible to scholars in the future. Faculty members are also involved in the direction of the African American Choral Ensemble, the African American Dance Company, and the IU Soul Revue. These performing groups are not extracurricular activities; they generate course enrollments.

During the 1980s, the department's enrollments increased dramatically from eleven hundred students per year in 1982 (which had been the standard since 1972) to fifteen hundred in 1986, and rose above two thousand in 1990. In 1985 the department had fifteen majors, but the numbers exceeded one hundred in the early 1990s. Enrollments and majors increased because the major was revised to allow students to double major, to create joint majors with other disciplines (interdepartmental majors) and to minor in Afro-American Studies and other disciplines. Graduate enrollment also increased from nine students in 1981 to thirty-six in 1989.

The department's proposal for a master's in Afro-American Studies was approved by all university committees, and by the Indiana Commission on Higher Education early in 1998. The department began advertising for student enrollments in February 1998. Eight students are currently enrolled in fall 1999. The department also offers the Ph.D. minor for students who are admitted to doctoral programs at the university; twelve students are currently enrolled in this program.

The faculty members and the one administrator interviewed by the consultant saw the approval of the master's program as an important step for the department, a powerful indication of its institutional stability. But the Associate Dean noted that most departments at Indiana have Ph.D. programs. In other words, the absence of a doctoral program is a serious weakness relative to other departments—even other new university programs. Nonetheless, as Professor Dean Peterson commented, "It's my sense that Afro is here to stay."

As to issues threatening stability, the CIP noted the staffing issues likely to arise with implementation of the new master's program; this, given the increased demands required by graduate level research and methodology and field study seminars. The report also cautioned the department about the risk of "drain[ing] already stretched resources from the existing undergraduate program."[13] Other issues raised were the aging of the full and at least one of the associate professors, the administrative responsibilities associated with the archival projects and performance ensembles related to the department. Such programs mean that the faculty carry significant and fairly complex curricular and administrative responsibilities in addition to their research roles.

As to enrollment, data generated by the university shows the department's to be comparable to Art History, Religious Studies, and to surpass enrollments of majors in Philosophy and Comparative Literature. In the number of graduating majors, in 1997, Afro-American Studies compared favorably with Art History, Philosophy, and Religious Studies. The department could, however, enlarge its enrollment still further by targeting an increased number of minors.[14]

Recommendations from IU Faculty

Several faculty members mentioned plans to develop a Ph.D. program. The Chair expects to have an M.A. and Ph.D. program within ten years and a faculty of sixteen or seventeen. He feels there is urgency to developing the graduate program because their window of opportunity is closing.

Reviewers' Recommendations

The department faculty members need to address gender inside and outside the classroom, as well as in their relations with the Gender Studies program; it was an important factor shaping the interactions and conflict around the Black Atlantic Seminar. Indeed, significant changes seem to have occurred since this review was initiated. In making final additions to this report, the consultant found that Maultsby and Burnim were no longer listed as faculty on the department's Web site but are now listed as faculty in the Department of Folklore and Ethnomusicology. Professor Valerie Grim remains a faculty member in the Department of Afro-American Studies. Staffing does seem as if it will be an issue in sustaining the master's program.

University of California, Berkeley

The Project

Entitled "African Diaspora Studies, Multiculturalism, and Identity Construction: The Development of a Comprehensive Multidisciplinary Framework," the Ford project at the University of California at Berkeley had two primary components. The first involved the development of critical methodologies and analytical frameworks for African American Studies, particularly from an African diasporan perspective. The main institutional platform for this portion of the project was the Department of African American Studies new doctoral program, the initial year of which coincided with the first year of the Ford funding. The second component of the project involved the building and strengthening of networks within and without the university, as well as the allocation of support for scholarly resources on campus, technological and otherwise.

Although the unit itself is called the Department of African American Studies, its new Ph.D. program has, by design, a decidedly African Diasporan orientation; one distinguished by a strong Caribbeanist strain. In addition, there has been a willingness to set this Diasporan focus within a comparative analytical framework—that is, within one informed by the recognition that the field of Diaspora Studies is not limited to scholarship on African populations. Accordingly, the faculty in African American Studies has been giving a great deal of attention in the 1990s to how such critical approaches to African American Studies, as a discipline, might be institutionalized—especially in terms of a graduate program. The Ford project was conceived, in part, to support efforts on this front.

One practical manifestation of this approach was the attempt to nurture faculty and graduate student research, especially when it involved faculty-student collaboration. Three such joint faculty-student efforts were to be supported with allocations of $5,000 per year. A related component of the Ford project was the establishing of monthly faculty and graduate student working-paper colloquia on the theme "Multiculturalism, Identity, and Diaspora." Modeled on the department's St. Clair Drake Forum, these regular meetings were intended to enhance graduate student training, bring together faculty members with common research interests, and formalize links among three key units on the UCB campus: the Department of African American Studies, the Department of Ethnic Studies, and the Center for the Teaching and Study of American Cultures. Ford funds also provided for a graduate research assistant who could aid the members of the department in their work on this project. Finally, the project supported an African American Studies faculty seminar that focused on "doctoral program curriculum development" and that generated a four hundred page course reader.

This Ford project reflected the department's commitment to nurturing connections with individuals and academic units outside of Berkeley. Ford funding supported a "Conditions in the African Diaspora" lecture series that brought to campus two foreign scholars per year. The Ford grant also enabled the convening of "African Diaspora Studies on the Eve of the 21st Century," a major conference in the spring of 1998. This conference was proposed to "bring together scholars with disparate understandings of the field and with different theoretical and analytical perspectives in an attempt to begin to develop some comprehensive understanding of African Diaspora Studies and what it encompasses." Another important element proposed for this conference (as it applied to African American Studies) was the "coordination of the resources, efforts and offerings of all the campuses of the University of California." This had already begun "through the formation of the African American Studies Inter-

Campus Council [which] emerged out of two working group meetings of the U.C. system-wide African and African American Studies faculty."[15]

Imaginatively designed and successfully executed (a member of the review team attended a portion of this event), the conference was divided into two parts. The first day of the conference centered on a number of workshops that addressed the current state of African and African American Studies and that drew upon faculty members and administrators from relevant units throughout the University of California system. The second day involved a series of panels on topics touching upon a number of disciplines and constructed to encourage comparative discussions. This conference presented an excellent range of scholars from around the world and attracted a large, diverse audience. The conceptualization of the first day's events, in particular, might serve as a useful model for other such meetings that Ford might support across the country.

The Berkeley project also involved communication and dissemination components. One example was the formal relationship established between the department and *Social Identities: Journal for the Study of Race, Nation, and Culture*, a British publication. Although no Ford funds were used directly for the journal, this connection was part of a larger effort on the part of the department to facilitate intra-institutional and international scholarly exchange, an effort that was central to the Ford project. Ford funding did go toward the purchase and maintenance of computer equipment that, in turn, was used to set up the department's newsletter, *The Diaspora*, as an online journal and to upgrade the technological resources available to the department's faculty and students. Finally, the Ford project included a library support component which allowed for acquisition by Berkeley of key African American collections that would facilitate ongoing faculty and student research.

African American Studies at the University of California, Berkeley

The history and current institutional situation of African American Studies at the University of California at Berkeley are complex. California's racially and ethnically heterogeneous population means that the African American Studies unit is in a potentially competitive environment with regard to shaping curricular and intellectual developments in Ethnic Studies and African American Studies at Berkeley. The unit began in 1970 as a program within Ethnic Studies. In 1975, it became the only one of four Ethnic Studies programs to achieve departmental status. Since then, African American Studies, though independent, has remained closely allied with the Ethnic Studies department—particularly through the doctoral program in Comparative Ethnic Studies that was created in 1984.

In 1997, the Department of African American Studies began offering its own Ph.D. program in African Diaspora Studies, with specializations in two areas: Issues of Development in the Diaspora and Cultural Studies. The department has grown into one of the strongest, most competitive research universities in the country, if not the world. Therefore, the unit's focus has been national, as well as international, with a significant number of study abroad opportunities for its students. However, the department's capacity to promote its faculty to tenure has been particularly difficult since its early years. Its faculty, for examples, does not hold joint appointments in other major departments and thus cannot chair dissertations of students in those departments even though they can serve on their doctoral committees, sometimes to an extraordinary extent.[16] In general, the department must attend to a more complex intellectual, administrative, curricular, and developmental agenda than do programs at some of the other institutions examined.

The African American Studies department also has ties with the Division of International and Area Studies (IAS), which includes the Center for African Studies. Headed by a dean, IAS oversees an undergraduate degree program with roughly 700 majors drawn from both the social sciences and the humanities. The unit is well networked within the university and apparently healthily funded. (Recently, it has received a Rockefeller grant for faculty development.) It is important to note, however, that undergraduate degrees are offered by IAS in Asian Studies, Latin American Studies, Middle Eastern Studies, but not African Studies. Moreover, there are M.A.

and Ph.D. degree programs in Asian Studies and Latin American Studies—not in African Studies.

In terms of its course offerings, the African American Studies department maintains a somewhat uneasy relationship with the Center for the Teaching and Study of American Cultures, which oversees the approval of courses that can be used to satisfy the breadth requirement in American Cultures that Berkeley instituted in 1991. A sizable number of the department's regular offerings are on the list of approved American Cultures courses, which has resulted in an increase in enrollment. At the same time, it is unclear whether a significant portion of the resources allocated to the American Cultures Center to support the creation and reworking of courses has flowed to the African American Studies department.

Possibly as a result of the decreasing enrollment of African American Studies students in the wake of anti-affirmative action legislation in California, there appears to be a drop in the number of African American Studies majors; meanwhile, enrollments in the department's courses remain high as students take them to fulfill their breadth requirements. There is some apprehension that should this trend continue, the department would gradually become something akin to a service unit. Some faculty members also noted the change in classroom dynamics as a result of the influx of non-major students who might never have enrolled in the department's courses were it not for the American Cultures requirement. That courses approved for this requirement have to be comparative has likely affected the design of some offerings in Ethnic Studies and African American Studies as well.

What is clear amidst these intricate, interlocking institutional networks is that the faculty in Ethnic Studies generally and in African American Studies in particular are mightily overworked. The Ethnic Studies department, which houses fifteen FTE, has the highest student-faculty ratio in the Social Sciences Division. The faculty in African American Studies is likewise stretched quite thin. For example, the Chair of the department teaches five courses a year to help staff the curriculum.

One part of the problem is the sheer volume and diversity of the academic workload that the department has to bear. In 1996–97 the unit mounted ninety-seven courses with a total enrollment of 2,533. In early 1998, there were forty-three African American Studies undergraduate majors, and the first two cohorts in the new Ph.D. program brought in twenty graduate students. This is not to mention the Ph.D. students in Ethnic Studies and other departments, many of whom work with faculty in African American Studies. (The proposal for the department's Ph.D. Program estimated that there would be approximately fifty students enrolled by the year 2000, assuming that ten students were admitted annually.) That the department's faculty members carry more than their fair share of administrative demands (as occurs at a number of campuses) only exacerbates the crisis.

In addition to workload, there is a lack of sufficient FTE in African American Studies. Between 1992 and 1998, four faculty were added to the department. In 1998–99, the unit held six full professors, two associate professors, two assistant professors, and two lecturers. Not only is this number (10 FTE) inadequate to handle the current teaching demands but it inevitably leaves massive gaps in the curriculum that are not consistently covered by faculty in other departments. Perhaps the two most dramatic examples are the absence of a specialist in Caribbean history and a West Africanist. This latter absence is especially striking, indeed. As of early 1998, Berkeley did not have a single regular faculty member who specialized in West Africa, regardless of field. The department also lacks a senior faculty member in African American history, one of the more volatile and interesting areas in African American Studies, and one populated by a sizable pool of scholars. The consequences of this staffing problem on both the undergraduate and graduate curricula in African American Studies are obvious. (The department's hiring priorities include these other fields: History of Science, Communications, Ethnomusicology, Social Theory, Psychology, Film, and Linguistics.) That the unit must compete for FTEs with larger departments within a division (Social Sciences) already strapped for faculty resources suggests that the problem will not find an easy solution.

As African American Studies faculty members have achieved senior status at Berkeley and in their careers, they are called on to carry additional responsibilities both within and without the university. For example, Margaret Wilkerson—former Chair of both the Theatre and the African American Studies departments and Director of the Center for the Study, Education, and Advancement of Women—is now on a leave as a Program Director with the Ford Foundation.[17] In addition, Charles Henry is on leave from the department while he works with the Chancellor to develop faculty hiring and student recruitment programs. Both of these individuals have played key leaderships roles in African American Studies over the past decade or two. (Earl Lewis's move from Berkeley to Michigan in the early 1990s constituted a major loss as well.)

Indeed, with the inevitable faculty departures, leaves, and retirements, African American Studies could find itself in the near future in an even more desperate situation. The administration's reluctance to allocate additional FTEs to the department after faculty have retired, as well as the recent migration of a faculty member from African American Studies (on whose FTE she was hired), to English, with apparently no compensation provided in return, point up a lack of institutional support for the unit that must change if the department is to survive, much less thrive. That the university faculty has been limited to a fixed size for some time means that growth in any one department requires the subtraction of faculty from another unit. When tenured faculty retire, their FTEs frequently return to the university's Senate Budget Committee, which makes recommendations to the Vice Chancellor about where to allocate these resources. This practice only worsens the staffing problems faced by African American Studies.

Not surprisingly, some of the concerns voiced by African American graduate students in interviews conducted as part of this review reflect anxiety about these staffing problems. Specifically, students bemoaned the absence of specialists in both African and African American History; some anticipated problems fulfilling core course requirements in light of the faculty shortage. Particularly frustrating for a few students were the institutional barriers that prevented their taking advantage of relevant faculty resources in other departments. For example, the English department had just recently brought in a distinguished visiting scholar to teach a graduate seminar. Because doctoral studies in African American Studies were not members of the department sponsoring this professor's course, they felt unable to benefit from her presence on campus. Some mentioned that they did not even know about the seminar; much less have a chance to enroll in it. (These and related anxieties on the part of students in Ethnic Studies climaxed at the end of the 1998–99 academic year with a protest and sit-in that received little major media coverage but which was commented on widely in academic channels.)

That said, the Department of African American Studies is to be commended not only for maintaining ambitious undergraduate and graduate degree programs, but for overseeing a striking number of important and diverse outreach efforts. Among the most noteworthy (and one that holds a key place in the department's regular undergraduate curriculum) is Professor VeVe Clark's "Their University or Ours." This orientation to academic culture at Berkeley has reportedly had a positive impact on the retention of first-year students and might be usefully replicated at other schools. In addition, the department sponsors African American Studies workshops for high school and community college teachers. It participates in the Ford-funded "Diversifying African Studies" project in collaboration with Stanford University, and it supports "Break the Cycle," an after-school math tutorial program staffed by Berkeley students. The department has also initiated an overseas studies program, which sponsors faculty-supervised, student travel to Barbados, Zimbabwe, and Kenya. And, in what is surely among the most ambitious and wide-reaching international networks maintained by the African American Studies units under review, the department has developed institutional links with the University of Namibia, University of Warwick, University of the West Indies, University of Western Ontario, and the University of Zimbabwe.

Another notable achievement is the inauguration of the department's Ph.D. program, certainly a difficult and substantial undertaking. The department has positioned itself as possessing the only such graduate program in the state—a status none of the other U.C. campuses apparently intend to match. Given the department's close affiliation with the Ethnic Studies department and with the Center for the Study and Teaching of American Cultures, the African American Studies Ph.D. program is well-situated to address such key African Diasporan issues as multiculturalism, race and ethnicity, and identity formation.

In sum, the African American Studies department at Berkeley is one of the most active such units in the country in terms of both curriculum development and outreach. The department is a national leader in scholarly publication and research in the field which, in turn, help to fuel its new doctoral program. The department also plays a central role in a number of important campus-wide initiatives. Yet, it is evident that the department is entering a period of extreme vulnerability and potential scarcity of resources. That this is occurring just as the already considerable demands on its faculty are likely to increase should be cause for no small alarm. It is also impossible to overstate the impact of anti-affirmative action legislation and regent policies on the university generally and on African American Studies at Berkeley specifically. These developments have limited the ability of the university to recruit ethnic minority students, faculty, and administrators, and it is expected that this will lead to a downward shift in enrollments in the department's courses. It has effectively required administrators at all levels to attempt to reconstruct what had always been a work in progress. Still, the Department of African American Studies has established a distinguished record as a leader in the field on a number of fronts. Without a major commitment of funds and faculty positions by the university administration, it is uncertain whether the department will be able to build on this strong record.

Recommendations from UC Berkeley Faculty and Students

These recommendations came from students in the doctoral program:

1. The department needs a computer lab and a full-time staff person to support its technology needs.
2. The department should hire an academic professional dedicated to the administration of the Ph.D. program.
3. Additional hiring is definitely needed, particularly for a West Africanist (preferably an historian). In this latter case, the department might usefully collaborate with the Center for African Studies.

Phyllis Bischoff suggested that a Library Science focus be developed within the African American Studies degree program. Given the growth in the field and the revolution in how libraries function based on dramatic changes in information technology, these proposals seem especially apt. The Cooperative Africana Microform Project, currently underway, is a collaboration of more than thirty libraries. Administered by the University of Chicago and the Center for Research Libraries, it digitizes newspapers and journals for use as online resources.

Reviewers' Recommendations

The department might address the extent to which its faculty is overworked by monitoring its FTEs more effectively. One complicated aspect of this problem involves the use of its faculty to support graduate work in other departments that have neither joint appointments nor permit African American Studies faculty to chair dissertation committees. Before the department had its own doctoral program, this sort of unrewarded service on the part of its faculty was understandable. However, it constitutes a major drain on faculty time when the African American Studies doctoral program is going to constitute an increasing demand for faculty attention. Perhaps some negotiation with other departments might prove fruitful.

University of California, Los Angeles

Cultural Studies in the African Diaspora Project

UCLA's Ford-funded Cultural Studies in the African Diaspora Project (CSADP) set out to "encourage an extensive dialogue between humanists and social scientists working in African American Studies, . . . Cultural Studies, and African Studies" envisioning them as clearly compatible. "Ideally," wrote Valerie Smith and Marcyliena Morgan, "both areas challenge disciplinary boundaries, situate cultural processes and productions within the context of social and political relations, and expand the body of texts available for scholarly consideration." Ideally, too, both endeavored "to encourage scholarly activity on people of African descent and to provide a framework to increase collaborative and interdisciplinary study of the African Diaspora."[18] Year One of the Project focused on "Race, Culture and Citizenship"; Year Two concentrated on "Changing Constructions of the Black Middle Class"; and Year Three on "Race and Science."

Several activities were carried on across all three years of the project, which began in 1996–97. The project sponsored an annual colloquium series and conference related to the specific topic for each year's projects, as well as travel grants, interactive media collaboration, interdepartmental course development, and collaborative programming in the Los Angeles area. In 1996–97 the grant sponsored a conference "Race, Class and Citizenship" in Western Europe and the United States. In spring 1998 the conference was "'Put Your Hands Together': Representation, Interpretation, and Black Spirituality," which brought UCLA faculty and Los Angeles religious institutions together for discussions. Scholars presented research on "Black Religious Practices in the African Diaspora." The "Power Moves Hip-Hop" conference sponsored in May 1999 fostered dialogue among academics in critical theory and Ethnomusicology; music executives; and music performers about the creation of new forms of expression, and hip-hop's role as a cultural and political voice for young people. The grant provided support for faculty awards for course development and travel, as well as student awards for research and travel. The grant from Ford was to be allocated over three years; funding support also came from UCLA.

The project used information technology innovatively as an integral part of all activities. One of the prominent features of the grant was the requirement that graduate students create Web sites as part of their participation. Co-Principal Investigators Valerie Smith and Marcyliena Morgan required their graduate students to create Web sites on which to locate their research.

This work was being done in 1996–97 when Web-based technology was relatively new to most departments and certainly to most African American Studies programs around the country. The CSADP also collaborated with local and international groups. Working with a scholar from England, the Project cosponsored a scholarly symposium in October 1998

"Rhapsodies in Blax: The Blaxploitation Movement and the Harlem Renaissance" in conjunction with an exhibition on the Harlem Renaissance at the Los Angeles County Museum of Art. It has worked with KAOS Network, a Los Angeles broadcaster and corporate sponsor of a program that exposes urban youth to computer and advanced media technology. This project reflected the importance of Cultural Studies in the humanities, and the growing interest in specific cultural innovation within Black communities while reaching out for a broader understanding of forces shaping communities of African descent transnationally. Research was explored in twenty-five different topics including gender and identity, immigration, youth, culture, and foodways.

The Center for African American Studies at the University of California Los Angeles

Founded in 1969, the Center for African American Studies (CAAS)[19] is one of the leading research units in the field in the nation. It has an elaborate administrative structure with significant support from the University and has the capacity to raise considerable external support through research and development activities. CAAS has also made productive use of the creation, in 1972, of the Institute of American Cultures, which "promotes the development of Ethnic Studies at UCLA by providing a structure for coordination of the four Ethnic Studies centers on campus."[20]

The University has continued to support CAAS evolution and development, and the Center has reached the point where departmental status is at least a possibility. Its research, faculty, and curriculum at the graduate and undergraduate levels are clearly among the strongest in the nation. At the same time, however, it contends with ongoing problems related to leadership of the Center, faculty stability, and the intellectual, political, and administrative demands associated with managing such a complex academic enterprise. The political issues surrounding attacks on affirmative action within the state of California by one of the University's own Regents, Ward Connerly, an African American businessman, poses perhaps the most serious threat in reducing the size of the African American student population attending the University.

CAAS is an Organized Research Unit (ORU) under the U.C. system. It includes a number of other units across a range of academic fields in addition to Ethnic Studies. Such ORUs normally have a fifteen-year life span after which they are subject to administrative review and renewal. The Ethnic Studies centers were, however, not reviewed after their first fifteen years of operation; they will be reviewed in the fall of 2000.[21] CAAS and the other Ethnic Studies ORUs (Asian American, American Indian, and Chicano Studies) report to the Vice Chancellor for Academic Affairs—currently Claudia Mitchell-Kernan, a former Director of the Center.

There are also interdisciplinary degree programs (IDPs) that overlap and interact with the ORUs, but they report to a different administrative structure. The IDP known as the Afro-American Studies Program directs an undergraduate major with a required concentration in Anthropology, Economics, English, History, Philosophy, Political Science, Psychology, or Sociology and a master's program in the same disciplines with the exception of Economics. Some students elect to double major in the undergraduate program, combining Afro-American Studies with another field. The IDP has set up a pilot coordinated degree program linking the M.A. in Afro-American Studies with the graduate program in the School of Education. A similar arrangement with the School of Law is being explored.

CAAS (the ORU) reports to Vice Chancellor Mitchell-Kernan, and the Afro-American Studies Program (the IDP) reports to the Dean of the Social Sciences, Scott Waugh, in the College of Letters and Sciences, an arrangement which creates interesting tensions and challenges. The Area Studies programs have recently been shifted to the College of Letters and Sciences and will report directly to the Provost (the head of the College). Yarborough also reports that "the possibility of departmentalization is even on the table for the centers, something that would not likely have happened five years ago."

As of 2000, Mitchell-Kernan will no longer serve as Vice Chancellor but will retain her position as Dean of the Graduate Division;[22] the positions had previously been held by two different individuals. Acting Director Yarborough notes that the centers have been asked to decide where within the university infrastructure they should be located—for example, the

Chancellor's office (where they are presently located), the Provost's office which heads the College of Letters and Science, or a specific division headed by a dean, such as Social Sciences or Humanities, within the College.[23]

When CAAS and the other Ethnic Studies centers were originally created, there was opposition to Ethnic Studies units having departmental status so they were designated ORUs.[24] The various Ethnic Studies programs are integrated into an overarching structure, the Institute of American Cultures. Mitchell-Kernan reported that while the Institute was created in 1972, preceded by the Ethnic Studies centers in 1969, the overarching structure wasn't fully implemented until 1976–77. The activities for all of the centers include outreach, predoctoral and predoctoral fellowships, faculty grants, programmatic activities, and conferences and symposia.[25] The centers each receive approximately half of their budget annually from University funds.

The University-designed structure of an overarching institute, which houses similarly structured Ethnic Studies centers, seems to have been an especially successful one. All of the UCLA centers are nationally prominent in their respective fields, and they conduct important research and community activities and projects within the greater Los Angeles area. CAAS defines its mission in terms of five divisions: research, academic program and scholarship, publications, library, and special projects. In all of these areas, CAAS is unusually prominent. Its faculty and their research are active in the social sciences (Larry Bobo, Walter Allen, Edmond Keller, Franklin Gilliam, Robert Hill, and Brenda Stevenson among others); the humanities (Richard Yarborough, Valerie Smith, Harryette Mullen, and Jacqueline DjeDje); and the arts (musician Kenny Burrell).

In addition, they are nationally and even internationally known. In fact, UCLA has been hard-pressed to hold on to faculty. Melvin L. Oliver, former Director of UCLA's Center for the Study of Urban Poverty left to become Vice President of the Ford Foundation (1996–2004)), and is currently Dean of Social Sciences at University of California, Santa Barbara. Bobo, formerly the Tishman-Diker Professor of Sociology and of African and African American Studies at Harvard, is now the Martin Luther King, Jr. Centennial Professor at Stanford University. Marcyliena Morgan, his spouse and one of the co-Principal Investigators (PIs) on the UCLA Ford grant, formerly a faculty member in the African and African American Studies at Harvard and founder of the HipHop Archives there, is currently Associate Professor of Communication and Executive Director of Stanford's HipHop Archive. There is no reason to think that this competition will not continue.

The Center has its own library that supports CAAS's academic programs and many research projects. The CAAS Special Projects Division directs cultural and scholarly programming such as the annual Thurgood Marshall Lecture on Law and Human Rights, and coordinates increasing fundraising activity. In this latter area, the University has within the last several years designated a development staff member who works specifically with the Ethnic Studies centers to assist them in fundraising efforts. The Center has published books and monographs for at least two decades and includes several series in addition to internal and external publications that report on CAAS activities.

The Ford Foundation and UCLA co-sponsored a previous CAAS project, Afro-American Studies Program for Interdisciplinary Research (ASPIR) from 1988–92. The project supported research that incorporated "a research paradigm that more fully reflected the complexities of the African-American experience."[26] There are a number of institutional challenges that have shaped the current project and the Center. This issue takes the shape of infrastructure versus indirect costs; the very complexity and size of CAAS make it somewhat vulnerable. External support is more important in this form than in the departmental model where costs are more closely linked to faculty support. Since the faculty members in CAAS have previously been budgeted primarily in their departmental units, the Center has grown through external support, as well as through increases in state funds. CAAS has a relatively significant infrastructure, and it has need for additional faculty positions and for research projects. The Center has begun to conduct some development work, but it is in the early stages. On the other hand, it is geographically well-situated to take advantage of its proximity to the film and entertainment industry.

The program is facing an important challenge in terms of leadership. As this report is being completed, it is conducting a search for a new director. A search, two years previously, that had resulted in an offer to a faculty member from the University of Pennsylvania was unsuccessfully concluded. A new search began in fall 1998 and an offer was made to then Sociology Professor Larry Bobo. By fall 1999 Bobo had decided not to accept the offer and departed to become a member of the Department of Afro-American Studies at Harvard. As acting director since January of 1997, Richard Yarborough reports that he is holding the reins but had expected to hold them for a relatively short time. In fact, he has overseen faculty searches and recruitment, curricular expansion, the renewal of the Ford grant that funded the CSADP, the growth of new development activities, and the hiring of two Assistant Directors for Research who were responsible for managing CAAS research programs and extramural grants.

Leadership of Afro-American Studies departments and Centers is a complex task because there are so many different processes to be balanced simultaneously. UCLA faculty M. Belinda Tucker quoted Vice Chancellor Mitchell-Kernan as saying that the role of Director of Afro-American Studies is "psychologically more difficult than being Vice Chancellor."[27] Leadership within the broader university is also an issue. There are two senior Black administrators in the University (Winston Doby and Mitchell-Kernan) who have played leadership roles for the last thirty years, but who are edging closer to retirement. There are no clear successors. Mitchell-Kernan is also a powerful presence within CAAS, having spent the first part of her administrative career as director of the Center. It was also under her direction that the Center's formal administrative structure, created in 1969, was so well and creatively implemented. Faculty members Belinda Tucker and Eugene Grigsby each served a term as Director of the Center before Yarborough assumed the directorship on an acting basis in 1996, while external searches have been conducted.

Another challenge facing CAAS is its relationship with the other Ethnic Studies programs. CAAS has an unusual setting in that it is structurally related to Chicano Studies, American Indian Studies, and Asian American Studies under the umbrella of the Institute of American Cultures. The Directors of the respective programs meet on a regular basis although it is unclear how often they engage in collaborative programming.

Another aspect of this issue intersects with the changes brought on by Proposition 209. All of those interviewed—faculty, students and administrators—mentioned the situation facing the state, the University system (including UCLA), Proposition 209, and the determination of conservatives to end affirmative action as we know it. Mitchell-Kernan called, it "the most demoralizing experience of my career"; she also reported that the new Chancellor had invested a lot in recruitment and retention, but that the framework would erode without aggressive affirmative action. Most expect the number of Asian American students to rise, and that of African Americans and Latinos to fall; a downturn that will pose problems for the centers. Financial competition is a likely possibility without careful communication and collaboration.

Recommendations

These are key points that arose in meetings with faculty, staff, and students:

1. An M.A. program in Afro-American Studies and Computer Science. This idea arose from the Web sites produced through the Cultural Studies of the African Diaspora Project.
2. There is a clear, even desperate, need for program leadership and for additional faculty.
3. CAAS is the product of organizational innovation at its beginning; it is important that the Center continue to innovate organizationally. The academic responsibilities are handled separately in the IDP from the research, programming, and intellectual center activities carried out by the ORU. This arrangement makes it possible to sustain a greater range of academic research projects than is typically possible in a departmental setting in which both the academic and curricular programs are centered in one administrative unit.
4. An American Studies Program might be created that integrates the various Ethnic Studies programs.
5. Enhanced support for the master's program could be added through research and teaching assistantships.[28]

University of Pennsylvania

The Project

The proposal submitted by the University of Pennsylvania in conjunction with Princeton University, was entitled "Reshaping Afro-American Studies: Transnationalism and a New Cultural Studies for the Americas." The three-year initiative was co-directed by Houston A. Baker, Director of the Center for the Study of Black Literature and Culture at the University of Pennsylvania, and Arnold Rampersad,[29] Director of the Programs in American Studies and in African American Studies at Princeton University. Its goal was to work collaboratively toward "a productive and scholarly redefinition of America and the Americas as a whole" by developing "interdisciplinary, transnational models for the study of the Americas" (specifically, the United States, the Caribbean, and Latin America).

In format, this project involved the convening of a series of seminars held at the two universities. As determined by an advisory group of faculty from the two schools, the first year featured two major lectures—one on the Atlantic Diaspora and the other on Chicanos in Chicago. (A third seminar on New Orleans was canceled due to the illness of the presenter.) In the second year, there were six seminars on one theme: "Interconnections and Flows of Religion between Latin America and the United States." The third year's seminars addressed Native American, Caribbean, and Canadian identity. Although Penn and Princeton provided many of the seminar's faculty participants, there was significant representation from other local schools—Temple, Swarthmore, Bryn Mawr, Haverford, and Villanova, among them. In addition, a number of graduate students attended the meetings, and Ford funds were used each year to employ a graduate student who oversaw "seminar logistics" and served as a research assistant for the project.

It is noteworthy that this Ford project appears to be the only one under review that involved a multi-ethnic comparative perspective. In addition, it was the only one with a primarily Western Hemispheric focus. It is a foregone conclusion that, as it enters the new century, African American Studies will increasingly have to incorporate an international perspective. The inevitable redefinition of African American Studies in the wake of a broadening of one's sense of the term "America" will play a key role in that conceptual reorientation. The African American Studies project funded by Ford at the University of Pennsylvania appears to constitute an ambitious step in that direction.

In the short term, the Ford seminars have reinforced interinstitutional ties between Penn and Princeton. (Note that there is already an agreement in place that allows their graduate students to take a limited number of courses at both universities.) To a lesser extent, the Ford project has similarly nurtured such ties among the several local schools whose faculty members attended the seminars. The move to develop a "transnational perspective" that informed the seminars has likely had an impact on faculty and graduate students research projects and approaches to teaching. However, the long-term impact of the Ford project is unclear. There are no readily apparent sources of funds that would permit the schools to continue to convene these seminars.

African American Studies at the University of Pennsylvania

The field of African American Studies at the University of Pennsylvania is institutionalized in two ways. First, there is the Afro-American Studies (AAS) Program, an interdepartmental degree-granting unit created in 1970 that administers a major and minor in the field. At the time of the review, the head of the program was Herman Beavers (English). Because Afro-American Studies does not have departmental status, its primary activities involve mounting courses and generating special programs. And while it appears to have no formal links with the Center for the Study of Black Literature and Culture (CSBLAC) on campus, it co-sponsors CSBLAC guest lectures and other events (for example, a graduate student conference). CSBLAC was established in 1987 and was designed to serve as the institutional nexus for research in African American Studies at the university. Some of its early success was underwritten by a grant from the Xerox Foundation in 1988 that funded a symposium and a summer program for high school teachers. Additional extramural moneys supported other CSBLAC initiatives including predoctoral fellowships (via funds from Rockefeller and Kodak) and the Richard Wright Lecture Series named for the celebrated African American author (via funds from the William Penn Foundation).

As of 2000, the Center appears to be in a period of transition. Not only has outside funding shrunk, but also Houston Baker (CSBLAC's founder and a major figure in African American Studies at Penn for years) has recently relocated to Duke. During our review, Professor Baker was on leave; English professor Michael Awkward was Acting Director of CSBLAC.

It is critical at this time that the University of Pennsylvania reaffirm its support for both the Center and the (poorly funded) Afro-American Studies Program. Under the leadership of President Judith Rodin, Penn has embarked on a multimillion-dollar development initiative with the goal of assuring "minority permanence" at the university. Given the involvement of the Afro-American Studies Program in undergraduate student support—most notably through a summer institute for "pre-freshmen"—in order to achieve this ambitious end, the administration would be well-served to draw upon the expertise of both the CSBLAC and the AAS Program; in turn, it should provide both units with additional resources. Another potentially fruitful sign has been the generation of a proposal to develop a graduate unit in Afro-American and American Cultural Studies in CSBLAC. Finally, there has been some discussion of creating a Ph.D. program that would draw upon the strengths of both Afro-American Studies and African Studies at the university. In order to exploit these opportunities, CSBLAC and the Afro-American Studies program will have to continue their history of close collaboration. The weighing in of other related units—the African Studies Program and the Du Bois Collective, a faculty research group—could prove useful.

University of Virginia

The Project

The Carter G. Woodson Institute for Afro-American and African Studies at the University of Virginia (UVa) has been reinvigorated and reconceptualized in the short time since Reginald Butler was named Director in 1996. The Ford-funded seminar originally proposed by Butler as the "Chesapeake Regional Seminar in Black Studies" is now titled "Rethinking African American Studies: The Chesapeake Regional Scholars Summer Seminar." The seminar brought twelve faculty fellows from the Chesapeake region to the University of Virginia for three-week seminars in 1997, 1998, and 1999 "Rethinking African American Studies" considered how changing conceptions of race will reshape African American Studies and was led by faculty in Anthropology, Architecture, Archaeology, English, History, and Music.

The participants—faculty who teach the humanities in small liberal arts colleges and universities, primarily HBCUs—studied the Chesapeake region with scholars and historians specializing in the area. They were introduced to the research projects that those scholars developed and the electronic technology many of them had begun using. The "annual three-week seminar include[d] lectures, workshops, field trips, and hands-on training in the use of World Wide Web resources and the creation of online teaching materials."[30] The Chesapeake scholars have since used electronic mail and the World Wide Web to continue their discussions and communication after the seminars. Notably, in 1999, the seminar was titled "Rethinking African American Studies: Archival Research in the Digital Age."

As director, Butler notes that the model for the program grew from "the success of a long-term partnership between [the Woodson Institute] and the Southeastern Regional Seminar in African Studies (SERSAS) [which] was organized in the early 1970s by the Social Science Research Council (SSRC) as one of a series of regional seminars intended to provide a new generation of African Studies pioneers with regular opportunities for interaction with their peers."[31] Indeed, the Woodson Institute hosted several SERSAS meetings, even after SSRC funding had ended. The Chesapeake Regional Seminar, conceived by Butler, operated under the direction of an advisory board.

To expand its resources and outreach, the seminar routinely invited scholars and historians to discuss their research with the Chesapeake Fellows[32]—effectively integrating the work of UVa scholars using the Web to interact with others around the country in innovative ways. An Emerging Scholars Program created in UVa's History department to train undergraduates in historical research methods and digital history worked on the Holsinger Project (an archive of nine thousand images from a nineteenth century photographer's collection in Charlottesville) and the Venable Lane Project (a study of Charlottesville's African American community in the nineteenth century). Other Woodson, predoctoral (two year), and postdoctoral (one year) fellows, and visiting scholars also provided an intellectual resource for the Woodson seminars.

The University of Virginia is interested in a regional consortium, what Butler calls "a springboard for other collaborative ventures"[33] between the Woodson Institute and such participating institutions as Virginia State, Hampton, Norfolk State, Virginia Commonwealth, Virginia Union, Fayetteville State, Salisbury State, and Delaware State Universities. As a permanent regional consortium, these schools would share resources and develop programs related to African and African American Studies.

The Carter G. Woodson Institute at the University of Virginia

The Woodson Institute is an interdisciplinary research center founded in 1981 in honor of Carter G. Woodson, the African American Virginia-born scholar who pioneered African American and African Studies. Faculty members have joint appointments and are tenured in departments. In 1995, when the Institute's director, Armstead Robinson, died at age 49, the faculty reported their concern about the status and survival of the Institute. Paula McClain, former Chair of the Department of Government and Foreign Affairs, chaired the search committee for Robinson's replacement and, along with her committee, nominated Reginald Butler as Director. She reported that faculty had been quite concerned about the status of the Institute.

Associate Professor of History Butler has proven to be a forceful and effective director. He has been an intellectual leader in conceptualizing such programs as the Chesapeake Seminar. He responded to the Foundation's "Crossing Borders: Revitalizing Area Studies" initiative with a proposal titled "Changing Cultures of Race in the Pan-Atlantic World." Although that proposal was unsuccessful, Butler has offered Program Officer Margaret Wilkerson an alternative proposal under the Afro-American Studies initiative. He has forged new interactions with Women's Studies including cross-listed courses, and restored relations with History, Government, and Foreign Affairs and other departments with which the Institute had ceased to interact.

With "Changing Cultures of Race in the Modern World," Butler's leadership has "institutionalized a forum for the cross-disciplinary exchange of ideas among university faculty, graduate students, visiting scholars, and Woodson research fellows."[34] The Race seminar discussed new scholarly approaches to race and gender on a level that has, according to Butler, "given scholarly discussions of race greater visibility."

With the College of Arts and Sciences providing two years of support for this seminar, Butler has been impressive in what he has accomplished in a very short time. He has rejuvenated and enriched the complex institutional environment of the Woodson Institute with its multi-tiered research and visiting scholar programs.

Butler is fortunate to have a well-designed environment in which to support an extraordinary array of institutionalized research projects. They include the ongoing work research of doctoral candidates and postdoctoral fellows on African and African American subjects, and faculty research projects in History ("The Valley of the Shadow"), Anthropology, and other fields. The Woodson Institute directs work on the Venable Lane/Catherine Foster nineteenth-century African American family burial site (discovered on UVa property in 1993); the Holsinger Studio Photograph Research Project; "The Culture of Desegregation in the Upper South, 1940–1970"; and the Central Virginia Social History Project.

Butler has strengthened existing projects and added a number of important new ones. In addition, the "Director and Assistant Director of the Woodson Institute serve as advisors to the Booker T. Washington National Monument in Franklin County, Virginia, and the Monticello/Thomas Jefferson Memorial Foundation in Charlottesville. The National Park Service has asked the Woodson Institute to cosponsor a conference on the Underground Railroad and Slave Resistance in the year 2000."[35] A conference and edited volume on the Sally Hemings–Thomas Jefferson relationship were developed in the wake of the controversy on the findings on the genetic evidence on their descendants. The University Press of Virginia also publishes a series in African and African American Studies.

The Institute directs the African American and African Studies Program at the University in which "more than fifty students major or minor." The program tracks courses "offered by more than a dozen departments and area studies programs" and offers courses through the Institute. The 1997–98 annual report took specific note of "our need for a full-time programming specialist to [develop] curriculum, electronic teaching resources, seminars and conferences." What had been handled by three people in the mid-1990s, as of May 1998 was handled by Scot French, the assistant director, who also has a half-time teaching load. The University had also halved its contribution to the Institute for part-time instructor salaries—allowing for only two courses. Butler (and another member of the History department) also proposed and led the Emerging Scholars Program, based first in the history department and now in the Woodson Institute, to mentor minority students and introduce them to the scholarly world at an early stage. He has also won approval from the University for the new Distinguished Majors Program for undergraduate majors in African American Studies within the Woodson Institute.

Virginia's Woodson Center seems to have a much more enriched research environment than schools that organized around projects and programs, rather than research-based activities. Many of Virginia's research activities also intersect with each other and with the Ford-funded Chesapeake Seminar; they are redundant but in their redundancy is their power.

Butler and Assistant Director French, an instructor in History, carry the bulk of the load of the Institute's workload, but it is unreasonable to expect this arrangement to continue indefinitely. Several issues are involved. This report has already mentioned the substantial reduction in administrative staff in the Institute since 1996—from three full time administrators to .5 FTE. It was clear to the Ford investigator that the Associate Dean with whom she met seemed fairly unsympathetic to the Institute's need for additional administrative support. The complexity and the volume of the research-based projects associated with the Institute might lead, after a number of years, to burnout. The untimely deaths of Robinson and, within a short period, the director of University of Iowa's program (who was also about fifty) should send clear signals to University administrators and leaders in the field. Maintaining these programs is not only intellectually demanding, it is physically and psychologically stressful.

In sum, the Institute's activities are impressive because the Director and his faculty and staff are engaged in a variety of development efforts. Butler and the Woodson have been unusually effective in their search for financial support. They have applied to foundations as well as to internal university sources for support. The University has also been supportive of the Institute's efforts, integrating the Institute into its fundraising efforts and supporting the "Changing Cultures of Race in the Modern World" seminar. The Institute's proposals for a Distinguished Major and the Emerging Scholars Program have also been supported.

The University is conducting a $750 million capital campaign which began in July 1993 and concludes in July 2000. The campaign includes a specific focus—presented in its brochure—on giving for interdisciplinary programs (including Afro-American and African Studies) in the College of Arts and Sciences. During the Ford consultant's one-and-a-half-day visit, the Director of Corporate Foundation Relations and Communications spent most of the first day in presentations made about Woodson Institute activities. It can be said, therefore, that the university has been supportive of the intellectual developments within the Woodson. But it has been unwilling to provide ongoing support for the administrative infrastructure to manage those activities.

While this is not unusual and other universities have displayed similar reluctance in these areas, the array of research projects fostered by the Woodson Institute and the loss of one director makes this resistance somewhat puzzling. One characteristic of the Institute is that the faculty and various fellows are strongly, although not exclusively, concentrated in the field of History. The density of the research focus in History, mixed well with anthropologists, English faculty, occasional political scientists, and scholars of African American Studies seems to yield a creative research and teaching environment. As well, faculty in History and the Woodson Institute are unusually committed to learning about and using new electronic technology in their research, teaching, and scholarship. One example is a proposal from the Woodson to the Faculty Senate to create an online guide to African American and African Studies teaching resources at the University of Virginia. Many of the research projects previously described also have important electronic and Web-based aspects to them.

Recommendations

The Institute has had difficulties making and holding appointments in fields such as Economics and Psychology. The Foundation might address this difficulty through a consortium of the Foundation, disciplinary associations, and the National Research Council. Since this consultant (Pinderhughes) has encountered similar difficulties in her own home institution, and it seems that this is a national problem, different strategies will need to be used to place and maintain faculty.

University of Wisconsin

The Project

The Ford-funded project administered by the University of Wisconsin is the Midwest Consortium for Black Studies.[36] It brings together four schools: Carnegie Mellon University, Michigan State University, the University of Michigan, and Wisconsin. The project's goals were to "consolidate the institutional presence of Black Studies" at the participating universities; encourage networking among the Consortium schools and historically Black colleges and universities (HBCUs); provide for the dissemination of research findings in the field; and to supply younger faculty and graduate students with research support. With the possible exception of outreach to the HBCUs, the itemized goals appear to have largely been achieved.

This Ford project convened year-long seminars at the University of Wisconsin and Carnegie Mellon University, followed by a major interdisciplinary conference at the University of Michigan. Although scholars from a diverse range of fields were involved in the project, there was a determination made at the outset to emphasize the public policy implications of the research under consideration. Along these lines, another aim of the project was to facilitate links between scholars in "cultural and historical studies" and those "in the quantitative and policy-oriented social sciences." (African American Studies units at each participating university, with the exception of Carnegie Mellon, had previously received Ford grants.)

The first seminar was "Black Women's Seminar: Culture, History, Social Policy," directed by Stanlie James at the University of Wisconsin in 1996–97. The second seminar was "African American Urban Studies: Culture, Work, Social Policy"; it was directed by Joe W. Trotter, Jr. and convened in 1997–98 at Carnegie Mellon. The theme of the culminating conference at the University of Michigan in 1998–99 was "Black Agenda for the Twenty-First Century." Note that, with the help of the Ford Foundation in the spring of 1995, Michigan State University had hosted a conference on "Comparative History of Black People in the Diaspora." Although this event at Michigan State preceded the particular Ford project under review, it clearly shaped the decision to focus in the 1996–99 cycle on the other schools in the Midwest Consortium and should be viewed as a key part of the Consortium's overall agenda.

Because our site visit was to the University of Wisconsin, most of the following comments will be drawn from information gathered at that institution. At Wisconsin, the Ford seminar had an important, though hardly the most significant, impact on the field. The seminar was targeted primarily to students with academic course credit earned for participation. Twelve guest speakers were brought in and the seminar readings and assignments were shaped around these presentations. One advantage of this approach was the role that it played in supporting the graduate curriculum in the Afro-American Studies department. However, its student focus had some drawbacks as well.

Perhaps the most serious drawback, according to Professor James, was that this year-long seminar occasionally ended up in conflict with the competing demands of the students' academic programs—especially for the graduate students involved. As a result, not all of the students were able to carry on through both semesters of the seminar: Professor James suggested that shortening this seminar to one academic term might have helped to alleviate this problem. For their part, the students interviewed attested to the benefits of the experience and noted that the lectures of the guest speakers were well-attended (these events were apparently open to the public). The outreach component mentioned in the Consortium's proposal to Ford seemed moderately successful at Wisconsin. Specifically, interviews with three of the guest speakers in the seminar were conducted and broadcast through the Madison affiliate of Wisconsin Public Radio.

In terms of overall impact, other facets of the Ford initiative at the University of Wisconsin may well prove to have a greater long-term effect than the year-long seminar. Faculty members mentioned the benefits of the release-time and research and travel funds that were distributed (both to faculty and some graduate students) under the auspices of the Ford grant. A number of faculty members were particularly grateful for the opportunity to employ graduate students as research assistants, a use of the Ford funds that provided support to both faculty and students simultaneously.

Unlike most of the other institutions visited in this review, Wisconsin committed a sizable portion of its Ford funding to building a significant collection of audiovisual materials designed to support both research and teaching in the Afro-American Studies department. Perhaps the most notable purchase in this regard was the large number of compact disks covering the areas of jazz, blues, hip hop, and rap—"African American musical modernism," as one member of the department termed it. This same faculty member noted that there needs to be some regular supervision of the collection as well as a listening room to facilitate its use. Nonetheless, faculty and students have already begun to draw upon the materials in their teaching and research projects. A collection of videotaped films relating to African American Studies has also been purchased using Ford funds.

Ford funds have also played a role in the building of an exceedingly ambitious and elaborate African American art Web site. Developed under the auspices of Professor Frieda Tesfageorgis, this project involves scanning images of hundreds of art works. The pedagogical benefits of having such material readily available via the Internet would be considerable. Professor Tesfageorgis noted that the Afro-American Studies department's Ford funds enabled her to pay for a computer aide in a course that she taught using these digitized images.

African American Studies at the University of Wisconsin

At the University of Wisconsin, the African American Studies unit has departmental status with (at the time of the review) approximately fifteen faculty members; over sixty-five undergraduate majors, and up to twenty M.A. students. The undergraduate program particularly benefits from the existence on campus of an Ethnic Studies requirement; at the time of the review, approximately 40 percent of the Ethnic Studies courses at the university were African American Studies offerings. (One obvious result of this fact is the large size of many of the department's classes.) The curriculum is organized into three foci: culture, history, and society, with the last area perhaps less strong than the first two in terms of faculty resources. Indeed, with a sizable portion of the department rapidly approaching retirement age, faculty development is a major concern.

As at a number of institutions, faculty recruitment over the next five to ten years will be critical if African American Studies is to maintain its current strength, much less grow. A cause for concern at Wisconsin, according to several faculty members, is the apparent slackening of administrative commitment to diversity in hiring over the past decade; such commitment being critical to the future of the unit, despite its departmental status.

The department is also constrained by ongoing budgetary problems, which affect its programming as well as how it must staff its courses. For instance, it offers few, if any, courses that are restricted to graduate students. At present, Ph.D. students carry a portion of the teaching load in the department. And while this practice, in itself, is not necessarily a problem, it is clear that the department at Wisconsin is understaffed.

Finally, a word must be said here about the Wisconsin State Historical Library, which is located on campus even though its funding is separate from the state allocation to the university. Among its most notable holdings is the largest collection of African American serials in the world (a collection for which the Historical Library has also received Ford funding). Having such a remarkable repository of archival materials within easy reach constitutes a real benefit to faculty members and students in African American Studies at Wisconsin.

The University of Michigan Conference

In March of 1999, the third and final major component of the Midwest Consortium's Ford initiative—an interdisciplinary conference—was convened at the University of Michigan. Although a formal site visit to Michigan was not conducted, both reviewers attended this meeting and later met with key figures involved in the institutionalization of African American Studies at the university. Entitled "Black Agenda for the 21st Century: Toward a Synthesis of Culture, History, and Social Policy," this conference constituted an apt and well-planned capstone to the three-year series of projects funded by the Ford Foundation at the four Midwest Consortium schools. Perhaps the most notable strength of the meeting was the diversity of scholars in attendance. The speakers and invited participants were not restricted to Consortium institutions and the presence of faculty members from non-elite schools was especially gratifying. The format was also conducive to thorough engagement with an issue and to open exchange of opinions. Each session was built around a paper submitted by a single scholar and involved formal responses to that scholar's presentation. Particularly timely was a session dedicated to technology that leads one to recommend an entire conference on the topic.

The overview of the three-year Midwest Consortium initiative presented as part of the conference at the University of Michigan filled in many of the gaps in our review of this multi-institutional Ford project. For instance, although the format of the seminar at Carnegie Mellon University (CMU) was similar to that at Wisconsin, the graduate student participants were not limited to those from Consortium schools. Specifically, the CMU seminar included students from the University of Pittsburgh. Professor Trotter, the director of the CMU seminar, also noted plans to add a comparative ethnicity component to such courses in the future.

The Michigan conference ended with an extraordinarily valuable open discussion of the future of African American Studies—again, with the emphasis on public policy-related research. (Points made during this portion of the meeting will make their way to the list of recommendations that will conclude this review.)

After the conference, the reviewers met with representatives from three of the four Consortium schools (Michigan, Carnegie Mellon, and Wisconsin). This exchange provided first-hand information on the impact of the Ford project at each school. For instance, it quickly became clear that Carnegie Mellon might have made the most progress with the help of Ford funding in terms of institutionalizing African American Studies on campus. Specifically, postdoctoral fellowships were generated, graduate programs were strengthened, and outreach to the nearby University of Pittsburgh was encouraged. Carnegie Mellon had made a commitment to fund an African American Studies junior scholar speaker series modeled along the lines of the Ford seminar convened there. That said, it is also true that Carnegie Mellon had perhaps the furthest to go of the four Consortium schools, with its Black Studies program having just been created in 1990.

At Wisconsin, the initiative strengthened the department's overall standing in a university where there is great emphasis placed on the successful raising of soft money. This could have a positive role in the development of the field at Wisconsin, given a new Diaspora Studies proposal that raises the possibility of interdisciplinary cluster hires.

An even more ambitious faculty recruitment effort in African American Studies appears to be taking place at the University of Michigan, where plans are underway to generate approximately fifteen new joint faculty hires. Some discussion has taken place about possibly moving the Center for Afroamerican and African Studies from program to departmental status. The Ford grant supported these developments on a number of fronts. First, the allocation funded a student-mentoring program. In turn, it was argued, the strength and number of the students in an area help to legitimize a given program. Secondly, the initiative facilitated links between the Black Studies unit on campus and the professional schools. And, finally, in solidifying collaboration among the Midwest Consortium institutions, the Ford funds contributed to building "a stable platform" for graduate training in the field. It is critical to note here that, in addition to a strong institutional base for African American Studies, Michigan is fortunate enough to have Earl Lewis as the Dean of Graduate Studies. Although one person can rarely make a sustained difference at a university (especially a huge state school), that Lewis is both an established African American scholar and also an aggressive advocate for the field provides Michigan with an advantage that few, if any, of the other institutions under review can claim.

Summary and Recommendations

One fundamental question confronting the Ford Foundation at this point is whether it should continue its aggressive support of African American Studies as a specific discipline.

Can a case be made that African American Studies merits Ford funding more than other Ethnic Studies, Women's Studies, or Area Studies? In theory, the answer may be probably not. In practice, however, the answer depends upon the specific goals driving Ford's ongoing investment in African American Studies. We can identify three such related goals. The first involves nurturing African American Studies as a field of scholarship. In terms of the work being produced and materials making their way into curricula in many mainstream disciplines, one can say that the field, in general, is as healthy as it has ever been, if not more so. (This judgment must be adjusted, of course, as we shift from one discipline to another; for example, from History to Economics, where departments are fairly reluctant to support faculty whose research focuses specifically on racial policy issues. Economists who study race are more likely to be located in policy schools and Schools of Social Work than in Economics departments.)

The second goal involves the building of African American Studies institutionally; and with the exception of a scant handful of units, the future of the field on this front is hazy. One problem evident to varying degrees at every university visited is that of leadership development. Another is the extent to which African American Studies faculty carry inordinate teaching, mentoring, and administrative roles at most schools. (Suffice it to say that they are usually not rewarded accordingly.) Overwork is related to joint appointments; significant graduate degree supervision (or the recent addition of graduate programs to an already busy faculty and administrative overload) and administrative staffing problems associated with small, and often, shrinking budgets. The size of most of the units is fairly small, which makes a loss of even a single faculty member—through an outside offer, retirement, or movement to another unit within the university—highly destabilizing. As of 1997–98, many of the units hold tenured or tenure-track faculty of twelve or fewer. Harvard has seven, Indiana twelve, Berkeley ten, and Wisconsin fifteen. Only UCLA had a faculty as sizable as twenty. Although these individuals are affiliated with the Center for African American Studies, their institutional homes are in other university units (usually, other departments). CAAS "owns" only six FTE, and the Afro-American Studies degree program at UCLA has only recently been authorized to participate in joint appointments.

It is also crucial to grasp the wide range of environments in which these departments and centers function. Berkeley's African American Studies department is one of the more complex institutional settings. It holds departmental status and coexists with a Center for African Studies and an Ethnic Studies department, which contains subfields in Asian American, Native American, and Chicano Studies. Berkeley has recently added a new American Studies program, which has depended upon African American Studies faculty and course offerings without, it appears, contributing additional resources to the department. In contrast, at Harvard, the Afro-American Studies department's faculty are jointly appointed. Furthermore, there exist two competing Ethnic Studies units on campus with African Studies holding subordinate status as a committee administered by faculty who are generally affiliated with African American Studies. With such complexities as these, it is not unimaginable that some African American Studies units might wither away from lack of aggressive, committed leadership or from a lack of faculty willing to make the professional sacrifices necessary to keep such units functioning.

Finally, the third goal can be viewed in the context of Ford's long-standing interest in stimulating the pipeline supplying African Americans (and ethnic minorities, in general) to the academic profession. Although significant strides have been made in this regard, we could very well be on the brink of a significant decrease in the number of African Americans entering the professorate. Key factors here are the spreading assault on affirmative action and the accompanying attack on Ethnic Studies. The upshot of these trends is that we might well see the day—in the not too distant future—when an African American Studies unit could exist on a given campus and yet have few, if any, African Americans on its faculty.

There are certainly other relevant issues that deserve attention here— for example, the decrease in African American undergraduates at many campuses. The bottom line is that much work remains to be done—and done urgently—if the gains in terms of institution building and diversifying faculty are to be maintained, much less built upon. Just how many resources the Foundation may wish to dedicate to these efforts in the wake of the sustained funding that it has already invested in African American Studies departments and programs is a crucial policy decision that must be addressed. Our recommendation is that the dedication of a reasonable amount of funds to African American Studies is more than justified at this point. At the very least, new RFPs that are designed to target a broader institutional audience or for collaborative projects should allow for a central role for African American Studies.

The problem of leadership is much broader than simply a question of finding individuals who are willing and able to head African American Studies units. Rather, our site visits brought home at every turn the crucial importance of informed, supportive administrators to ensure the health of African American Studies on a given campus. The roles played by such figures as Neil Rudenstine at Harvard (President), Earl Lewis at the University of Michigan (Dean of the Graduate School and Vice Provost for Academic Affairs-Graduate Studies), and Claudia Mitchell-Kernan at UCLA (Vice Chancellor for Academic Affairs and Dean of the Graduate Division) have a great deal to do with the relative strength of African American Studies at those three schools. And given the institutional vulnerability of most African American Studies departments and programs, even a well-meaning but uninformed or unaggressive dean, provost, or chancellor can undermine such units in short order.

These administrators are so crucial primarily because of their control of resource allocation. Nearly every unit visited looked to be understaffed in terms of tenure-track FTE and some expressed scant hopes of receiving relief in the near future. Although providing FTE to African American Studies units is a critical way for administrators to be supportive, they must also be willing to work to ensure the retention and promotion of AAS faculty. Moreover, they may need to monitor closely and ultimately police the handling of joint appointments involving AAS and other departments and programs. At three universities under review, faculty members "walked away" from African American Studies, as it were, taking their FTE with them as their appointments migrated to other departments. In each case, it is unclear that the department was compensated for its significant loss of staff.

If it is clear that high-level administrators need to be committed to and educated about African American Studies at their campuses, the same applies to development officers at these schools. Although it constitutes something of a unique case, Harvard is perhaps the best example of how much can be accomplished in a relatively short time with a supportive development office. A more modest model (but only in comparison to Harvard) might be UCLA, where the four Ethnic Studies units have for the past two years shared the services of a dedicated development officer. No other institution under review had created similar development staff support focusing specifically on Ethnic Studies units. The emphasis on fundraising at the department and program level will only increase over time, and development officers will need to learn how to maximize the potential of African American Studies units to raise extramural funds.

Likewise, African American Studies faculty must be willing to play major roles in such fundraising efforts. However, the extraordinary workload of most AAS professors makes it difficult for them to dedicate still more time and energy to an activity from which faculty traditionally shy away. One strategy might be to make fundraising considerably more transparent early in the educational process, so that graduate students are aware of its necessity and of how it is done. This is clearly an administrative priority that deserves continued attention.

Given the critical nature of all these factors to the institutional health of African American Studies units, Ford might consider ways it might educate administrators and development officers to the particular needs and institutional value of African American Studies departments and programs.

For example, Ford might convene a meeting of development officers from universities with major African American Studies units to discuss fundraising strategies.

The Foundation might want to play a similar role in facilitating interinstitutional exchanges among African American Studies units, for it is clear from our review that there is far too little consistent communication between these programs.

In our research, we encountered several platform models that Ford might support in order to encourage such exchange. One was the conference entitled "Black Agenda for the 21st Century: Toward a Synthesis of Culture, History, and Social Policy" and convened at the University of Michigan. Drawing primarily but not exclusively upon scholars from the four member institutions of the Midwest Consortium for Black Studies, this meeting focused upon African American Studies and public policy issues and thus, by design, had little humanities contact. Nonetheless, its format of formal papers followed by respondent commentary and open discussion worked well and spawned some constructive conversations.

A second model was the "African Diaspora Studies on the Eve of the 21st Century" conference held at the University of California at Berkeley. The first day of this two-day event involved a number of workshops to which AAS faculty throughout the University of California system were invited.

A third example is the Committee on Institutional Cooperation (CIC) meeting to be convened at the University of Illinois. The CIC is the Midwestern association of public institutions known as the "Big Ten" and Penn State University. It coordinates interinstitutional exchanges among deans, unit heads, and administrators at a variety of levels. These meetings allow peers at eleven institutions the opportunity to compare notes on such issues as curriculum, administration, research, development, and organizational strategies. Directors of Afro-American Studies programs in the Big Ten met twice over the last ten years, but meetings have not been organized in some time due to scheduling difficulties. Dianne Pinderhughes (Chair of Afro-American Studies at the University of Illinois) has worked with the CIC administrator to resume these meetings. One will be held in May 2000, and another should follow in the 2000–01 academic year. Similar working groups of the African and African American Studies faculty in the University of California system generated the conference on the "African Diaspora Studies on the Eve of the 21st Century" at Berkeley in May 1998.

What all of these gatherings have in common is the goal of generating scholarly exchange across institutional lines but within a relatively narrowly defined region. All are designed to facilitate the flow of administrative, curricular, and research-planning information. Such events certainly need to occur at the national level as well, but too little attention has been paid to extending these meetings to the local level. The national meetings tend to enable individual scholars to establish professional networks; they do not consistently enable the building of links among universities and colleges in which these scholars labor.

What appears to be desperately needed at both the national and local levels is sustained and open conversation regarding the growing number of advanced degree programs in African American Studies. At present, there has been no real attempt to keep track of such programs and, more importantly, there is no clearinghouse of information such as course syllabi, curriculum designs, and program proposals through which schools might learn from each other's experiences.

On one hand, the diversity of M.A. and Ph.D. programs is such that what might work for one may not work for another. On the other hand, if a coherent field called African American Studies can be said to exist, then it behooves those active in it to strive for some coherence in the training of future scholars. One option is the accrediting system proposed by the National Council for Black Studies. Given the independence of these graduate programs, such a system is doomed to failure without universal approval, which is simply not reasonable to expect. Another less prescriptive step, and one that Ford could facilitate, would be the convening of a meeting of the heads of African American Studies graduate programs for a discussion of goals and strategies for dealing with student financial aid, collaboration with other departments on campus, curricula, introductory courses, job placement, research planning, and the like. One can envision the benefits to be gained from a published volume of papers from such a meeting—especially one appended with syllabi and program descriptions.[37]

Finally, the Foundation might itself take on the creation and maintenance of a database of information regarding AAS graduate programs or, in the alternative, provide the funds necessary for an AAS program to set up such a database. In sum, greater intellectual consistency will be crucial in order to facilitate and sustain the construction of graduate programs that will produce scholars promote the field across narrow disciplinary lines.

The response to the renaissance of the Department of Afro-American Studies at Harvard raises the issue of intellectual consistency. First, there is no single or dominant disciplinary organization. Faculty participates in the National Council for Black Studies (NCBS), the Association for the Study of Afro-American Life and History (ASALH), the American Studies Association, and national disciplinary organizations. These groups reflect generational differences, philosophical distinctions, and differently designed intellectual approaches. In a number of cases, we found that units had their own networks but did not consistently interact with each other. In other cases, the Ford grant stimulated outreach. UVa's Woodson Center reached out to regional HBCUs; Cornell's Africana Studies and Research Center partnered with regional colleges and universities, and an HBCU several states away. And, at Wisconsin, an African American Studies consortium was created linking Midwestern universities: Carnegie Mellon Michigan, and Michigan State. The University of Pennsylvania and Princeton University have also formed an alliance, inspired by a Ford grant.

Another important collaboration that we encountered in our review involved linkages being established between large research universities and small colleges. The Woodson Institute at the University of Virginia had taken a leadership role in developing a regional consortium "of schools interested in sharing resources and developing programs related to African and African American Studies." This consortium grew out of the Ford-funded Chesapeake Seminar of 1997–99, which attracted faculty from HBCUs in the Chesapeake region. At Cornell, the ASRC's Ford project linking upstate New York–based consortium with Baltimore's Morgan State University, was particularly impressive for its use of teleconferencing, distance-learning technology, and its onsite "common seminar."

The relationship between the institutionalization of African American Studies and the diversifying of faculty at schools where such units exist is a complex one—particularly with the diminished commitment to ethnic diversity at all levels at a number of major universities and colleges. The building of African American Studies units in the late 1960s and early 1970s created a mechanism, a highly strategic one, for adding blacks to college faculties that had long been segregated by race and also by gender. Although some of these African American Studies units are now celebrating their 25th and 30th anniversaries, this approach to diversifying faculties has a mixed record in recruitment, retention, and promotion of Black professors. We see a high point of sorts on this front in the early and mid-1980s, when many schools earmarking funds for the hiring of African American faculty members. The effectiveness of this strategy depended upon an institutional commitment to what came to be known as "Target of Opportunity" appointments. Unfortunately, such appointments too often became the only way in which departments would hire individuals from underrepresented racial and ethnic groups (and in some cases, women). Over the past decade, the faltering interest in building an ethnically diverse faculty has been reflected by the drying up of Target of Opportunity funds or, at some institutions, by the use of such moneys to support spousal hires or the appointment of white males in particularly desirable specialization.

A related issue involves the decision a unit must make about pursuing junior versus senior faculty appointments in African American Studies. On the one hand, hiring at the junior level is risky for a number of reasons, the most obvious of which is that it takes at least six years before the faculty member is tenured (if he or she is promoted at all) and thus becomes a stable factor in the curriculum and research agenda of the unit. This process is both time-consuming and uncertain. On the other hand, making senior appointments can be problematic. In many cases, mainstream departments undervalue the work of African American Studies scholars, thereby rendering it difficult to muster the support necessary to conduct an effective recruitment. In cases where departmental support for certain distinguished individuals is forthcoming, the market value of established, well published African American Studies scholars (especially, if they happen to be Black) can be inflated beyond the means of the given college or university. Even when the administration is willing to provide the requisite resources to make such appointments, senior faculty members in the given department can sometimes resent the steps that would have to be taken to bring in the African American Studies scholar and undermine the recruitment effort. That said, it is critical to note here that the exaggerated competition for high-profile African American Studies scholars applies to but a small fraction of those who work in the field.

For Afro-American Studies programs it will also be important to make strategic choices in a number of new areas. Library Science, Computer Science, cultural and entertainment programming are but a few fields being shaped by radical changes in information technology. The needs of educational institutions and of the African American community suggest that these areas would be prime ones for innovative curricular alliances. UCLA, for example, has created a collaboration between graduate programs in Afro-American Studies and the School of Education; a similar arrangement is being pursued with the School of Law. Links between Afro-American Studies and the new sectors being created by the information technology economy can generate exciting alliances. Harvard's Afro-Am Listserv is just one such example. For curricular as well as developmental purposes, programs will need to consider the feasibility of such academic alliances.

Notes

[1] In the Pinderhughes-Yarborough report, the authors collectively refer to African American Studies programs, departments, institutes, etc., as "units."

[2] Robert L. Harris., Jr., Darlene Clark Hine, and Nellie McKay, *Three Essays: Black Studies in the United States* (New York: The Ford Foundation, 1990), pp. 7–14. Also included in the current volume, see pp. 100–137.

[3] Harris, Hine, and McKay, pp. 15–16.

[4] For the sake of convenience, we will use the term "Black Studies" when discussing the field generally.

[5] There are currently 8 universities that offer the Ph.D. in Black Studies: Clark Atlanta (Africana Women's Studies), Harvard, Michigan State, Northwestern,

Temple, UC Berkeley, University of Massachusetts at Amherst, and Yale. A full list of Black Studies programs funded by the Ford Foundation can be found in Appendix A.

[6] Civil Rights Act of 1964, Title VI, 42 U.S.C. § 2000d et seq. Prohibits discrimination on the basis of race, color, and national origin in programs and activities receiving federal funding.

[7] The library is named for the noted African American historian who helped establish ASRC curriculum and taught Black History at Cornell in the 1970s.

[8] The Institute was renamed the W. E. B. Du Bois Institute for African and African American Research in the 2003–04 academic year.

[9] An Invitation to The Ford Foundation to Make a Grant in Support of Indiana University's Afro-American Studies Summer Seminar Program (1996–1998), January 1995.

[10] *Ford Foundation Interim Report,* Black Atlantic Seminar, Indiana University/Bloomington, August 1997.

[11] Departmental Mission Statement from the Indiana University Department of Afro-American Studies Web site, July 1998.

[12] Brochure. *Department of Afro-American Studies at Indiana University.* Bloomington, August 1997.

[13] *CIP Humanities Study Group Report,* Department of Afro-American Studies, April 6, 1998, Indiana University Document, conveyed by Associate Dean, M. Jeanne Peterson, College of Arts and Sciences, October 15, 1998.

[14] Indiana University Documents on faculty teaching, departmental degree recipients, majors, enrollments, etc., through the 1996–97 academic year.

[15] "African Diaspora Studie—Multiculturalism and Identity Construction: The Development of a Comprehensive Multidisciplinary Framework." Percy C. Hintzen and Margaret B. Wilkerson, Co-Principal Investigators, Proposed Project September 1995–1998, submitted to the Ford foundation, *n.d.*

[16] Barbara Christian reported that she was on forty-three Ph.D. committees; Percy Hintzen notes that he served on sixteen. Since the African American Studies doctoral program had only just begun when this review was conducted, most, if not all, of these committees were for students in departments other than African American Studies.

[17] In 1998, Margaret Wilkerson became Program Officer for Education and Scholarship; she was promoted to Director of Media, Arts and Culture in 2000.

[18] *A Cultural Studies in the African Diaspora Project: A Proposal Submitted to the Ford Foundation.* Valerie Smith and Marcyliena Morgan, Center for African American Studies, UCLA, undated document.

19 CAAS has since been renamed the Ralph J. Bunche Center for African American Studies in honor of the diplomat and first African American Nobel Peace Prize laureate.

20 "CAAS. The UCLA Center for African American Studies, History and Mission," UCLA Web site, July 10, 1998.

21 No follow up was done to see whether the reviews took place.

22 Mitchell-Kernan continues to serve as Dean of the Graduate Division.

23 E-mail correspondence, December 3, 1999.

24 Interview with M. Belinda Tucker, July 23, 1998.

25 Interview with Vice Chancellor for Academic Affairs Claudia Mitchell-Kernan, July 23, 1998.

26 *ASPIR, Afro-American Studies Program for Interdisciplinary Research,* Final Report, UCLA Center for Afro-American Studies, 1991, p. 2.

27 Tucker Interview, July 23, 1998.

28 In 2002 CAAS received a $700,000 grant from the Ford Foundation's Affirmative Action initiative to develop research on the impact of Proposition 206 on UCLA admissions.

29 Arnold Rampersad is currently at Stanford University, where he is the Sara Hart Kimball Professor in the Humanities, the Cognizant Dean for the Humanities, and a Professor in the English department.

30 Letter from Carter G. Woodson Center Director Reginald Butler to Alison Bernstein, Vice President of the Ford Foundation, April 14, 1998.

31 *A Proposal for Support of the Chesapeake Regional Seminar in Black Studies,* Principal Investigator: Reginald D. Butler, Department of History, The University of Virginia. Undated document provided by Butler and the Woodson Institute, p. 3.

32 [In the original report,] . . . the first week of the three-week 1999 program is included for illustrative purposes in an appendix following this portion of the report. The seminar included a fascinating array of scholars with a wide range of methodological training and substantive research interests, including, for example, Peter Wood, Abdul Alkalimat, and Sharon Harley. Lecturers in the 1997 and 1998 programs were comparably talented. [The appendix has not been published in this version of the report.]

33 *1997–98 Annual Report,* Carter G. Woodson Institute for African American and African Studies; May 1, 1998, pp. 7–8.

34 *1997–98 Annual Report,* Woodson Institute, *op. cit.,* p. 9.

35 *The Carter G. Woodson Institute for Afro-American and African Studies: An Introduction and Overview.* Document prepared for Dr. Dianne Pinderhughes, Ford Foundation Representative, July 27, 1998.

[36] As of 2006, while the Consortium continues to do collaborative activities, no autonomous Web site exists; information is housed within the African American Studies Web sites of participating institutions.

[37] Two such texts in other disciplines are *Reconstructing American Literature: Courses, Syllabi, Issues,* edited by Paul Lauter (1983) and *Women of Color and the Multicultural Curriculum: Transforming the Classroom,* edited by Liza Fiol-Matta and Miriam K. Chamberlain (1994). This latter volume included materials generated in the course of the Ford Foundation initiative on curriculum development focusing on ethnic women.

PART FIVE

Epilogue:
Continuing Challenges
(2006)

Farah Jasmine Griffin

As Black Studies comes of age in the twenty-first century, it still has important intellectual and institutional challenges to confront. Although there are those who will forever question the legitimacy of African American Studies as an intellectual discipline, the field itself must move beyond such tiresome debates and focus instead on its continued growth and development. The wide range of ideologies, perspectives, and stances is testament to the continued evolution of the field. Indeed, the legitimacy of such traditional disciplines as History and English is not questioned simply because diverse perspectives and emphases exist—sometimes within the same department. Sociology and Anthropology have undergone profound internal struggles over their direction and purpose, yet they continue to exist as legitimate and important areas of study.

Why is Black Studies under such scrutiny? Certainly, African American Studies scholars need not respond to such diversions every time a journalist[1] decides it's time to write about a "crisis" in the field? To do so takes away from the important work that remains to be done.

The Foundation recognizes the need for African American Studies to exist in American institutions of higher learning. For over 25 years, it has provided support to African American Studies departments and programs at a limited number of institutions. It has also spread its resources beyond that number through the support of consortia that include a range of institutions, and graduate programs whose graduates go on to teach at diverse institutions. The Ford Diversity (formerly Minority) Fellowships program helps to sustain a diverse professoriate, many of whom go on to make contributions to African American Studies. The documents in this volume demonstrate how Foundation support extended to a variety of institutional arrangements that fostered creativity in formal and informal structures to benefit African American Studies and the university at large. These arrangements provide examples of not just "best practices" but working practices that ensure the long-term stability of this vitally important academic field. The reports also speak to the fact that many college students who take African American Studies courses go on to become teachers, journalists, activists, lawyers, and doctors committed to a more democratic society. These students—and their professions—have benefited greatly from African American Studies.

The Foundation's most significant contribution can be found in the partnerships it established through its grant making with individual scholars, institutions of higher education, professional organizations, film makers, and others committed to advancing African American Studies toward the substantive transformation of American higher education to become more diverse and inclusive.

Although the last report Ford commissioned to analyze its grant making in African American Studies was completed seven years ago in 2000, the Foundation has not wavered in its continued commitment to Black Studies. Between 2000 and 2006, the Foundation made grants totaling $12.5 million dollars to support academic departments and programs, special initiatives and research in the field of African American Studies.

From the beginning of its commitment to the field, Ford has funded institutionalization as a critical and substantial area in need of support. This prioritization is consistent with what Robert L. Harris predicted seventeen years ago in his essay, "The Intellectual and Institutional Development of Africana Studies."[2] In what Harris described as "the fifth stage in the development of African American Studies," he anticipated that we would witness the creation of a national network of Ph.D. programs, leading to greater professionalization of the field. Indeed, there are now eight universities[3] that offer the Ph.D. in African American or Africana Studies. Despite precarious funding scenarios at public higher education institutions in particular, a number of institutions that have programs and departments plan to establish Ph.D. programs.[4]

There is no question that African American Studies has significant issues and challenges it must face if it is to survive. Many of these have been enumerated in the various reports over time, and continue to resurface, indicating the need to give them attention and support. Some of the core challenges that require attention and support are discussed below.

African American Studies and the Challenge of Identity

> We must draw a distinction between the health of African American
> Studies as a scholarly field of study and the status of African American
> Studies programs and departments within specific institutions. Although
> the two are related, they are distinct. While the scholarly field of African

American Studies is thriving, and while African American Studies departments and programs at elite schools appear to be healthy and flourishing, such is not the case at many public higher education institutions where programs and departments no longer receive support from university administrators. In fact, programs at many public institutions and smaller private colleges appear to be struggling for their existence. A purposeful effort is needed to ensure that these programs have the resources and support necessary to thrive as viable academic and pedagogical units.

African American Studies and the Challenge of Black Communities

None of us can forget the images of Hurricane Katrina's devastation, but what the world was unprepared for was the stark division between the haves and the have-nots that emerged along racial lines. Given the continued crises facing Black communities worldwide, African American Studies as a field must reevaluate its commitments to issues and communities outside of the academy. From its inception, African American Studies has articulated the need for a relationship between scholarship and a social and political agenda that advances the interests of Black people. As those interests and identities became transformed, and as the field itself sought academic legitimacy, this relationship between scholarship and activism (though still articulated as a central goal of the field) has become more complex, and has, in some cases, ceased to exist.

African American Studies and the Challenge of Gender and Sexuality

African American Studies has yet to fully embrace scholarship on gender and sexuality, especially the latter. Black women scholars have yet to receive widespread recognition for their scholarship and leadership. Yet, they are among the field's hardest and most devoted workers. There is a great deal of anecdotal evidence about the price Black women have paid in terms of their health and the sacrifice of their own scholarship, and an emerging body of literature is beginning to document these claims.[5] Further investigation is needed in this area and programs to remedy the situation must be put in place.

African American Studies and the Challenge of Globalization

As the demographics of the United States change so too does the composition of the Black student population. The field needs to become more inclusive to reflect the multidimensional histories and cultures of that population while not losing sight of the history and specificity of Black experiences and struggles both locally and globally.

African American Studies and the Challenge of Technology

Today, African American Studies, like the rest of higher education, must confront the transformations brought on by technology.[6] Increasingly, faculty are asked to incorporate new technological tools into their teaching. African American digital texts point to new directions in the teaching and presentation of Black Studies. It is essential that doctoral programs in Black Studies incorporate technology as a necessary tool of the trade, and look to ways in which technology can be used to enhance research and pedagogy in the field, and build stronger linkages to Black communities.

African American Studies and the Challenge of the Pipeline

One of the most pressing issues facing the field is that of an adequate pipeline of scholars. As a consequence of the challenges to affirmative action programs, the number of African American students entering and completing doctoral programs is still very low. Ironically, this phenomenon may influence the racial diversity of African American Studies.

It is important to note, however, that although there are far too few young people of color pursuing academic careers, the problem of the pipeline has become a convenient excuse used by departmental and university administrators who are resistant to diversifying the faculty. There is a history in higher education of departments dismissing qualified interdisciplinary Black candidates for not meeting the criteria of the individual discipline. Oftentimes such scholars who would be highly sought after by African American Studies because of the intellectual contribution they make to the field are less attractive to traditional disciplines. This is a problem African American Studies shares with a number of other interdisciplinary programs and is one of the primary reasons that many call for autonomy in the hiring and tenuring of faculty.

African American Studies and the Challenge of Leadership Succession

Leadership development is necessary to ensure sustainability in any field. Historically, African American Studies programs and departments have relied on the long-term leadership of a few charismatic individuals. Generational shifts require the emergence of a new cadre of intellectual and institutional leadership to ensure the stability and longevity of the field.

African American Studies and the Challenge of Collaborations and Partnerships

The relationship and tensions between African American Studies and African Studies requires further thoughtful analysis. In some institutions these two fields have established collaborative relationships; in others they can be quite contentious. The very different intellectual origins of the two projects are of importance here: nineteenth- and early twentieth-century scholars of the Black experience insisted upon the importance of Africa to the experiences of Africans in the Diaspora, as did the students and faculty who helped to establish the first academic programs in the late 1960s.

As Huggins noted in his report,[7] contemporary African American Studies departments and programs emerged from an environment of broader social change, protest, and struggle. In contrast, many African Studies programs were founded during the period of decolonization as area studies programs, some of which were funded by the U.S. government. Continued exploration of the relationship between African American and African Studies is needed as more African American Studies programs seek to broaden their perspectives to include Africa and the African Diaspora. It is also necessary to understand the institutional and intellectual relationship between African American Studies and Ethnic Studies as both fields continue to grow.

African American Studies and the Challenge of Building a Professional Network

> As the number of Ph.D.s continues to grow, it is incumbent upon the field to consider what type of national organizational structure is needed to evaluate programs and departments and provide a space for scholars of African American Studies to gather and chart new directions for the field. This is by no means a call for a common curriculum; the issue here is the strengthening of professional networks.
>
> Currently, there are at least two national organizations that might serve this purpose: the National Council for Black Studies (NCBS), and the Association for the Study of African American Life and History (ASALH). While NCBS has as one of its goals to "establish standards of excellence," ASALH has established collaborations with such organizations as the American Historical Association with which it grants book prizes. Further, ASALH's journal is comprised of an editorial board that reflects ideological and methodological diversity. Support is needed to build the capacity of these organizations as they face fluctuating memberships, as they struggle to keep abreast of emerging technology, and as they reflect on how best to serve their members and the field.

As the reports have all affirmed, there is little question that sustainability is perhaps the greatest challenge and most important goal currently facing African American Studies. Although most would agree that the interdisciplinary nature of African American Studies is one of its strongest assets and that it is important to maintain ongoing dialogue and debate with traditional disciplines, if the field is to survive, it must be able to stand on its own feet institutionally. In many institutions this means departmentalization and the ability to hire and tenure faculty without having to rely on other departments for joint appointments. Furthermore, African American Studies units will need strong and permanent financial footing. To do so will require a coalition of support including foundations. Most importantly, it will require committed university administrators who are in the position to direct their development offices to work with African American

Studies units to create a compelling message, and identify and nurture potential donors.

Since its modest beginnings, African American Studies has stood at the forefront of cutting-edge approaches and interpretations. As the field is strengthened, it will greatly influence and enhance the position of all interdisciplinary units within the arts and sciences. The intellectual future of the field is bright. To realize this potential, a strong institutional future for the field of African American Studies is a necessity.

Notes

1 See "Black to the Future: Where Does African American Studies Go From Here?" by Chanel Lee. New York: The Village Voice, Fall Education Supplement 2005.

2 See current volume, Part II: pp. 106–115.

3 The institutions that award the Ph.D. in Black Studies are Clark Atlanta (Africana Women's Studies); Harvard; Michigan State; Northwestern; Temple; University of California, Berkeley; University of Massachusetts, Amherst; and Yale. A full list of African American Studies Programs funded by the Ford Foundation that were evaluated for these reports can be found in Appendix A.

4 Both Boston University and the University of Iowa offer concentrations in Black Studies at the Ph.D. level. Also, there are numerous M.A. programs in Black Studies.

5 See also DuCille, Ann. "The Occult of True Black Womanhood: Critical Demeanor and Black Feminist Studies." In Female Subjects in Black and White: Race, Psychoanalysis, Feminism, eds. Elizabeth Abel, Barbara Christian, and Helene Moglen, Berkeley: University of California Press, 1997. Originally published in Signs: Journal of Women in Culture and Society 19, no. 3 (1994), pp. 591–629. Reprinted in The Second Signs Reader, (Chicago: University of Chicago Press, 1996).

6 Consult Report to the Ford Foundation on Black Studies and Technology by Abdul Alkalimat, University of Toledo, June 5, 2006.

7 See current volume, Part I: pp. 10–92.

Contributors

Farah Jasmine Griffin is Professor of English and Comparative Literature and African American Studies at Columbia University where she served as Director of the Institute for Research in African American Studies from 2003–2006. A graduate of Harvard College and Yale University, Griffin is the editor of numerous volumes and the author of *Who Set You Flowin': The African American Migration Narrative* (1995); *If You Can't Be Free, Be a Mystery: In Search of Billie Holiday* (2001); and (co-author with Salim Washington) the forthcoming *Clawing at the Edges of Cool: Miles Davis and John Coltrane, 1955–1961*. She is currently a fellow at the Dorothy and Lewis B. Cullman Center for Scholars and Writers at The New York Public Library.

Robert Harris Jr. is currently a Professor of African American history in the Africana Studies and Research Center at Cornell University. He also serves as the Vice Provost for Diversity and Faculty Development. Harris is the author of *Teaching African American History* and the co-editor of *The Columbia Guide to African American History Since 1939*. In 2003 he was awarded the Carter G. Woodson Scholars Medallion for distinguished work in the field of African American life and history.

Darlene Clark Hine, a historian of the African American experience and one of the founders of the field of black women's history, is currently the Board of

Trustees Professor of African American Studies and History at Northwestern. She is a past president of the Organization of American Historians and the Southern Historical Association. Her publications include *The African American Odyssey; Hine Sight: Black Women and the Re-Construction of American History; A Question of Manhood: A Reader in U.S. Black Men's History and Masculinity;* and *A Shining Thread of Hope: The History of Black Women in America.*

The late **Nathan Huggins** (d. 1989) was the Director of the Harvard University W. E. B. Du Bois Institute at the time he wrote the Ford report. His writings on Black historical and contemporary figures included both academic prose and shorter books for young adults. He was the author of *Black Odyssey: The Afro-American Ordeal in Slavery* and editor of *W. E. B. Du Bois: Writings; Malcolm X: Militant Black Leader; Marcus Garvey: Black Nationalist Leader; Alex Haley;* and *Alice Walker.*

The late **Nellie Y. McKay** (d. 2006) was the Evjue Professor of American and African American Literature at University of Wisconsin–Madison, where she helped to establish an African American literature curriculum in the department of Afro-American studies. She received many teaching awards, including honors from University of Wisconsin System and Phi Beta Kappa. She was also the president of the Midwest Consortium of Black Studies and helped to develop similar organizations. Professor McKay published more than 60 essays and book and journal articles on important figures in black women's literature. She is the author of *Jean Toomer, Artist: A Study of His Literary Life and Work, 1894–1936* (1984), the editor of *Critical Essays on Toni Morrison* (1988), and the co-editor *The Norton Anthology of African-American Literature.*

Robert O'Meally is the Zora Neale Hurston Professor of English and Director of the Center for Jazz Studies at Columbia University. He is the author of *The Craft of Ralph Ellison; Lady Day: The Many Faces of Billie Holiday; Tales of the Congaree,* and the editor of *The Jazz Cadence of American Culture* and *Uptown Conversation: The New Jazz Studies.* His work as co-producer on the CD box-set, *The Jazz Singers,* earned him a Grammy nomination. O'Meally has also written the liner notes for a Sony/Columbia re-release of Louis Armstrong's *Hot Fives and Sevens,* and for a Duke Ellington box-set called *The Duke.*

Dianne M. Pinderhughes was the Director of Afro-American Studies and Research Program at the University of Illinois at Urbana-Champaign from 1991 until 2000. In fall 2006 she joined the faculty at the University of Notre Dame where she is Professor in the departments of Political Science, and Africana Studies. Her articles include: "A Reflection on Mathew Holden at 25: Toward Black Regrouping and the Next Five Years: Morale and Objective Capacity," *National Political Sciences Review;* "Voting Rights Policy and Redistricting: An Introductory Essay," Symposium: Race and Representation, *National Political Science Review;* and *Race and Ethnicity in Chicago Politics: A Reexamination of Pluralist Theory.* In 2006 she became the President-Elect of the American Political Science Association, and is the first African American woman to hold this position.

Valerie Smith is currently the Woodrow Wilson Professor of Literature and Director of the Program in African American Studies at Princeton University. She is the author of *Self-Discovery and Authority in Afro-American Narrative; Not Just Race, Not Just Gender: Black Feminist Readings;* and the editor of *African American Writers; Representing Blackness: Issues in Film and Video;* and *New Essays on Song of Solomon.* In 2002 she co-edited a special issue of Signs with Marianne Hirsch (2002) and a special issue of *Black American Literature Forum* (now *African American Review*) on black film (1991) with Camille Billops and Ada Gay Griffin.

Richard Yarborough is currently an Associate Professor of African-American Literature and Culture and American Literature at University of California, Los Angeles. He was awarded a Distinguished Teaching Award in 1987, and received a commendation from the City of Los Angeles in 1990. He is the co-editor of the *Norton Anthology of African American Literature; the Heath Anthology of American Literature, 2nd ed.;* the *Heath Anthology of American Literature: Colonial Period to 1800;* and the *Heath Anthology of American Literature: Early Nineteenth Century.*

Appendix A

Black Studies Programs
Funded by the Ford Foundation

School	Names of Departments and Web Site Address	Chair of Department (as of September 2006)	Ford Evaluations	Institutionalization Timeline: Degrees Offered and Ford Grant History*
Cornell University	Africana Studies & Research Center www.asrc.cornell.edu	Salah M. Hassan	O'Meally-Smith, 1994 Pinderhughes-Yarborough, 2000	1970: BA 1971: MPS 1991: $261,643 1999: $250,000 **Total $ 511,643**
Harvard University	African and African American Studies www.aaas.fas.harvard.edu W. E. B. Du Bois Institute for African and African American Research http://dubois.fas.harvard.edu/index.html	Henry Louis Gates, Jr.	O'Meally-Smith, 1994 Pinderhughes-Yarborough, 2000	1968: Faculty Committee on African and Afro-American Studies formed 1969: Department established and Institute proposed 1969: Undergraduate concentration program established 1975: Institute established 1995: $250,000 2001: Ph.D. program established **Total $250,000**
Indiana University	African American and African Diaspora Studies www.indiana.edu/~afroamer	Valerie Grim	O'Meally-Smith, 1994 Pinderhughes-Yarborough, 2000	1970: Department established 1975–6: BA 1983: Ph.D. minor 1990: $300,000 1997–9: M.A. 2006: Developing Ph.D. **Total $300,000**

School	Names of Departments and Web Site Address	Chair of Department (as of September 2006)	Ford Evaluations	Institutionalization Timeline: Degrees Offered and Ford Grant History*
Michigan State University	African American and African Studies http://www.msu.edu/~aaas/	Gloria Stephens Smith	O'Meally-Smith, 1994	1990: $316,000 1991: $180,125 2002: Ph.D. 2002: Established under-graduate program, which is a specialization in Black American and Diasporic Studies **Total $496,125**
University of California, Berkeley	African American Studies http://violet.berkeley.edu/~africam/	Stephen A. Small	O'Meally-Smith, 1994 Pinderhughes-Yarborough, 2000	1970: Program established within ethnic studies 1970: B.A. 1975: Department established 1991: $300,000 1999: $350,000 2000: $35,000 **Total $685,000**

School	Names of Departments and Web Site Address	Chair of Department (as of September 2006)	Ford Evaluations	Institutionalization Timeline: Degrees Offered and Ford Grant History*
University of California, Los Angeles	Afro-American Studies www.afro-am.ucla.edu Ralph J. Bunche Center for African American Studies at UCLA http://www.bunchecenter.ucla.edu/frames/index.html	Brenda Stevenson	O'Meally-Smith, 1994 Pinderhughes-Yarborough, 2000	1969: Center for African American Studies established (later became the Bunch Center) 1974: Department established 1974: B.A. 1980: M.A. 1988: $312,000 1996: M.A./J.D. dual degree 1999: $250,000 **Total $562,000**
University of Michigan	Center for Afroamerican and African Studies www.umich.edu/~iinet/caas	Kevin Gaines	O'Meally-Smith, 1994	1966: Center established 1970: Undergraduate students can have a minor or concentration 1988 (8800473) 300K 2005: Graduate certificate **Total $300,000**
University of Pennsylvania	Center for Africana Studies www.sas.upenn.edu/africana	Tukufu Zuberi	O'Meally-Smith, 1994 Pinderhughes-Yarborough, 2000	1970: Program established 1970: B.A. or minor 1991: $326,700 **Total $326,700**

School	Names of Departments and Web Site Address	Chair of Department (as of September 2006)	Ford Evaluations	Institutionalization Timeline: Degrees Offered and Ford Grant History*
University of Virginia	Carter G. Woodson Institute for African-American and African Studies www.virginia.edu/woodson	Scot French, Interim Director	O'Meally-Smith, 1994 / Pinderhughes-Yarborough, 2000	1981: Institute established / 1981: B.A. or minor / 1981: Predoctoral and postdoctoral program / 2004: $300,000 / **Total $300,000**
University of Wisconsin	Afro-American Studies http://polyglot.lss.wisc.edu/aas/	Craig Werner	O'Meally-Smith, 1994 / Pinderhughes-Yarborough, 2000	1970: Department established / 1970: B.A. / 1980: $300,000 / 1983: M.A., Ph.D. minor / **Total $300,000**
Yale University	African American Studies www.yale.edu/afamstudies	Robert Stepto	O'Meally-Smith, 1994	1969: Department established / 1969: B.A. and concentration / 1969: $184,000 / 1978: M.A. / 1989: $300,000 / 2000: Ph.D. / **Total $484,000**

*The grants listed here were specifically earmarked for institutionalization projects and curriculum development.

Midwest Consortium on Black Studies

Currently, there is no Web site information available for the Midwest Consortium.

Index

Note: Page references in italics refer to illustrations.